Workbook
for

Architecture
residential drawing and design

by

Clois E. Kicklighter
Dean, School of Technology and
Professor of Construction Technology
Indiana State University
Terre Haute, Indiana

Joan C. Kicklighter, C.H.E.
Co-author of *Residential Housing*
Terre Haute, Indiana

INTRODUCTION

This workbook is designed for use with ARCHITECTURE, Residential Drawing and Design. The questions, problems, and activities are aimed at helping you master the subject matter given in the text. The many drawing problems guide you in developing a certain amount of skill in creating architectural designs and constructing drawings in an accepted manner.

Each chapter in this workbook corresponds to a chapter in the text. After studying a chapter in the text, try to complete as many questions as you can without referring to the text. Then, search out answers to the remaining questions. Study the examples and material in the text to work the problems.

The workbook includes several types of questions, problems, and activities. In some instances, you will be required to identify the parts shown in an illustration. Other activities require that you collect materials or prepare a notebook. Many tasks require that you complete a drawing or make a typical construction drawing. Several types of questions have been included: multiple choice, matching, completion, short answer/listing, and calculations.

Workbook problems will require the use of the following architectural drawing equipment: pencils; eraser; erasing shields; T-square, straightedge or drafting machine; 30-, 60-, 45-degree triangles; protractor; engineer's scale; architect's scale; case instruments; irregular curves; pencil pointing devices; assortment of quarter scale templates; and drafting tape. Most of the problems are to be completed on the workbook page. Others, however, will require larger sheets which you must provide. Two standard sizes of tracing vellum — "B" size (12 x 18 in.) and "C" size (18 x 24 in.) — will be required. "B" and "C" size drawings may be drawn in the traditional manner or drawn on a CADD system. Several workbook-size sheets are included in the back for other problems designed by your instructor.

After studying each text chapter and successfully completing the workbook, you will have developed a solid background in the design and drawing of residential structures. Further expertise can be developed through the design of more complex structures, further study of building codes, and research in material applications and building recommendations.

Clois E. Kicklighter
Joan C. Kicklighter

CONTENTS

Chapter 1

THE WORLD OF ARCHITECTURE

Text Pages 7-24

Name _____   Course _____

Date_____   Score _____

PART I: MATCHING: Match the correct house style with the characteristics listed below. Place the corresponding letter on the blank at right.

<table>
<tr><td>A. Cape Ann</td><td>E. New England Gambrel</td></tr>
<tr><td>B. Cape Cod</td><td>F. Ranch</td></tr>
<tr><td>C. Contemporary</td><td>G. Salt Box</td></tr>
<tr><td>D. Garrison</td><td>H. Southern Colonial</td></tr>
</table>

1. The long, low roofline which gently slopes from roof peak to eaves helps to combat bitter winter winds. The name of this house style is derived from containers used for food storage.

    1. _____

2. This house style has a large, centrally located chimney and a gambrel roof. The attic may be converted to living or sleeping space.

    2. _____

3. An unique feature of this house style is the overhanging second story. This style also has a steep pitched roof and narrow siding.

    3. _____

4. Ornate woodwork, iron trim, three-story chimneys, upper and lower balconies, large columns and porticoes are some unique features of these elegant homes.

    4. _____

5. The features of this popular house style include a gable roof with the top of the windows near the roofline, a central chimney, and shutters on the windows.

    5. _____

6. A low-pitched roof with gables and overhanging eaves is characteristic of this one-story home. Some homes are "L" shape and have an attached garage.

    6. _____

7. These homes vary in design and use of materials. Some borrow ideas from past designs while others are completely innovative. Plans are designed to please the homeowner.

    7. _____

8. The name of this house style came from one of its features. It is found in most sections of the country. Two advantages of this style include usable space as a result of the roof design and shorter rafters.

    8. _____

PART II: COMPLETION: Complete each sentence with the proper response. Place your answer on the blank in the right column.

1. Some homes are designed for particular settings such as a _____, seashore, or a steep cliff.

   1. _____

2. The trends in architecture are to design homes to complement the site, _____, and retain privacy.

   2. _____

3. _____ architectural design combines traditional and contemporary characteristics and is reminiscent of past styles.

   3. _____

4. New materials and techniques help homes to be _____ and weather resistant.

   4. _____

5. Older, structurally solid homes may be _____ to their original beauty.

   5. _____

6. The _____ is made from fiberglass-skin wedges which have an R-value of 25.

   6. _____

PART III: SHORT ANSWER/LISTING: Provide brief answers to the following questions.

1. The distinguishing construction technique of the Garrison home has three advantages. List each:

   A. _____

   _____

   B. _____

   _____

   C. _____

   _____

2. List three trends in residential architecture which are prevalent today.

   A. _____

   B. _____

   C. _____

   _____

PART IV: PROBLEMS/ACTIVITIES

1. Start a notebook of architectural designs. Collect pictures from magazines, newspapers, advertising pamphlets, or use your own photographs to illustrate the various traditional and contemporary house styles. Include pictures of the current trends in architecture as well. Label the style in each picture and list the identifying features of each design.

Chapter 2

BASIC HOUSE DESIGN

Text Pages 25-36

Name _____   Course _____

Date_____   Score _____

PART I: MULTIPLE CHOICE: Select the best answer and place its letter in the blank at right.

1. Which of the following is a feature of the one-story ranch design?
   A. Minimal heating costs.
   B. Economical to build.
   C. Easily adapted to indoor-outdoor living.
   D. Limited hall space.

1. _____

2. Which of the following basic house designs is suitable for older or handicapped persons?
   A. One-story ranch design.
   B. One-and-one-half-story design.
   C. Two-story design.
   D. Split-level design.

2. _____

3. Outside maintenance is generally easy on a one-story ranch design because of:
   A. Small outside wall area.
   B. Low-pitched roof.
   C. It is built on a sloping lot.
   D. All of the above.

3. _____

4. Dormers are usually added to this design to achieve more livable space.
   A. One-story ranch design.
   B. One-and-one-half-story design.
   C. Two-story design.
   D. Split-level design.

4. _____

5. Advantages of the one-and-one-half-story design include:
   A. Attic may be expanded to achieve more livable space.
   B. Dormers may be added for light and ventilation.
   C. Heating costs are minimized.
   D. All of the above.

5. _____

6. Which of the following best describes a two-story design?
   A. Little hall space is needed, and the sleeping, living, and service areas are on different levels.
   B. About one-third of the ceiling is directly under the roof, so adequate ventilation and insulation should be provided.
   C. It is economical to build, requires a smaller lot, and has a small roof and foundation area compared to interior space of most other designs.
   D. It is built on one level. Thus, patios, porches, and terraces are possible outside any room.

6. _____

9

7. Advantages of the two-story design include:
   A. Heating is relatively simple and economical because heat naturally rises from the first to the second floor.
   B. This style is popular today because many variations on the basic design are possible.
   C. Exterior maintenance is simple and requires no special equipment.
   D. The design easily meets the needs of a retired couple or newly married couple.

7. _____

8. This house design lends itself to easy cooling since the ceiling is not directly under the roof. Several windows provide effective ventilation.
   A. One-story ranch design.
   B. One-and-one-half-story design.
   C. Two-story design.
   D. Split-level design.

8. _____

9. Which of the following house designs takes advantage of a sloping or hilly lot?
   A. One-story ranch design.
   B. One-and-one-half-story design.
   C. Two-story design.
   D. Split-level design.

9. _____

10. The family room, garage, and shop are commonly found on this level in a split-level design:
    A. Basement level.
    B. Intermediate level.
    C. Living level.
    D. Sleeping level.

10. _____

11. Which of the following is a feature of the split-level design?
    A. Easily accommodates patios and terraces on more than one level of the house.
    B. The design makes efficient use of space.
    C. May be built with either a basement or crawl space.
    D. All of the above.

11. _____

PART II: SHORT ANSWER/LISTING: Provide brief answers to the following questions.

1. Without proper design and planning, heating may be a problem in a split-level design. What steps may be taken to solve the problem?

   _____

   _____

2. Name the three variations of the split-level design.

   A. _____

   B. _____

   C. _____

3. Which variation of the split-level design is most suitable for a lot that is high in front and low in back?

   _____

4. What is unique about the entry of a traditional split-level?

   _____

Name _____

5. Traffic circulation should be planned for maximum efficiency. Explain why the foyer and garage play an important role in planning a house.

_____

_____

_____

_____

_____

6. Name the four basic house designs.

A. _____

B. _____

C. _____

D. _____

PART III: PROBLEMS/ACTIVITIES

1.

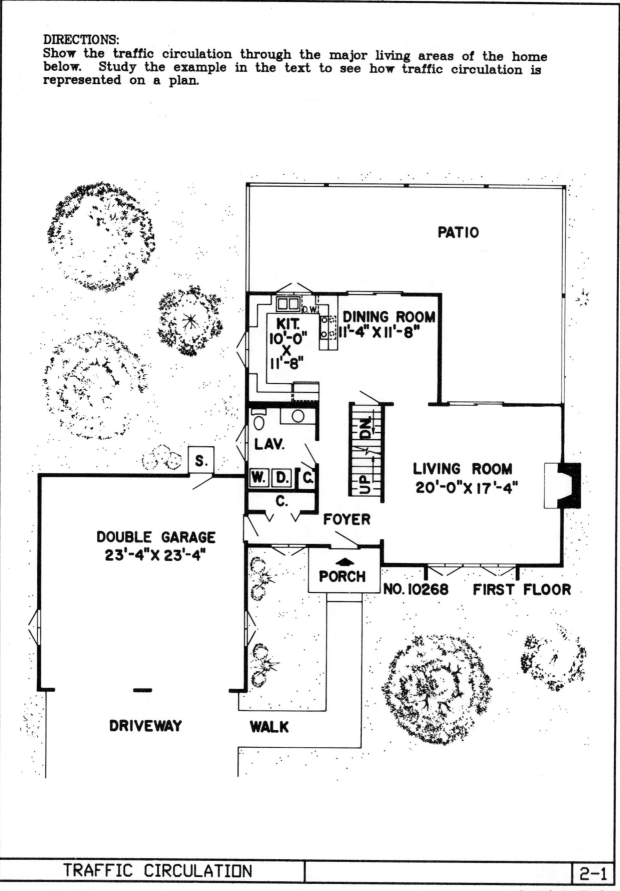

DIRECTIONS:
Show the traffic circulation through the major living areas of the home below. Study the example in the text to see how traffic circulation is represented on a plan.

PATIO

KIT.
10'-0"
X
11'-8"

D.W.

DINING ROOM
11'-4" X 11'-8"

LAV.

DN.

UP

LIVING ROOM
20'-0"X 17'-4"

S.

W. D. C.

C.

FOYER

DOUBLE GARAGE
23'-4"X 23'-4"

PORCH

NO. 10268   FIRST FLOOR

DRIVEWAY   WALK

TRAFFIC CIRCULATION   2-1

Name _____

2. Collect pictures or photographs of the four basic house designs you have studied in this chapter. Add them to your notebook which you began in Chapter 1. Write a brief description of each style.

3. From magazines or newspapers select a floor plan showing good traffic circulation. Write an explanation of why the plan represents good traffic path design.

Chapter 3

PRIMARY CONSIDERATIONS

Text Pages 37-48

Name _____   Course _____

Date_____   Score _____

PART I: COMPLETION: Complete each sentence with the proper response. Place your answer on the blank in the right column.

1. The house is the biggest item in terms of home investment. The _____ ranks second and should be evaluated carefully to realize its potential as part of the home and surroundings.

   1. _____

2. A _____ design is better suited to a hilly or sloping site.

   2. _____

3. The structure should appear to be part of the _____.

   3. _____

4. A competent attorney should examine the deed and _____ before the site is purchased.

   4. _____

5. _____ ordinances determine whether commercial, multi-family, or single-family structures may be built on the intended site.

   5. _____

6. The type of house which can be built on any given site is subject to local _____ codes.

   6. _____

7. Information on permit costs, inspections, or regulations may be obtained from the local _____ inspector or local building department.

   7. _____

8. The _____ is just as important as size of the lot in determining construction possibilities.

   8. _____

9. Family _____ is a major consideration in house design.

   9. _____

10. Several considerations in planning a residential structure include exterior design, size, and _____ as well as salability.

    10. _____

11. A home designed around _____ sizes results in less wasted material.

    11. _____

12. The size of plywood and paneling is generally _____.

    12. _____

13. Exterior walls should be modular lengths or multiples of 2 or _____ ft.

    13. _____

14. Plan interior rooms around standard sizes of carpeting which are available in widths of 12 or _____ ft.

    14. _____

15. The _____ of living provided by the structure is a measure of the architect's success in solving a problem.

    15. _____

PART II: MATCHING: Match the correct term with its description listed below. Place the corresponding letter on the blank at right.

A. Building codes
B. Deed
C. Easements
D. Modular construction
E. Restrictions

F. Specifications
G. Surveyor
H. Title search
I. Topographical drawings

1. It determines if there are any legal claims against the property.

1. _____

2. This document shows any restrictions or easements attached to the property.

2. _____

3. May specify style and size of house which can be built on the property, as well as landscaping and overall cost of the house.

3. _____

4. May allow utilities to cross the property or may prevent the filling in of a low area which must remain for drainage purposes.

4. _____

5. Involves plumbing, electrical, and building standards.

5. _____

6. A professional who checks measurements and lot lines to determine lot boundaries.

6. _____

7. Illustrates slope, contour, size, shape, elevation, trees, rocks, and soil conditions.

7. _____

8. Uses building materials based on 4 in. units of measurement.

8. _____

9. Describes the quality of materials and workmanship.

9. _____

PART III: MULTIPLE CHOICE: Select the best answer and place its letter in the blank at the right.

1. This plan locates switches, convenience outlets, ceiling outlet fixtures, TV jacks, service entrance location, panel box, and general information concerning circuits and special installations.
   A. Foundation plan.
   B. Plumbing plan.
   C. Plot plan.
   D. Electrical plan.

1. _____

2. These drawings include specifics of kitchens, stairs, chimneys, fireplaces, windows and doors, foundation walls, and items of special construction.
   A. Construction details.
   B. Elevations.
   C. Pictorial presentation.
   D. Furniture plan.

2. _____

3. Which of the following items will be found on a plot plan?
   A. The direction of joists and major supporting members.
   B. A description of how the structure has been designed to accommodate future expansion.
   C. Location of the house on the site, utilities, topographical features, site dimensions, and other buildings on the property.
   D. Exterior and interior walls, doors, windows, patios, walks, decks, fireplaces, mechanical equipment, built-in cabinets and appliances.

3. _____

Name _____

4. Which of the following best describes the foundation plan?
   A. Typical orthographic projection showing the exterior features of the building such as placement of windows and doors, type of exterior materials used, steps, chimney, roof lines, and other exterior details.
   B. Shows size and material of the support structure. May serve as the basement plan. Gives information pertaining to excavation, waterproofing, and supporting structures.
   C. Locates and identifies plants and other elements on the site surrounding the house.
   D. Shows rafters, ceiling joists, and supporting members.

4. _____

5. This plan shows such features as the hot and cold water system, waste lines, vents, storage tank, placement of plumbing fixtures, and cleanouts.
   A. Heating and cooling plan.
   B. Plumbing plan.
   C. Electrical plan.
   D. Expansion plan.

5. _____

6. A plan which illustrates all exterior and interior walls, doors, windows, patios, walks, decks, fireplaces, mechanical equipment, built-in cabinets, and appliances.
   A. Foundation plan.
   B. Furniture plan.
   C. Floor plan.
   D. Roof plan.

6. _____

PART IV: SHORT ANSWER/LISTING: Provide brief answers to the following questions.

1. The community is a key element in bringing satisfaction and happiness to a homeowner. List the points to be considered when evaluating a neighborhood.

   A. _____
   _____

   B. _____
   _____

   C. _____
   _____

   D. _____
   _____

   E. _____
   _____

   F. _____
   _____

   G. _____
   _____

   H. _____
   _____

(Continued)

I. _____

_____

J. _____

_____

K. _____

_____

2. List the factors that affect the price of a building site which should be evaluated.

A. _____

_____

B. _____

C. _____

3. What factors (in addition to those considered for a city lot) should be taken into account if the lot is out of town?

A. _____

_____

_____

_____

B. _____

_____

4. List the individual and family activities which should be provided for in the design of a house.

A. _____ I. _____

B. _____ J. _____

C. _____ K. _____

D. _____ L. _____

E. _____ M. _____

F. _____ N. _____

G. _____ O. _____

H. _____ P. _____

5. The set of construction drawings plus the specifications form the basis for a legal contract between the owner and the builder. Name the drawings commonly found in a set of plans.

A. _____

B. _____

C. _____

D. _____

E. _____

F. _____

G. _____

Name _____

PART V: PROBLEMS/ACTIVITIES

1. If you live in a city or town, evaluate your neighborhood on the following points.

   A. _____
   _____

   B. _____

   C. _____
   _____

   D. _____

   E. _____
   _____

   F. _____
   _____

   G. _____
   _____

   H. _____

   I. _____

2. Select a site where a new house is being built. (Seek permission before entering the site.) Sketch a site plan and show the prominent topographical features such as the contours, elevations, trees, property lines, etc.

3. Select a floor plan from a magazine, newspaper, or other source and record the square footage dedicated to the following activities.

A. Food preparation _____   I. Sleeping _____

B. Dining _____   J. Relaxing _____

C. Entertaining _____   K. Working _____

D. Recreation _____   L. Storage _____

E. Hobbies _____   M. Bathing _____

F. Laundering _____   N. Housekeeping _____

G. Studying _____   O. Planning _____

H. Dressing _____   P. Accommodating guests _____

Chapter 4

DRAWING INSTRUMENTS AND TECHNIQUES

Text Pages 49-72

Name _____   Course _____

Date_____   Score _____

PART I: MATCHING: Match the correct term with its description listed below. Place the corresponding letter on the blank at right.

A. Alphabet of lines
B. Burnish plates
C. CADD software
D. Computer symbols library
E. Data processing unit
F. Dimension lines

G. Drafting tapes
H. Grids
I. Illustration boards
J. Orthographic projection
K. Photoplotters
L. Technical fountain pens

1. Lines used to show size and location.

1. _____

2. A drafting aid representing areas of interest or emphasizing certain elements and may be used on vellum, plastic overlays, or illustration board.

2. _____

3. These drafting aids are useful in sketching idea plans, in modular construction drawings, or in drawing perspectives.

3. _____

4. An underlay device used to save time in drawing siding, bricks, trees, and roofing.

4. _____

5. A series of standard symbols specifically designed for use in architecture, engineering, and construction drawings.

5. _____

6. A means of representing an object from a point at infinity.

6. _____

7. Use for presentation plans.

7. _____

8. Used by the drafter to letter and draw straight and curved lines in ink.

8. _____

9. Executes the commands given the computer by the operator or through specific programs.

9. _____

10. Details the operations to be performed on the data by the computer.

10. _____

11. An output device which prints printed-circuit-board masters.

11. _____

12. The line symbols used in drawing.

12. _____

PART II: MULTIPLE CHOICE: Select the best answer and place its letter in the blank at right.

1. A standard drawing sheet size which measures 9 x 12 in. is designated by the letter:
   A. A.
   B. B.
   C. C.
   D. D.

1. _____

2. "C" size paper is what size?
   A. 12 x 18 in.
   B. 18 x 24 in.
   C. 24 x 36 in.
   D. 36 x 48 in.

2. _____

3. The procedure for drawing a horizontal line with a straightedge for a right-handed person is:
   A. Hold the blade with the right hand and draw from right to left.
   B. Clamp the blade to the drawing table and draw from right to left.
   C. Hold the blade with the left hand and draw from left to right.
   D. All of the above.

3. _____

4. In drafting terminology, a "half size" drawing means:
   A. 1/4" on the drawing equals 1'-0".
   B. 1/2" on the drawing equals 1'-0".
   C. The drawing is only half as large as the object in real life.
   D. None of the above.

4. _____

5. A modern computer-aided design and drafting (CADD) system can:
   A. Generate schedules.
   B. Generate analyses.
   C. Draft architectural designs.
   D. All of the above.

5. _____

6. CADD system hardcopy output devices include:
   A. Printers.
   B. Pen plotters.
   C. Electrostatic plotters and photoplotters.
   D. All of the above.

6. _____

7. Most residential architectural drawings require this size paper:
   A. "A".
   B. "B".
   C. "C".
   D. "D".

7. _____

8. Lines used to indicate features above the cutting plane, such as wall cabinets in a kitchen or an archway, are:
   A. Object lines.
   B. Border lines.
   C. Hidden lines.
   D. Center lines.

8. _____

9. Lines used to indicate symmetrical objects, such as windows and doors, are:
   A. Center lines.
   B. Hidden lines.
   C. Border lines.
   D. Object lines.

9. _____

10. Pencil lead normally used for lettering:
    A. 4H.
    B. 6H.
    C. H.
    D. All of the above.

10. _____

Name _____

11. Pencil lead generally used for construction lines and guidelines:　　11. _____
    A. 6H.
    B. 2H.
    C. 4H.
    D. H.

PART III: COMPLETION: Complete each sentence with the proper response. Place your answer on the blank in the right column.

1. The three principal views in orthographic projection are the _____, front, and right side views.　　1. _____

2. The front view of an object in mechanical drawing is the same as the _____ elevation in architectural drawing.　　2. _____

3. The hardness number is printed on the _____ of a wood pencil and along the _____ in mechanical pencils.　　3. _____

4. Most architectural drafters use tracing paper, _____, or drafting film.　　4. _____

5. T-squares are manufactured from wood, metal, _____, and combinations of these materials.　　5. _____

6. Drafting tables usually have a _____ machine or straightedge permanently attached to be used for drawing horizontal lines.　　6. _____

7. Metal protractors with a _____ scale will measure accurately to one minute.　　7. _____

8. The divisions of the architect's scale are based on _____ units to the foot, and the engineer's scale is based on ten units to the inch.　　8. _____

9. One-half scale means that _____ on the drawing is equal to 1'-0" on the object.　　9. _____

10. Use _____ or H lead in the compass and keep it sharpened to a fine point.　　10. _____

11. _____ devices are used when uniformity of letters is essential.　　11. _____

12. AEC stands for architectural, _____, and construction.　　12. _____

13. The _____ or control section of the computer contains programs that are currently in use or on-line.　　13. _____

14. A _____ plotter produces a very accurate drawing in ink on a variety of materials—paper, vellum, or polyester film.　　14. _____

15. Thin lines used to show that not all of the part is drawn are _____ break lines.　　15. _____

16. _____ lines or crosshatch lines are used to show that the feature has been sectioned.　　16. _____

17. Two lines that should be drawn lightly and are for the drafter's use only are guidelines and _____ lines. All other lines should be dark in order to reproduce well.　　17. _____

18. Capital rather than _____ case letters are commonly used in architectural lettering.　　18. _____

PART IV: SHORT ANSWER/LISTING: Provide brief answers to the following questions.

1. List the elevations which architectural drafters normally draw.

   A. _____

   B. _____

   C. _____

   D. _____

2. What are the factors to consider when choosing an eraser?

   A. _____

   _____

   B. _____

   _____

3. Triangles are used to draw lines that are not horizontal. Name the two triangles most commonly used by drafters.

   A. _____

   B. _____

4. Name the two different styles of common protractors used by architectural drafters.

   A. _____

   B. _____

5. What are the two most typical uses of dividers?

   A. _____

   B. _____

   _____

6. Explain the procedure for drawing arcs using a compass.

   _____

7. Explain the procedure for drawing a curve using an irregular curve.

   _____

   _____

8. The pen plotter is an output device popular with architectural drafters. What are the two different types of pen plotters?

   A. _____

   B. _____

9. What is the purpose of a drawing?

   _____

10. Name the heavy lines that are used to show where the object is to be sectioned.

   _____

11. What is a good rule to follow in spacing words?

   _____

1.

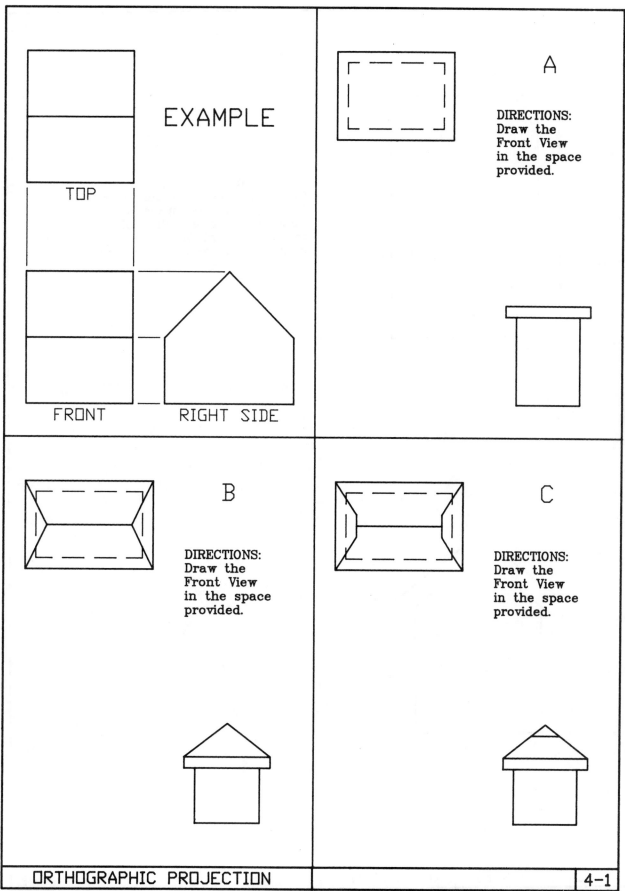

EXAMPLE

TOP

FRONT   RIGHT SIDE

A

DIRECTIONS:
Draw the
Front View
in the space
provided.

B

DIRECTIONS:
Draw the
Front View
in the space
provided.

C

DIRECTIONS:
Draw the
Front View
in the space
provided.

ORTHOGRAPHIC PROJECTION   4-1

Copyright Goodheart-Willcox Co., Inc.

2.

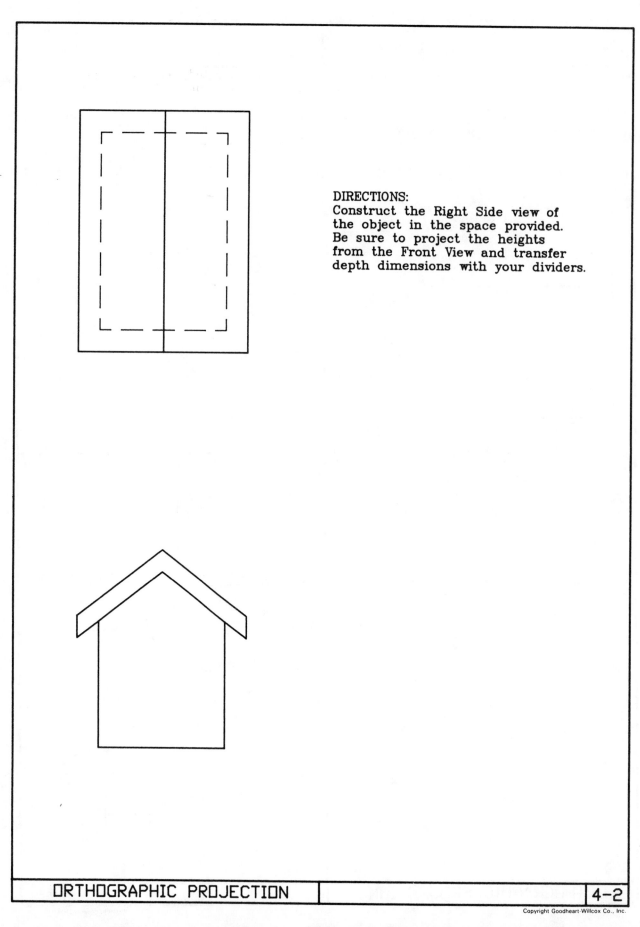

DIRECTIONS:
Construct the Right Side view of
the object in the space provided.
Be sure to project the heights
from the Front View and transfer
depth dimensions with your dividers.

ORTHOGRAPHIC PROJECTION | 4-2

3.

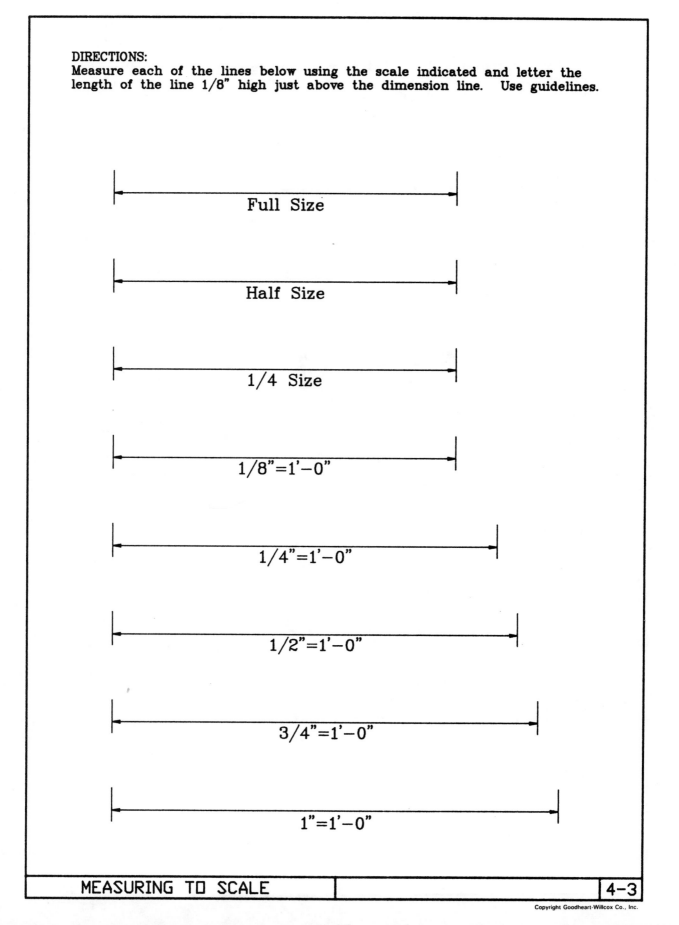

DIRECTIONS:
Measure each of the lines below using the scale indicated and letter the length of the line 1/8" high just above the dimension line.   Use guidelines.

Full Size

Half Size

1/4 Size

1/8"=1'-0"

1/4"=1'-0"

1/2"=1'-0"

3/4"=1'-0"

1"=1'-0"

MEASURING TO SCALE   4-3

4.

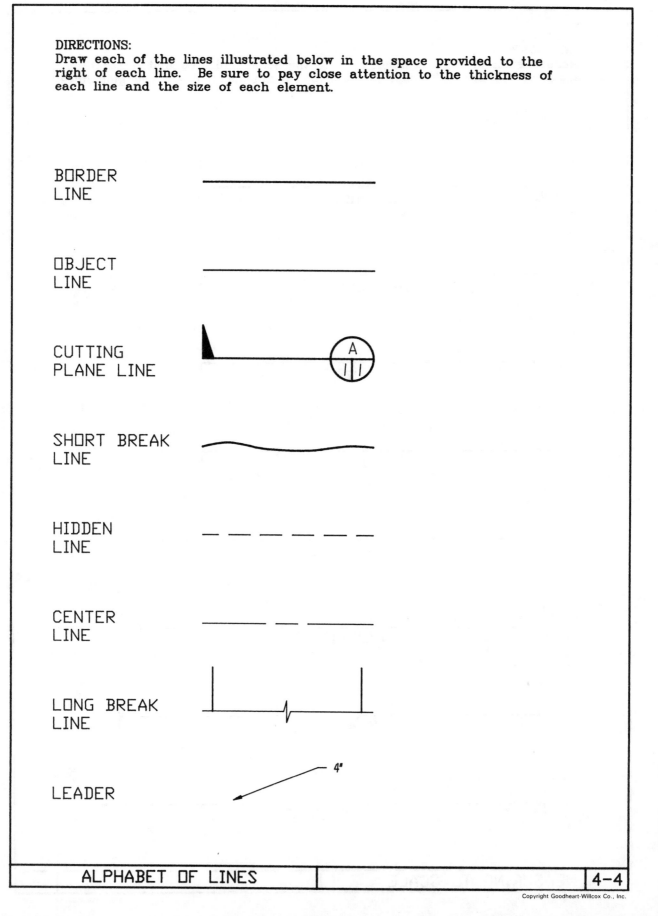

DIRECTIONS:
Draw each of the lines illustrated below in the space provided to the right of each line. Be sure to pay close attention to the thickness of each line and the size of each element.

BORDER
LINE

OBJECT
LINE

CUTTING
PLANE LINE

SHORT BREAK
LINE

HIDDEN
LINE

CENTER
LINE

LONG BREAK
LINE

LEADER

ALPHABET OF LINES   4-4

5.

DIRECTIONS:
Practice lettering the alphabet and numbers using a style similar to one illustrated in the text. Practice "your" style until it becomes a part of you and flows easily.

ARCHITECTURAL LETTERING | | 4—5

Chapter 5

ROOM PLANNING, SLEEPING AREA

Text Pages 73-88

Name _____   Course _____

Date_____   Score _____

PART I: MULTIPLE CHOICE: Select the best answer and place its letter in the blank at right.

1. Approximately _____ of the house is devoted to the sleep-
   ing area, which includes bedrooms, baths, dressing rooms, and
   nurseries.
   A. 1/2.
   B. 1/4.
   C. 1/3.
   D. 3/4.

   1. _____

2. The _____ normally determines the number of bedrooms
   a house will have.
   A. Size of the family.
   B. Size of the neighborhood.
   C. Number of guests.
   D. None of the above.

   2. _____

3. Generally, _____ homes have the most sales potential.
   A. One-bedroom.
   B. Two-bedroom.
   C. Three-bedroom.
   D. Four-bedroom.

   3. _____

4. In a split bedroom plan, the _____ is separated from the
   remaining bedrooms for additional privacy.
   A. Smallest bedroom.
   B. Nursery.
   C. Guest bedroom.
   D. Master bedroom.

   4. _____

5. The FHA (Federal Housing Administration) recommends that
   the minimum size for a bedroom should be _____ sq. ft.
   A. 50.
   B. 100.
   C. 150.
   D. 200.

   5. _____

6. The largest bedroom is usually the _____.
   A. Nursery.
   B. Children's bedroom.
   C. Master bedroom.
   D. Guest bedroom.

   6. _____

7. The minimum bedroom closet depth is _____ ft.
   A. 1.
   B. 2.
   C. 3.
   D. 4.

7. _____

8. The most desirable location for a closet is _____.
   A. On an outside wall.
   B. In the hall near the bedroom.
   C. Near the bedroom entrance.
   D. None of the above.

8. _____

9. Closet doors may be _____.
   A. Sliding.
   B. Bi-fold.
   C. Flush.
   D. All of the above.

9. _____

10. An ideal bedroom will have windows _____.
    A. On two walls.
    B. On one wall.
    C. Low on the wall.
    D. Evenly spaced on the walls.

10. _____

11. Bedroom doors should be _____ wide to accommodate a wheelchair.
    A. 2'-6".
    B. 2'-8".
    C. 2'-10".
    D. 3'-0".

11. _____

12. The best location for a bedroom door is _____.
    A. On a long wall.
    B. Near a corner.
    C. In the center of a wall.
    D. On an exterior wall.

12. _____

PART II: COMPLETION: Complete each sentence with the proper response. Place your answer on the blank in the right column.

1. Two-story, split-level, and ranch designs are more functional with at least _____ baths.

1. _____

2. A bath should be located near the living and _____ areas of the home.

2. _____

3. A water closet and lavatory comprise a _____ bath.

3. _____

4. A water closet, lavatory, and shower generally comprise a _____ bath.

4. _____

5. A minimum size bath is _____ by 8 ft.

5. _____

6. In addition to the lavatory, water closet, and tub, some bathrooms have a hygiene fixture called a _____.

6. _____

7. A well-lighted _____ should be placed above the sink.

7. _____

8. Provide space at least _____ wide for a water closet.

8. _____

9. The most popular size for a bathtub is _____.

9. _____

10. Prefabricated shower stalls are available in metal, _____, and plastics.

10. _____

Name _____

11. Marble, _____, and ceramic tile showers are usually more costly than prefabricated units.

11. _____

12. Storage and countertop space can be provided by installing sink cabinets or _____.

12. _____

13. Larger bathrooms may accommodate _____ or saunas.

13. _____

14. An _____ fan should be located near the water closet and tub.

14. _____

15. _____ should be placed out of reach from the tub.

15. _____

16. A _____ (ground fault circuit interrupter) receptacle should be installed in the bathroom.

16. _____

17. Bathroom doors are generally _____ or 2'-4" in width.

17. _____

PART III: SHORT ANSWER/LISTING: Provide brief answers to the following questions.

1. List the steps in planning the furniture arrangement of a bedroom.

   A. _____

   B. _____

   C. _____

   D. _____

   E. _____

   F. _____

2. Name three reasons why the decor of a bathroom should be well planned.

   A. _____

   B. _____

   C. _____

3. Name several considerations to provide safety in the bath.

   A. _____

   B. _____

   C. _____

   D. _____

   E. _____

4. In addition to the normal activities carried out in the bathroom, list two others a larger bath might accommodate.

   A. _____

   B. _____

5. Name three basic areas of a home.

   A. _____

   B. _____

   C. _____

1.

DIRECTIONS:
Using colored pencils, crayons, felt tip markers, or adhesive−backed (semi−transparent) overlays, shade each of the three basic areas of the house using three colors. Include a legend for clarity.

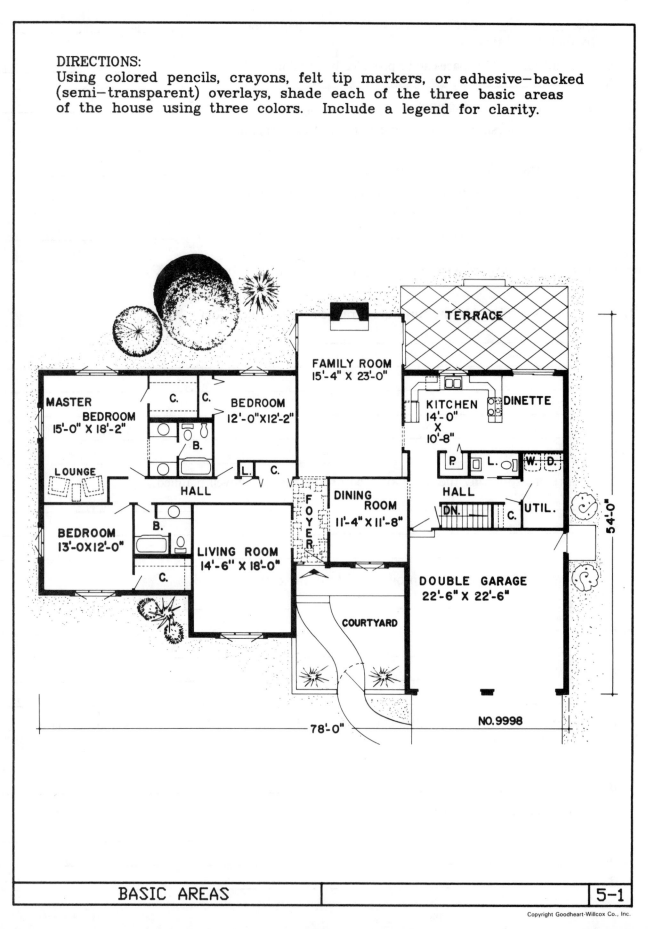

BASIC AREAS

5-1

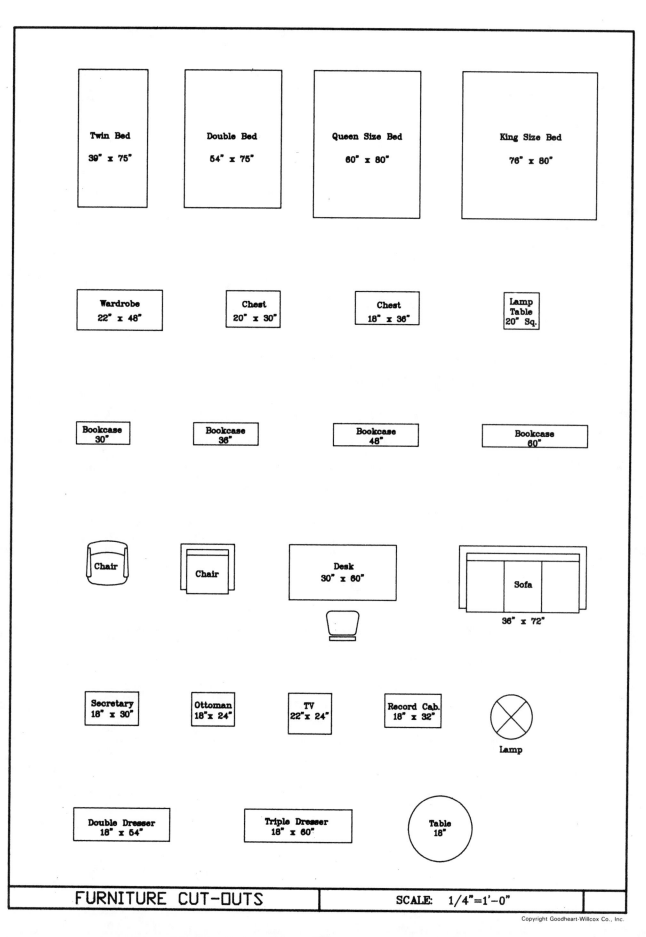

Twin Bed
39" x 75"

Double Bed
54" x 75"

Queen Size Bed
60" x 80"

King Size Bed
76" x 80"

Wardrobe
22" x 48"

Chest
20" x 30"

Chest
18" x 36"

Lamp
Table
20" Sq.

Bookcase
30"

Bookcase
36"

Bookcase
48"

Bookcase
60"

Chair

Chair

Desk
30" x 60"

Sofa
36" x 72"

Secretary
18" x 30"

Ottoman
18" x 24"

TV
22" x 24"

Record Cab.
18" x 32"

Lamp

Double Dresser
18" x 54"

Triple Dresser
18" x 60"

Table
18"

FURNITURE CUT-OUTS   SCALE: 1/4"=1'-0"

2.

DIRECTIONS:
Remove the "Furniture Cut-Outs" page from your workbook and
carefully cut out each furniture piece for use in this assignment
or use a furniture template. Plan a functional arrangement for
each of the bedrooms below using the cut-outs or template.
Observe the spacing shown in Fig. 5-12 in the text. Trace the
location of each item and label.

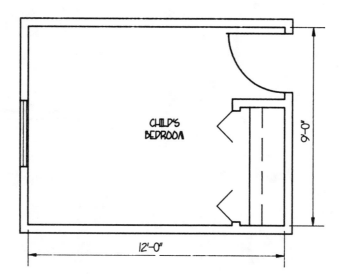

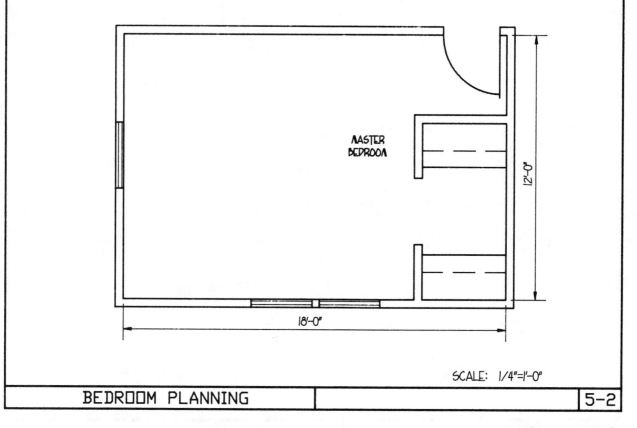

SCALE: 1/4"=1'-0"

| BEDROOM PLANNING | | 5-2 |

3.

DIRECTIONS:
Plan a functional arrangement of fixtures for each of the baths shown below. Study Figs. 5−30 through 5−34 in your text for arrangement ideas and clearances. Use a template to draw the fixtures.

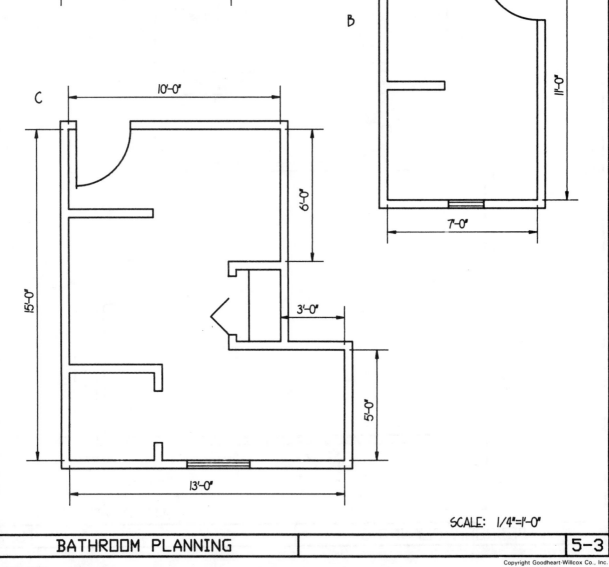

A

8'-0"

5'-0"

B

11'-0"

7'-0"

C

10'-0"

15'-0"

6'-0"

3'-0"

5'-0"

13'-0"

SCALE: 1/4"=1'-0"

BATHROOM PLANNING

5-3

4.

DIRECTIONS:
Plan a modern bathroom which meets the following specifications:
> Covers approximately 250 square feet of space
> Provides for storage and dressing
> Includes the standard fixtures——water closet, bathtub, sink cabinet or vanity, bidet, and shower stall
> Drawn at a scale of 1/4"=1'-0".

BATHROOM PLANNING | | 5-4

5. Collect pictures of bedrooms and bathrooms to add to your notebook. With each, attach a note stating what you like about the picture. This could be arrangement of the room, style of furniture or decoration, color scheme, etc.

Chapter 6

ROOM PLANNING, LIVING AREA

Text Pages 89-126

Name _____   Course _____

Date_____   Score _____

PART I: COMPLETION: Complete each sentence with the proper response. Place your answer on the blank in the right column.

1. An average size living room contains approximately _____ sq. ft.

    1. _____

2. Analyzing the functions to be performed in the living room helps determine the _____ needed.

    2. _____

3. To discourage "thru traffic," slightly raise or _____ the living room level.

    3. _____

4. Locating the living room at grade level lets activities flow to outside _____ or terraces.

    4. _____

5. Rather than opening up directly to an outside entrance, the living room should open up to a _____ or hallway.

    5. _____

6. Locate a living room on the _____ side of the house in warm climates to take advantage of shaded, cooler areas.

    6. _____

7. Using large windows or _____ glass doors increases a feeling of "spaciousness."

    7. _____

8. The living room should be located near the _____ room or the family room.

    8. _____

9. A _____ such as a flower planter, furniture arrangement, screen, or change in level may serve to separate the dining and living rooms.

    9. _____

10. To minimize the weak points and emphasize the good points of a room, use color, _____, and design.

    10. _____

PART II: MULTIPLE CHOICE Select the best answer and place its letter in the blank at right.

1. A small dining room would require approximately _____ sq. ft. to seat four people.
    A. 100.
    B. 120.
    C. 150.
    D. 175.

    1. _____

2. A medium size dining room should seat _____ people.
    A. 6 to 8.
    B. 8 to 10.
    C. 10 to 12.
    D. 12 to 14.

    2. _____

3. Allow _____ between the back of the chair and the wall for serving in the dining room.
   A. 1'-0".
   B. 2'-0".
   C. 3'-0".
   D. 4'-0".

3. _____

4. An ideal dining room location would be one between the _____ and the kitchen.

   A. Foyer.
   B. Master bedroom.
   C. Living room.
   D. Utility room.

4. _____

5. A(n) _____ makes the rooms appear larger.
   A. Two-story plan.
   B. Ranch-style plan.
   C. Closed plan.
   D. Open plan.

5. _____

6. The color scheme in the dining room is frequently the same as the _____.

   A. Living room.
   B. Kitchen.
   C. Bedroom.
   D. Bathroom.

6. _____

7. A house may have this type of entry.
   A. Main entry.
   B. Service entry.
   C. Special purpose.
   D. All of the above.

7. _____

8. A _____ entry should be impressive because it is the first part of the house that guests see. It should be centrally located to provide easy access to various parts of the house.
   A. Special purpose.
   B. Main.
   C. Service.
   D. Side.

8. _____

9. Glass side panels in the entry may provide _____.
   A. Visibility.
   B. Natural light.
   C. Design.
   D. All of the above.

9. _____

10. Courts may be used to _____.
    A. Direct traffic to various areas of the house.
    B. Divide the house into separate areas.
    C. Provide natural light to an interior part of the house which has no exterior wall space.
    D. All of the above.

10. _____

Name _____

PART III: MATCHING: Match the correct term with its description listed below. Place the corresponding letter on the blank at right.

A. Courts
B. Deck
C. Double doors
D. Entry
E. Family recreation room
F. Foyer
G. Foyer coat closet
H. Foyer decor

I. Foyer floor
J. Mirror wall
K. Mudroom
L. Patios
M. Play patio
N. Porches
O. Sliding doors

1. The lines of the house should be compatible with this area.

1. _____

2. To place more emphasis on the entry and increase its function, use these.

2. _____

3. Is commonly added between the service entry and the kitchen.

3. _____

4. Are generally used in special-purpose entries.

4. _____

5. Where guests are greeted and coats are removed.

5. _____

6. Materials used in this area should be able to withstand water and mud.

6. _____

7. FHA minimum size is 2 x 3 ft.

7. _____

8. An accessory used to create an open feeling in a foyer.

8. _____

9. Reflects materials and color scheme used in adjacent areas.

9. _____

10. Its purpose is to provide a place where the family can play or pursue hobbies.

10. _____

11. Located at ground level near the house, but not structurally connected to it.

11. _____

12. Generally designed for use by children and adults for physical activities that require more open space.

12. _____

13. Raised above grade level and structurally connected to the house.

13. _____

14. An uncovered porch.

14. _____

15. Areas totally or partially enclosed by walls or roof.

15. _____

PART IV: SHORT ANSWER/LISTING: Provide brief answers to the following questions.

1. Name rooms that are generally considered to be part of the living area.

A. _____

B. _____

C. _____

D. _____

E. _____

F. _____

2. List five factors you should consider when planning a living room.

   A. _____

   B. _____

   C. _____

   D. _____

   E. _____

3. What three factors affect the dining room size?

   A. _____

   B. _____

   C. _____

4. What pieces of furniture are frequently used in the dining room?

   A. _____

   B. _____

   C. _____

   D. _____

   E. _____

5. Name two ways in which protection from the weather can be provided in an entry.

   A. _____

   B. _____

6. List the factors that should determine the size of the foyer.

   A. _____

   B. _____

   C. _____

   D. _____

7. Name four places where a family recreation room is generally located.

   A. _____

   B. _____

   C. _____

   D. _____

8. When should rugs and deep pile carpeting not be used in a family recreation room?

   _____

9. Name four types of special-purpose rooms.

   A. _____

   B. _____

   C. _____

   D. _____

Name _____

10. What requirements should be considered when planning a darkroom?

    A. _____

    B. _____

    C. _____

    D. _____

11. List three types of activities normally performed on patios.

    A. _____

    B. _____

    C. _____

12. List some popular materials used in constructing patios.

    A. _____

    B. _____

    C. _____

    D. _____

13. Where should relaxing patios be located?

    _____

14. Will a living or entertaining patio most likely be located to the front or back of the house?

    _____

15. List some features which may be used to add beauty to a patio.

    A. _____

    B. _____

    C. _____

16. Where is a play patio most likely located?

    _____

    _____

17. What features are sometimes added to porches to increase their usefulness?

    _____

1.

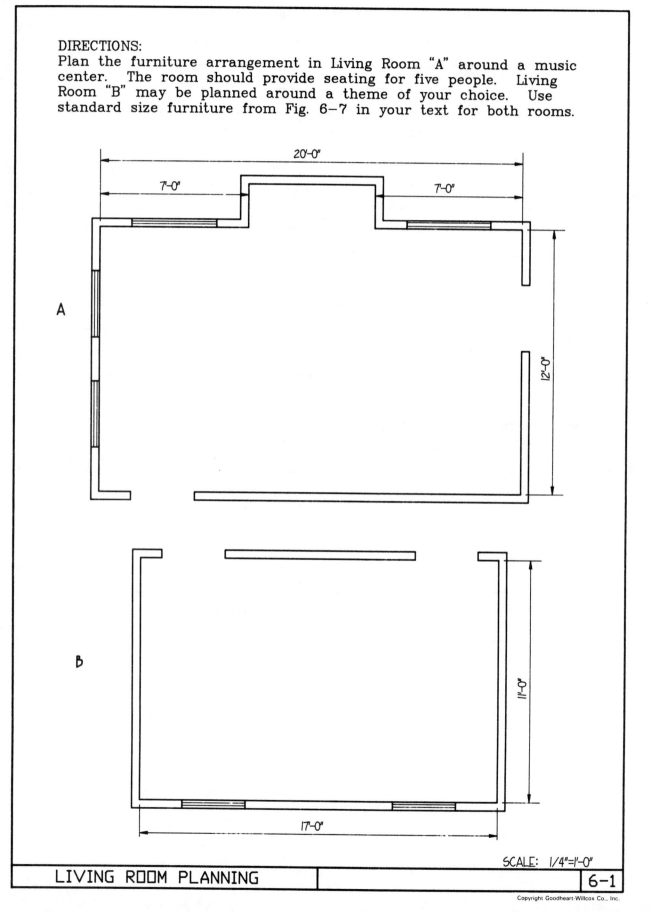

DIRECTIONS:
Plan the furniture arrangement in Living Room "A" around a music center. The room should provide seating for five people. Living Room "B" may be planned around a theme of your choice. Use standard size furniture from Fig. 6-7 in your text for both rooms.

A

B

SCALE: 1/4"=1'-0"

LIVING ROOM PLANNING

6-1

2.

DIRECTIONS:
Plan an arrangement of the following furniture pieces (table with 6 chairs, buffet, or china cabinet) in the dining room below. In the remaining space, design a medium size dining room (180—200 square feet) which provides seating for 8 and storage for dishes, table linens, silverware, and accessories.

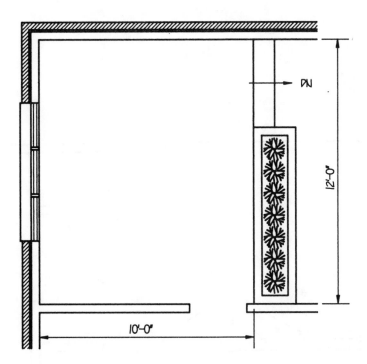

SCALE: 1/4"=1'-0"

DINING ROOM PLANNING   6—2

3.

DIRECTIONS:
Complete the entry/foyer below by adding the following: slate floor, brick veneer exterior, entry arrow, plant in foyer, and closet shelf and rod.

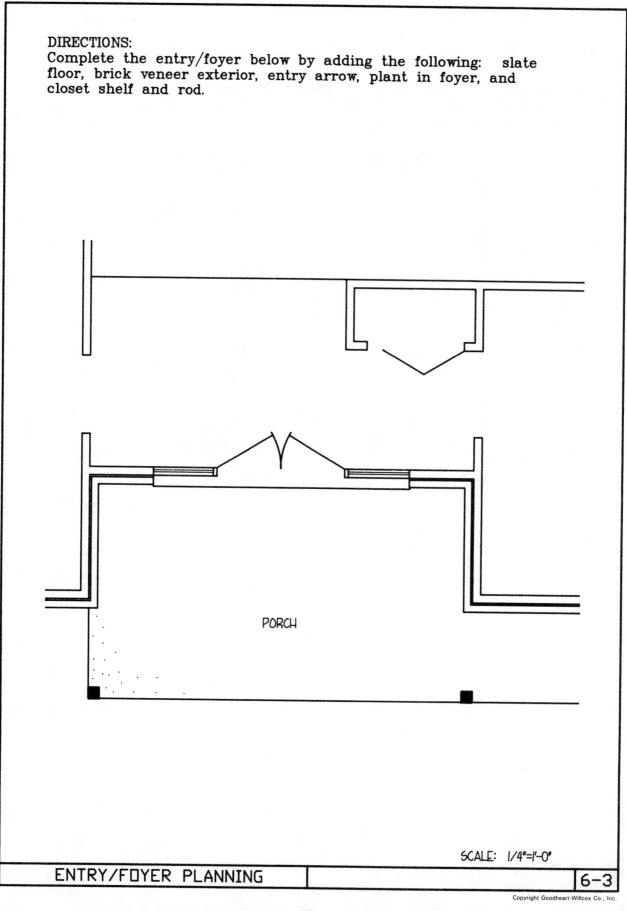

PORCH

SCALE: 1/4"=1'-0"

ENTRY/FOYER PLANNING | | 6-3

4.

DIRECTIONS:
Plan a functional arrangement of furniture in the Family Recreation Room below which includes a sofa, upholstered chair, coffee table, lamp table and lamp, and built—in cabinets along the wall opposite the fireplace. Draw an elevation view of the storage units in the space provided.

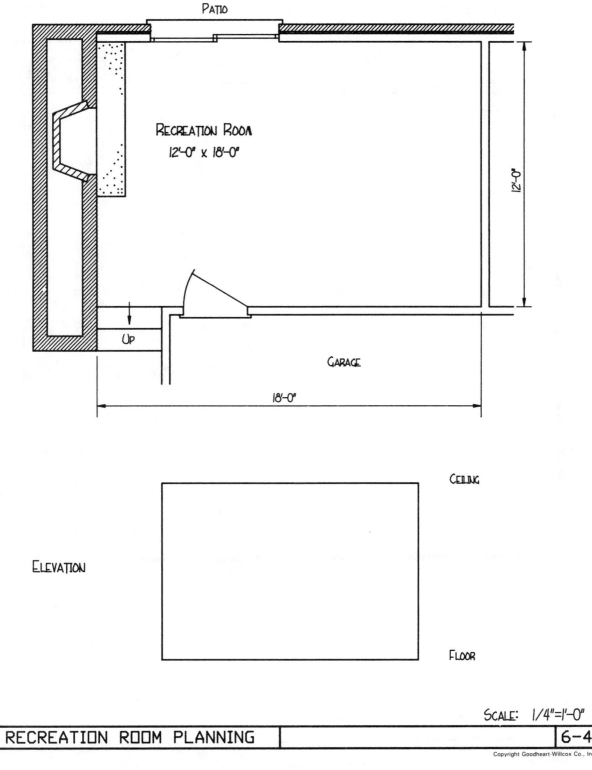

PATIO

RECREATION ROOM
12'-0" x 18'-0"

12'-0"

Up

GARAGE

18'-0"

CEILING

ELEVATION

FLOOR

SCALE: 1/4"=1'-0"

RECREATION ROOM PLANNING | 6-4

5.

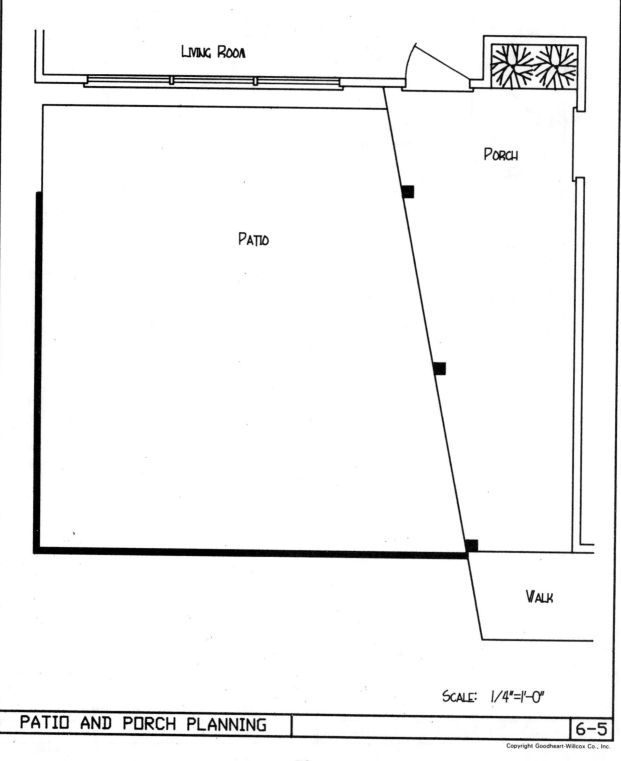

DIRECTIONS:
Complete the plan below (covered porch on the right and patio on the left). Include clay tile pavers on the porch, concrete patio divided into 4'−0" square grid, seating along long porch wall, two lounge chairs and round table on patio, plants along front privacy wall, hedge between living room and patio, and several plants in pots on the patio and porch.

LIVING ROOM

PORCH

PATIO

WALK

SCALE: 1/4"=1'−0"

PATIO AND PORCH PLANNING

6−5

Name _____

6. Collect pictures of living rooms, dining rooms, family recreation rooms, special-purpose rooms, foyers, and outside patios to add to your notebook. Indicate with notes what features you especially like about each selection.

Chapter 7

ROOM PLANNING, SERVICE AREA

Text Pages 127-150

Name _____   Course _____

Date_____   Score _____

PART I: MATCHING: Match the correct term with its description listed below. Place the corresponding letter on the blank at right.

A. Corridor kitchen	E. Peninsula kitchen
B. Garage or carport	F. Service area
C. Island kitchen	G. Straight-line kitchen
D. L-shaped kitchen	H. U-shaped kitchen

1. Supplies, equipment, and space for maintenance, storage, and service are found in this area.

1. _____

2. A popular kitchen design for cottages and apartments.

2. _____

3. A kitchen design located along two adjacent walls.

3. _____

4. This kitchen design is located on two walls opposite each other.

4. _____

5. This kitchen design maintains a high level of efficiency and is the most popular of the six kitchen designs.

5. _____

6. A compact work triangle, reduced traffic, and often joined to a dining room are features of this kitchen design.

6. _____

7. A variation of the straight-line, L-shaped, or U-shaped kitchen.

7. _____

8. Provides shelter for the family automobile(s).

8. _____

PART II: MULTIPLE CHOICE: Select the best answer and place its letter in the blank at right.

1. The standard kitchen base cabinet is _____.
   A. 36" high, 24" deep, in width increments in 2" multiples.
   B. 30" high, 25" deep, in width increments in 4" multiples.
   C. 36" high, 23" deep, in width increments in 3" multiples.
   D. 34 1/2" high, 24" deep, in width increments in 3" multiples.

1. _____

2. The kitchen should be located _____.
   A. Adjacent to the main entry.
   B. In a quiet part of the house.
   C. Near the service entrance and the dining room.
   D. Near the living room.

2. _____

3. Proper kitchen ventilation generally requires _____.
   A. A small wall fan.
   B. A hood with a fan.
   C. Exhausting fumes into the attic.
   D. All of the above.

3. _____

4. A clothes care center should _____.
   A. Be ventilated and well lighted.
   B. Have flooring which is resistant to water and easily cleaned.
   C. Have countertop area which is soil resistant and easily cleaned.
   D. All of the above.

4. _____

5. The space designed for a two-car garage should range in size from _____ to _____ ft.
   A. 11 x 19 to 16 x 25.
   B. 20 x 20 to 25 x 25.
   C. 12 x 18 to 14 x 24.
   D. 15 x 20 to 22 x 22.

5. _____

6. Storage for outdoor recreation equipment and gardening tools is generally provided in the _____.
   A. Garage.
   B. Attic.
   C. Family recreation room.
   D. Kitchen.

6. _____

7. Standard garage doors are available in _____.
   A. Wood and fiberglass.
   B. Plastics.
   C. Aluminum and steel.
   D. All of the above.

7. _____

8. A two-car garage door is generally _____.
   A. 16 ft. wide and 7 ft. high.
   B. 12 ft. wide and 7 ft. high.
   C. 8 ft. wide and 7 ft. high.
   D. 14 ft. wide and 8 ft. high.

8. _____

PART III: COMPLETION: Complete each sentence with the proper response. Place your answer on the blank in the right column.

1. The kitchen is usually the _____ (most/least) expensive area of the home per sq. ft. It receives more active use than any other room.

1. _____

2. The kitchen work triangle should not exceed _____ ft.

2. _____

3. Pots and pans should be stored in the _____ center.

3. _____

4. To adapt a kitchen design for a person in a wheelchair, provide toe space of _____ deep and 8 to 11 in. high under the cabinets.

4. _____

5. Most of the kitchen storage space is available in kitchen _____.

5. _____

6. On a drawing, wall cabinets are shown with a _____ line symbol, while base cabinets are shown as object lines.

6. _____

7. A kitchen eating area should be located outside the _____ area, but convenient to it.

7. _____

8. If chairs are to be used at a kitchen eating counter, the height of the counter should be _____ in.

8. _____

9. _____ are often built in warmer climates, while garages are more commonly built in colder climates.

9. _____

10. A covered walkway should be provided from a free-standing garage to the _____ entrance.

10. _____

Name _____

11. Recreational vehicles may require garage doors higher than _____ ft.

11. _____

12. The minimum driveway width is _____ ft.

12. _____

13. Rather than backing into the street from a garage or carport, a _____ should be provided.

13. _____

PART IV: SHORT ANSWER/LISTING: Provide brief answers to the following questions.

1. List the rooms or areas included in the service area.

A. _____

B. _____

C. _____

D. _____

E. _____

2. List the three work centers found in the kitchen.

A. _____

B. _____

C. _____

3. The work triangle is one measure of kitchen efficiency. Explain the procedure for measuring the work triangle.

_____

4. Where should lighting be provided in the kitchen?

_____

_____

_____

5. What is the purpose of a clothes care center?

_____

_____

6. Name three factors that determine the size and location of a garage or carport.

A. _____

B. _____

C. _____

7. List four factors to consider when designing or constructing garages.

A. _____

_____

B. _____

C. _____

D. _____

_____

1.

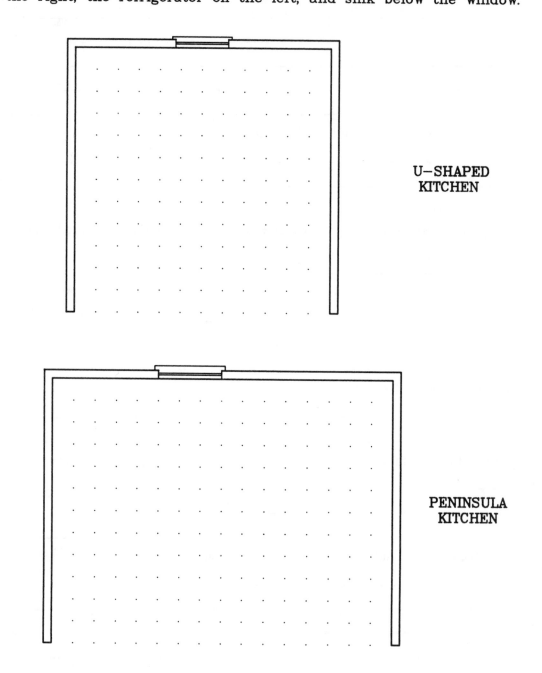

DIRECTIONS:
Draw the base and wall cabinets, appliances, and work triangle for each of the kitchens below. Use standard size units.
U—SHAPED KITCHEN: The available space is 12' by 12'. Include a 36" wide range on the right side wall, a 36" wide refrigerator on the left side wall, and a sink under the window. Label appliances.
PENINSULA KITCHEN: The available space is 12' by 16'. The peninsula is designed to accommodate four stools. The range is to be located on the right, the refrigerator on the left, and sink below the window.

U—SHAPED
KITCHEN

PENINSULA
KITCHEN

SCALE: 1/4"=1'-0"

| KITCHEN PLANNING | | 7-1 |

2.

DIRECTIONS:
Study the configuration of this large, complex kitchen to determine
the most functional layout. Include the following: refrigerator,
range, dishwasher, planning desk, sink, breakfast bar with cabinets
above and stools below. Show ceramic tile floor as 12" square
grid. Label appliances.

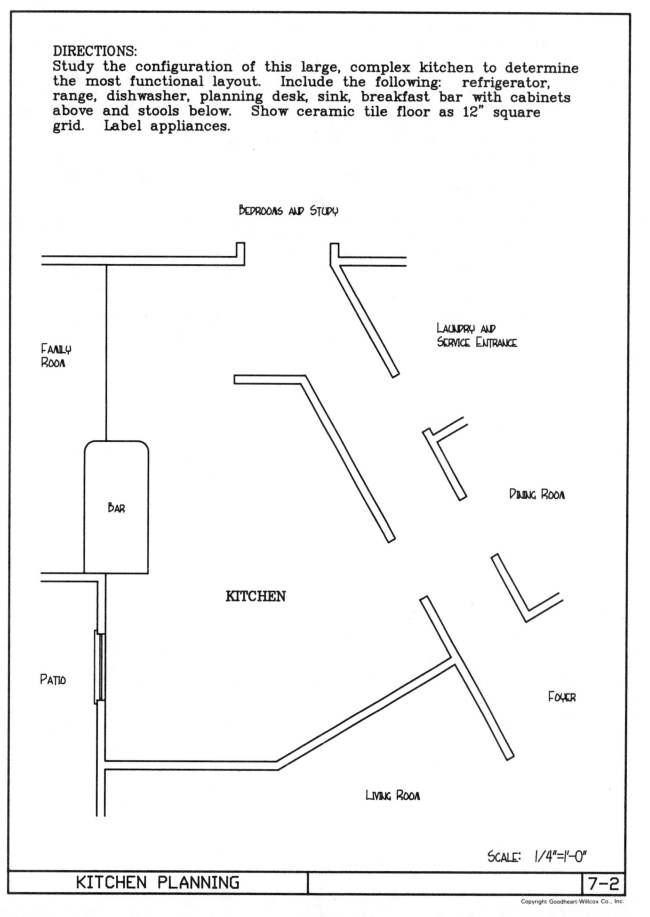

KITCHEN PLANNING

7-2

3. **Kitchen Design.** This assignment will be evaluated based on the following factors: quality of work; degree to which the design meets parameters; quality of communication through proper use of symbols, notes, and standard layout; and neatness of the print.

Directions: You are to design a modern U-shaped kitchen which applies the principles of good design described in the text. Present a floor plan, elevation of each wall, a typical section through the cabinets along one wall from floor to ceiling, and a cabinet and appliance schedule. Draw the plan view and elevations at 1/2" = 1'-0" scale and the typical section at 1" = 1'-0" scale. Make your drawings on two "C" size sheets divided into four 9 x 12 in. areas so that an eight-page package can be presented. Place one drawing in each of the 9 x 12 in. areas. Make a print of the completed drawings and cut into 9 x 12 in. sheets. Bind the pages along one edge. Use a title page as the cover.

Specifications. Include the following elements in your design:
- Utilize a floor area of between 125 and 200 sq. ft.
- Appliances should include cooking top and oven (separate or combined), refrigerator, sink, garbage disposal, and dishwasher.
- Use standard manufactured base and wall cabinets.
- Include a range hood over the cooking area and incorporate at least one window in the kitchen.
- Show the work triangle (not to exceed 22 ft.) and identify the total length.
- Dimension the finished wall to finished wall sizes on the plan view.
- Incorporate a soffit area above the wall cabinets for down lighting or a dropped ceiling.
- Show all appropriate dimensions on the typical wall section. See Fig. 7-24 in the text.
- Secure manufacturer's spec sheets for the specifications of cabinets and appliances. You must use real dimensions for this assignment. Prepare an appliance and cabinet schedule which includes: number of each item, manufacturer's identification, make or model, and price, if available.

4.

DIRECTIONS:

Plan a functional arrangement for the Clothes Care Center below which includes the following items: fold—down ironing board, washer, dryer, laundry tub, countertop space for folding and sewing with base cabinets below, wall cabinets for storage, and planning area. Draw an elevation of the wall (which includes the window) in the space provided. Label each component in the Plan View.

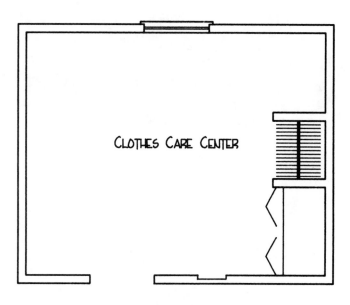

CLOTHES CARE CENTER

PLAN VIEW

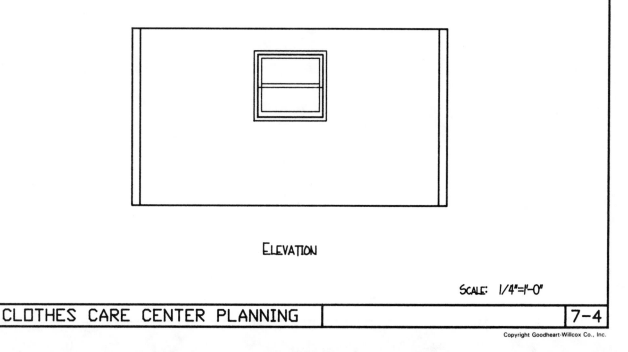

ELEVATION

SCALE: 1/4"=1'-0"

CLOTHES CARE CENTER PLANNING | | 7-4

5.

DIRECTIONS:
The pictorial below shows a detached garage of frame construction.
Draw a Plan View of this garage which assumes the following: garage
is 22'-0" long by 20'-0" wide, door is 16'-0" wide, a 3'-0" side door
leads to the house, garage has two windows on the left side, and
shelves at the rear of the garage. Garage walls are 5 1/4" thick.
Scale is 1/4"=1'-0".

GARAGE PLANNING		7-5

6.

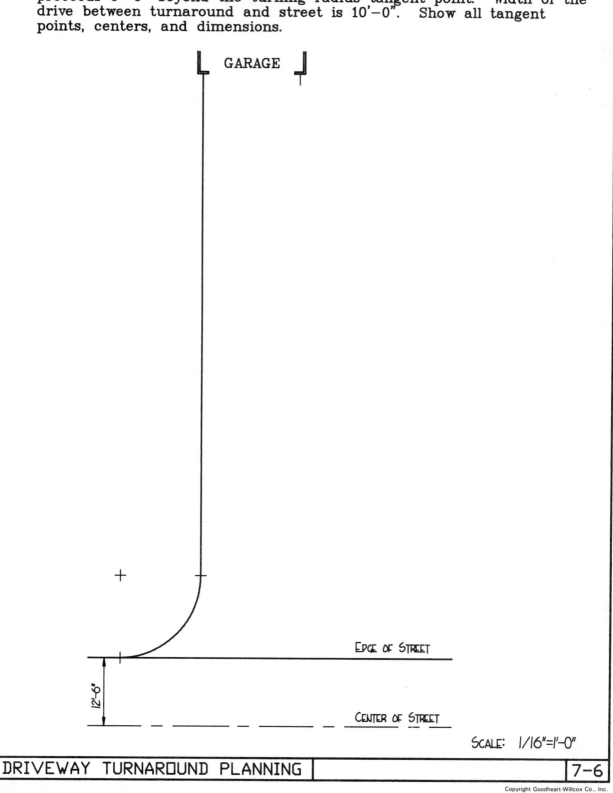

DIRECTIONS:
Plan a driveway with turnaround which meets the following criteria:
Drive is 18'−0" wide at garage with turning radius beginning 6'−0"
in front of garage on the right side.   Turnaround is 20'−0" wide and
proceeds 6'−0" beyond the turning radius tangent point.   Width of the
drive between turnaround and street is 10'−0".   Show all tangent
points, centers, and dimensions.

GARAGE

EDGE OF STREET

12'-6"

CENTER OF STREET

SCALE: 1/16"=1'-0"

DRIVEWAY TURNAROUND PLANNING   7-6

7. Collect photos of kitchens, clothes care centers, utility rooms, storage facilities, and garage and carport designs to add to your notebook.

Chapter 8

PLOT PLANS

Text Pages 151-160

Name _____   Course _____

Date_____   Score _____

PART I: MATCHING: Match the correct term with its description listed below. Place the corresponding letter on the blank at right.

A. Bearing angles
B. Bench mark
C. Blue
D. Closed contour lines
E. Contour interval
F. Contour line
G. Estimated contours

H. Green
I. Landscape plan
J. Meridian arrow
K. Plot plan
L. Property lines
M. Topographical features

1. Plan view drawing which shows the site and location of buildings on the property.

1. _____

2. These lines define the site boundaries.

2. _____

3. Recorded in degrees — and sometimes in minutes and seconds — from either north or south.

3. _____

4. Identified with a special symbol on a plot plan when a property corner begins or ends here.

4. _____

5. A line connecting points that have the same elevation.

5. _____

6. The vertical distance between two adjacent contours.

6. _____

7. Represents summits and depressions.

7. _____

8. Represented by a short dashed line similar to a hidden line.

8. _____

9. Includes trees, ground cover, railroad tracks, sewer lines, fences, water, and sand.

9. _____

10. This color represents water (streams, lakes, marshes, ponds) on topographical drawings.

10. _____

11. On topographical drawings, vegetation is represented by this color.

11. _____

12. Also known as the north symbol.

12. _____

13. Illustrates the type and placement of trees, shrubs, flowers, gardens, and pools on the site.

13. _____

PART II: SHORT ANSWER/LISTING: Provide brief answers to the following questions.

1. List the features found on a plot plan.

A. _____

B. _____

(Continued)

C. _____

D. _____

E. _____

F. _____

G. _____

H. _____

I. _____

J. _____

K. _____

L. _____

M. _____

2. Describe the procedure for drawing the property lines of a given site.

_____

_____

_____

3. What type of line is used to represent contours drawn as a result of a survey?

_____

4. What features on a topographical drawing are represented in black?

_____

_____

5. What does brown represent on topographical drawings?

_____

6. During the analysis of a site, what items must be considered to determine the location and placement of the structure?

A. _____

B. _____

C. _____

D. _____

E. _____

F. _____

G. _____

H. _____

I. _____

J. _____

K. _____

7. Name three methods of representing the house on the plot plan.

A. _____

_____

B. _____

_____

C. _____

Name _____

8. When following the procedure for drawing a plot plan, what step comes after you have lightly drawn the contour lines?

_____

9. At what point should contour lines be darkened in on a plot plan?

_____

10. What information is given on a landscape plan that is also given on a plot plan?

A. _____

B. _____

C. _____

D. _____

E. _____

F. _____

G. _____

PART III: COMPLETION: Complete each sentence with the proper response. Place your answer on the blank in the right column.

1. The plot plan is drawn from information supplied by a _____ and recorded on a site plan.

1. _____

2. Property line lengths are measured with a(n) _____ scale to the nearest 1/100 foot.

2. _____

3. _____ lines help describe the topography of a site by depicting the shape and elevation of the land.

3. _____

4. _____ elevations are usually acceptable in residential home construction.

4. _____

5. A _____ slope is indicated when contours are placed close together.

5. _____

6. When contours are smooth and parallel, the ground surface is _____.

6. _____

7. _____ contours indicate rough and uneven ground surface.

7. _____

8. Contours of _____ elevations do not touch.

8. _____

9. Contours cross watersheds and ridges at _____ angles.

9. _____

10. When the distance between the house and property line is critical, the _____ of the roof should be shown on the drawing.

10. _____

11. To dimension the location of the house on the site, dimension the distance from the _____ of the exterior wall to the property line.

11. _____

12. Scales commonly used in drawing plot plans range from 1/8" = 1'-0" to _____.

12. _____

PART IV: PROBLEMS/ACTIVITIES

1.

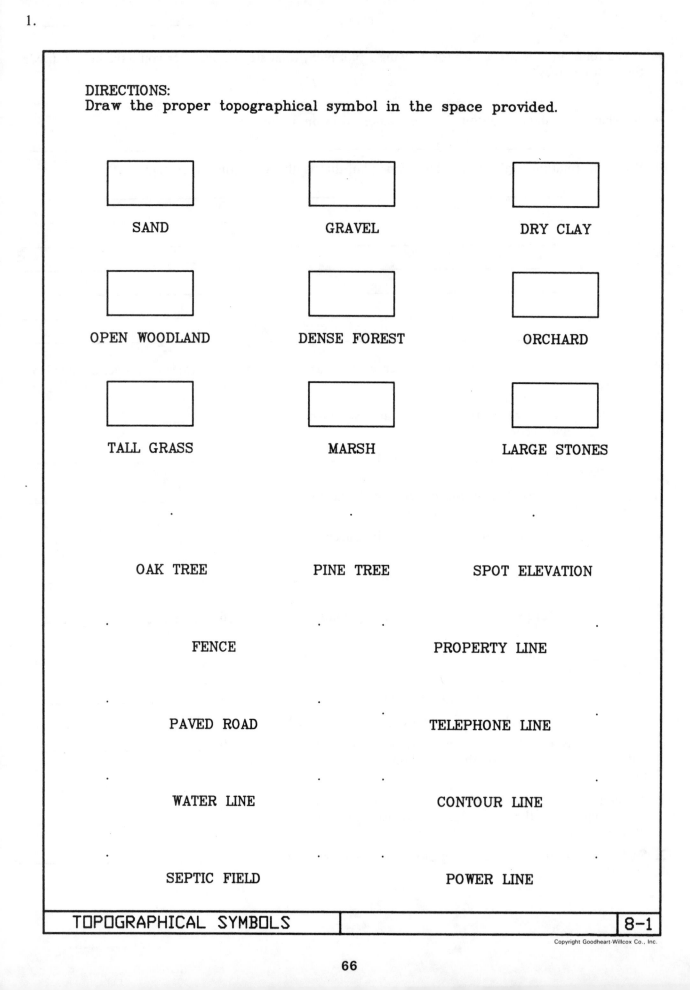

DIRECTIONS:
Draw the proper topographical symbol in the space provided.

SAND

GRAVEL

DRY CLAY

OPEN WOODLAND

DENSE FOREST

ORCHARD

TALL GRASS

MARSH

LARGE STONES

OAK TREE

PINE TREE

SPOT ELEVATION

FENCE

PROPERTY LINE

PAVED ROAD

TELEPHONE LINE

WATER LINE

CONTOUR LINE

SEPTIC FIELD

POWER LINE

TOPOGRAPHICAL SYMBOLS

8-1

2.

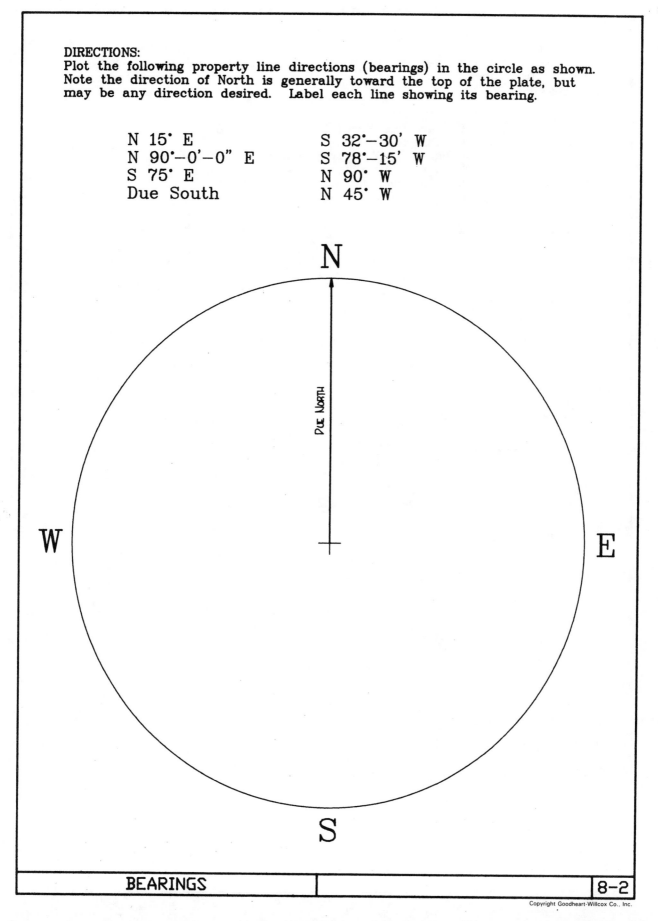

DIRECTIONS:
Plot the following property line directions (bearings) in the circle as shown.
Note the direction of North is generally toward the top of the plate, but
may be any direction desired.   Label each line showing its bearing.

N 15° E   S 32°-30' W
N 90°-0'-0" E   S 78°-15' W
S 75° E   N 90° W
Due South   N 45° W

N

DUE NORTH

W   E

S

BEARINGS   8-2

3.

DIRECTIONS:
Using the property line symbol and format shown in the example below,
locate the property boundaries described in the chart.   Note the scale and
direction of North.

> Begin at point "A".
> Line AB bears Due North for a distance of 150.0'.
> Line BC bears N 75° E for a distance of 112.5'.
> Line CD bears S 56° E for a distance of 45.0'.
> Line DE bears S 15° W for a distance of 142.5'.
> Determine the bearing and length of line EA.
> Label property lines and corners.

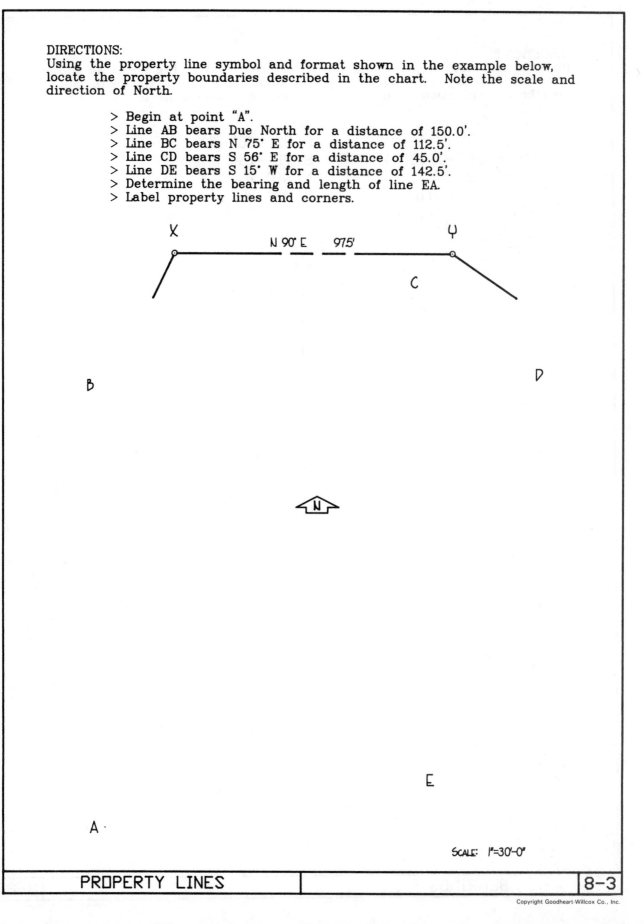

SCALE: 1"=30'-0"

PROPERTY LINES   8-3

4.

DIRECTIONS:
This assignment consists of two parts--plotting contour lines from an
elevation grid and showing a profile section defined by a cutting plane.
Using the elevation grid at the top of the page, plot the contour lines at
elevations 5, 10, and 15 feet. Use the proper contour line symbol and label.
Draw a profile section of the property defined by Section A,1,1 in the space
provided. Be sure to project the points from the grid above. Hatch the
sectioned area in the profile.

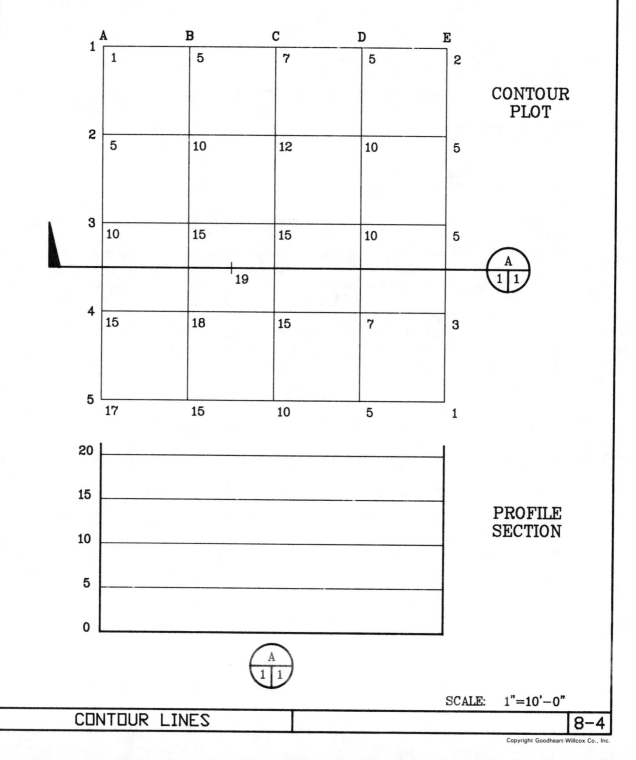

CONTOUR PLOT

PROFILE SECTION

SCALE: 1"=10'-0"

CONTOUR LINES

8-4

5. **Site Plans.** This assignment will be evaluated based on the following factors: accuracy of the property lines and symbols, neatness of work, and degree to which directions were followed. The assignment is to be presented on "B" size paper (12 x 18 in.). You will need two sheets. The plate will be oriented with the long dimension horizontal. Identify the plate as "Plate 8-5."

Directions. Locate point "A" 1 3/4 in. down from the top edge of the paper and 3 3/4 in. from the left edge. This is the beginning property corner and is at the water's edge of Sandy Lake. Now locate the tip of the north arrow down 2 in. from the top edge and 2 in. in from the right edge. North has a bearing of 15 deg. to the right of a vertical line. Draw the north symbol at the location described. Hint: Turn the plate so that North points straight up.

Property Lines. Proceed to identify and draw the property boundary lines described below using a scale of 1" = 20'-0".
- Begin at point "A".
- Line AB bears N 75° E for a distance of 200.0'.
- Line BC bears S 15° E for a distance of 112.0'.
- Line CD bears S 36° W for a distance of 70.0'.
- Line DE bears S 85° W for a distance of 154.0'.
- Determine the bearing and chord length of EA.

Point "E" is also on the water's edge of Sandy Lake. The lake shore follows roughly the contour lines provided for you on the elevation grid chart. Label all corners (A, B, C, D, and E) and assign the following elevations to each corner:
- Elevation of "A" is 100.0'.
- Elevation of "B" is 106.4'.
- Elevation of "C" is 108.6'.
- Elevation of "D" is 107.9'.
- Elevation of "E" is 100.0'.

Elevation Grid. On another "B" size sheet, lay out an elevation grid for the data shown on the elevation grid chart.

Grid lines are spaced 1/2 in. apart or 10'-0" at 1" = 20'-0" scale. Plot the contour lines at each one foot interval (101, 102, 103, etc.). Grid lines A-1 correspond to point "A" on the property line description. The 100.0' contour line should also pass through corner "E" of the site. Hint: The property boundary lines should fall inside the contour grid. Once you have located the contour lines, trace them on the sheet which contains the property lines.

Foliage and Features. Locate the following trees on the site:
- Oak 30 ft. dia. From "E" N 55° E 50.0 ft. to center of tree.
- Oak 20 ft. dia. From "A" N 90° E 80.0 ft. to center of tree.
- Oak 20 ft. dia. From "B" S 45° W 30.0 ft. to center of tree.
- Pine 15 ft. dia. From "C" N 90° W 15.0 ft. to center of tree.

Add the following features:
- Sandy beach from waters edge to the 102.0' elevation contour line.
- Lake name, lot #8, scale, title.
- Boat dock 3 x 20 ft. with posts every 10 ft. Begin at the 101.0' contour line anywhere along the beach.

Elevation Grid Data Chart for use with Assignment 8–5

	A	B	C	D	E	F	G	H	I	J	K	L	M	N	O	P	Q	R	S	T	U
1	100.0	101.3	103.2	104.4	105.2	106.0	106.5	107.0	107.5	108.0	108.4	108.8	108.6	108.3	108.0	107.5	107.1	106.8	106.7	106.5	106.4
2	99.8	101.1	102.7	104.0	105.0	105.8	106.4	106.8	107.4	107.8	108.3	108.7	108.8	108.6	108.2	107.6	107.0	106.8	106.7	106.6	106.6
3	99.4	100.8	102.2	103.5	104.6	105.8	106.3	106.7	107.3	107.7	108.2	108.6	109.0	108.7	108.4	107.8	107.2	106.8	106.7	106.7	106.8
4	99.2	100.5	101.9	103.2	104.2	105.2	106.1	106.5	107.0	107.8	107.9	108.4	108.7	108.8	108.5	108.1	107.4	106.9	106.8	106.9	107.3
5	99.1	100.4	101.7	103.0	103.7	104.8	105.7	106.3	106.7	107.4	107.7	108.2	108.6	109.0	108.5	108.2	107.7	107.3	107.2	107.3	107.5
6	99.1	100.4	101.8	102.7	103.5	104.5	105.3	106.0	106.5	107.0	107.4	107.9	108.5	108.8	108.7	108.2	107.7	107.6	107.4	107.5	107.7
7	99.2	100.4	101.5	102.6	103.4	104.3	104.8	105.6	106.3	106.7	107.3	107.8	108.4	108.7	108.8	108.1	107.7	107.7	107.7	107.7	107.9
8	99.3	100.5	101.5	102.5	103.4	104.2	104.7	105.4	106.0	106.6	107.2	107.7	108.3	108.7	108.8	108.1	107.8	107.8	107.9	108.1	108.2
9	99.5	100.4	101.5	102.4	103.3	104.0	104.5	105.1	105.8	106.4	106.9	107.6	108.2	108.7	108.8	108.3	108.0	108.1	108.2	108.3	108.3
10	99.6	100.3	101.6	102.3	103.2	103.9	104.5	105.0	105.7	106.3	106.8	107.5	108.1	108.6	108.8	108.5	108.3	108.3	108.2	108.3	108.4
11	99.7	101.0	101.8	102.4	103.5	103.8	104.4	105.0	105.6	106.2	106.7	107.4	108.0	108.5	108.9	108.7	108.5	108.5	108.5	108.5	108.5
12	100.0	101.2	102.0	102.5	103.4	103.8	104.4	105.0	105.6	106.1	106.7	107.4	107.8	108.4	108.8	108.9	108.7	108.7	108.7	108.7	108.6
13	100.4	101.3	102.2	102.6	103.4	103.4	104.4	104.9	105.5	106.0	106.6	107.3	107.6	108.2	108.5	108.8	109.0	108.9	108.8	108.8	108.8
14	100.7	101.6	102.4	102.7	103.4	103.4	104.4	104.8	105.4	105.9	106.5	107.1	107.4	107.8	108.2	108.5	108.7	108.6	108.8	108.8	108.9
15	101.0	101.8	102.5	102.9	103.4	103.9	104.3	104.7	105.3	105.8	106.3	106.7	107.3	107.6	107.9	108.3	108.4	108.5	108.6	108.7	108.7
16						104	104.3	104.7	105.2	105.7	106.0	106.5	107.0	107.3	107.5	107.9	108.2	108.3	108.4	108.5	108.6

EXPLANATION: The point where grid line "A" crosses grid line "1" is 100.0' elevation. The grid lines are drawn 1/2" apart or 10'-0" at the scale of 1"=20'-0". This is a chart of grid data and not the grid itself. You must draw the grid to scale and record the data on the grid before locating the contour lines.

6. **Plot Plans**. This assignment will be evaluated based on the following factors: proper placement of the house on the site; appropriate method of dimensioning the house on the site; correct size and location of drive, street, and utilities; neatness of work; and the degree to which directions were followed. The assignment is to be presented on "B" size paper (12 x 18 in.) using a standard border and title block. The plate should be turned with the long edge horizontal. Identify the plate as "Plate 8-6." Scale is 1" = 20'-0".

Directions. Using the site developed in Assignment 8-5, draw a plot plan that has the following elements:

A. Trace the property lines, contour lines, trees, dock, etc. from Assignment 8-5. (Be sure to correct any errors that you made on the assignment.)

B. Use the house and garage shown on the next page of your workbook as the house to be located on the site.

C. The house is 53'-0" across the front and the front should be parallel to the property line which has a bearing of S 15° E.

D. Draw the exterior walls (foundation only) and show them as 8 or 12 in. thick. Shade the wall thickness as though it were a single line. Omit windows, doors, and interior walls. Shade or hatch the interior space so the house space is highly visible on the plan.

E. Show the deck, porch between house and garage, and steps on the plot plan. (Show the boards.)

F. Locate the following features outside the property lines: Gas line, water, sewer, edge of street, and center line of street. Each of these items are dimensioned to the lot line which is parallel to the street. Use these dimensions:

Gas line: 8'-0"   Edge of street: 20'-6"
Water line: 18'-0"   Center of street: 33'-0"
Sewer line: 26'-0"

G. Lay out a paved drive 20'-0" wide at the garage, but 10'-0" at the street. Provide a turnaround using proper turning radii. Refer to Assignment 7-6.

H. Dimension the following:
   • Reference corner of house location.
   • Location of all utilities to the property line.
   • Drive dimensions and centers of all radii (show tangent points).

I. Label the following:
   • Elevation of house reference corner.
   • Drive.
   • Street name that you decide.
   • Include everything from the site plan (Problem 8-5).

J. Complete the drawing by adding the scale and title.

Floor Plan for use with Assignment 8—6

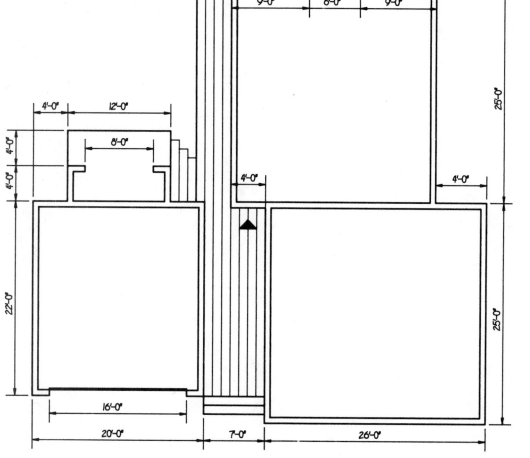

SCALE: 1"=10'—0"

Chapter 9

FOOTINGS, FOUNDATIONS, AND CONCRETE

Text Pages 161-182

Name _____   Course _____

Date_____   Score _____

PART I: COMPLETION: Complete each sentence with the proper response. Place your answer on the blank in the right column.

1. When staking out the house location, a surveyor's transit may be used for measuring angles other than _____ degrees.

   1. _____

2. The distances used to locate the corners of the house are taken from the _____ plan.

   2. _____

3. To lay out square corners, use the 9-12-_____ unit method.

   3. _____

4. _____ measurement checks the position of the corners for accuracy.

   4. _____

5. The location of the foundation is kept during excavation and construction by the use of _____ boards.

   5. _____

6. Batter boards are placed approximately _____ ft. outside the footing line.

   6. _____

7. To insure that each stake of the batter boards is placed accurately, a plumb _____ is used.

   7. _____

8. The corner having the highest elevation is normally selected for the _____ point.

   8. _____

9. The finished floor of the house should be a minimum of _____ in. above the grade.

   9. _____

10. Footings should be excavated at least _____ in. into undisturbed earth and a minimum of 6 in. below the average maximum frost penetration depth.

    10. _____

11. To obtain the minimum footing depth for any given area, check the local _____.

    11. _____

12. Where part of the footings bear on rock, remove approximately _____ in. of the rock and replace with compacted sand to equalize settling.

    12. _____

13. Only when soil tests prove that the earth is adequately compacted properly to sustain a building, should _____ be placed in filled or regraded soils.

    13. _____

14. Excavate a gentle back slope in _____ soil.

    14. _____

15. Excavation in _____ permits a steep slope.

    15. _____

16. Beams may be either metal or _____.

    16. _____

17. The _____ (top/bottom) flange on a steel post is larger.

    17. _____

18. Lintels should extend at least _____ in. into a masonry wall on either side of an opening.

18. _____

19. Sidewalks, driveways, footings, and basement floors require one part cement, _____ parts sand, and five parts aggregate.

19. _____

20. Vibrating or _____ poured concrete results in a more dense product and dislodges weak spots caused by air pockets.

20. _____

21. The size of a wide flange beam needed to span 59 feet, assuming that the weight of beam per sq. ft. is 53 lb., would be what size? _____. (Refer to the chart in your text.)

21. _____

PART II: SHORT ANSWER/LISTING: Provide brief answers to the following questions.

1. What is the purpose of a footing?

_____

_____

2. What material is normally used for the footings of residential structures?

_____

3. Generally, how thick and wide should the footing be made?

_____

_____

4. Why might a difference in settling occur for a structure resting on two or more different subsoils?

_____

_____

5. What can be done to reduce cracks caused by uneven settling? Remember that the weight of most residential structures lies on two rather than all four walls.

_____

_____

6. When would longitudinal reinforcing bars be used?

_____

_____

_____

7. How thick should the footing for a fireplace be?

_____

8. What can be done to prevent cracking where steps are located in horizontal and vertical footings?

_____

_____

9. Where do the foundation walls begin and terminate on a residential structure?

_____

_____

Name _____

10. Name the materials used to construct foundation walls.

    A. _____

    B. _____

    C. _____

    D. _____

    E. _____

11. Name the four basic types of foundation walls.

    A. _____

    B. _____

    C. _____

    D. _____

12. What factors determine the type of foundation to be used?

    A. _____

    B. _____

    C. _____

    D. _____

    E. _____

    F. _____

13. What are form boards and when are they used?

    _____

    _____

    _____

14. Should the foundation wall of a slab foundation extend below the frost line?

    _____

15. Name three advantages of a slab foundation.

    A. _____

    B. _____

    _____

    C. _____

    _____

16. Give three reasons why built-up wood beams are used more often than solid wood beams in residential construction.

    A. _____

    B. _____

    C. _____

17. Name two characteristics of solid wood beams.

    A. _____

    B. _____

18. Which has greater strength, the S-beam or the W-beam?

_____

19. What are live loads and give some examples.

_____

_____

_____

20. Define dead loads and give examples.

_____

_____

_____

21. List four materials from which lintels are commonly made.

A. _____

B. _____

C. _____

D. _____

22. List three places where contraction joints should be located.

A. _____

B. _____

C. _____

23. Identify the drawings of the different types of foundations commonly used in residential construction.

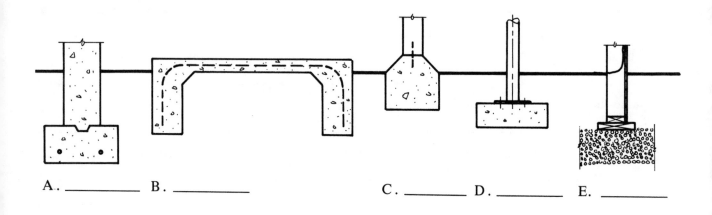

A. _____ B. _____   C. _____ D. _____ E. _____

Name _____

24. Identify these parts on the basement wall drawing: header, sill, drain tile, and expansion joint.

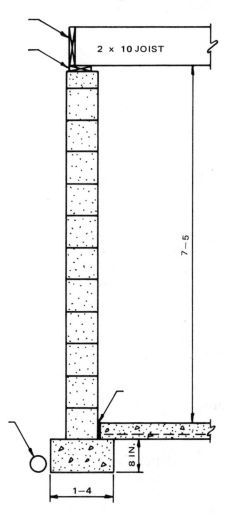

PART III: MULTIPLE CHOICE: Select the best answer and place its letter in the blank at right.

1. Posts used in post foundations are commonly made of:
   A. Masonry.
   B. Steel.
   C. Pressure-treated wood.
   D. All of the above.

1. _____

2. The wood foundation is particularly suitable in:
   A. A garage where the distance is too great to span with floor joists.
   B. Areas where the sea level is high.
   C. Climates where traditional concrete foundation work stops in freezing or rainy weather.
   D. None of the above.

2. _____

3. The trench excavated for a structure with a crawl space should be _____ deep.
   A. Less than 10 in.
   B. At least 12 in.
   C. 9 in.
   D. 6 in.

3. _____

4. When using a wood foundation for a basement:
   A. The site is excavated 12 in. deeper than the regular depth.
   B. A basement sump is installed in poorly drained soils.
   C. No foundation drainage is necessary.
   D. All of the above.

4. _____

5. Nails used in wood foundations should be made of:
   A. Hot-dipped zinc-coated steel.
   B. Copper.
   C. Silicon bronze.
   D. All of the above.

5. _____

6. The floor joists or trusses of a wood foundation are placed on the:
   A. Double top plate of the foundation wall.
   B. Inside of the foundation wall.
   C. Basement floor slab.
   D. None of the above.

6. _____

7. Backfilling for a wood foundation should be started:
   A. Before the floor joists or trusses are installed.
   B. Before the polyethylene film is applied.
   C. After the basement floor has cured and the first floor is installed.
   D. All of the above.

7. _____

8. The factor(s) that determine(s) the stability and strength of masonry or concrete basement walls include:
   A. Support from crosswalls.
   B. The size of the floor joists.
   C. The live load of the structure.
   D. All of the above.

8. _____

9. Basement walls generally are:
   A. A little shorter than first or second floor walls.
   B. The same height as first or second floor walls.
   C. Somewhat higher than first or second floor walls.
   D. Much shorter than first or second floor walls.

9. _____

10. Basement load bearing crosswalls should be attached to exterior walls by:
    A. Metal tiebars.
    B. A masonry bond.
    C. Anchor bolts.
    D. All of the above.

10. _____

11. If the wood sill bears on the outer and inner face shells of the block,:
    A. Cap the top course of block using 4 in. solid block.
    B. Capping may be omitted.
    C. Cores in the top course are filled with concrete or mortar.
    D. The top course may be capped with reinforced concrete masonry bond beam.

11. _____

12. Concrete block basement walls should be dampproofed to eliminate ground water from seeping through the wall. This is done by:
    A. Painting the outside of the blocks with oil base paints.
    B. Applying a 1/4 in. coat of fire clay.
    C. Applying two 1/4 in. thick coats of cement-mortar or plaster then a coat of bituminous waterproofing.
    D. All of the above.

12. _____

Name _____

13. To eliminate water damage to basements in wet or poorly
drained soils:
    A. Install a check valve in the floor drain to keep water from
    flowing in through the drain.
    B. Reinforce the floor slab to resist uplift from groundwater
    pressure.
    C. Install a sump pump to take away any water which seeps in.
    D. All of the above.

13. _____

14. To support a 4 in. masonry wall above an opening, use a
_____ piece of angle steel for a 10'-6" span. (Refer to Fig.
9-38 in the textbook.)
    A. 3 1/2 x 3 1/2 x 5/16 in.
    B. 4 x 4 x 5/16 in.
    C. 4 x 4 x 3/8 in.
    D. 6 x 4 x 3/8 in.

14. _____

15. A float is used in finishing concrete to:
    A. Put the final finish on the surface.
    B. Work fine aggregate to the bottom of the form.
    C. Condense mortar to the surface ready for final steel-
    troweling.
    D. All of the above.

15. _____

16. When ordering concrete, allow _____ cubic feet to the
yard.
    A. 24.
    B. 25.
    C. 26.
    D. 27.

16. _____

17. Concrete slabs are normally placed on a base of compacted
sand _____ in. thick.
    A. 4 to 6.
    B. 5 to 7.
    C. 6 to 8.
    D. 9 to 10.

17. _____

18. The actual size of a concrete block is _____:
    A. 7 5/8 x 7 5/8 x 15 5/8 in.
    B. 8 x 8 x 16 in.
    C. 8 5/8 x 8 5/8 x 16 5/8 in.
    D. 9 x 9 x 18 in.

18. _____

PART IV: MATCHING: Match the correct term with its description listed below. Place the corresponding letter on the blank at right.

A. ACA or CCA
B. AWWF
C. Bearing wall
D. Cement
E. Concrete
F. Contraction joints
G. Coarse aggregate
H. Float
I. Jointing tool
J. Kip

K. Lintel
L. PWF
M. Pier foundation
N. Plot plan
O. S-beam
P. Saw kerf
Q. Screed
R. Slab foundation
S. T-foundation
T. Trowel

1. This plan provides the dimensions to be used when staking out the location of the house on the lot.

2. Prevents movement of string along batter board.

3. The name of this foundation comes from its shape.

4. Sometimes called a thickened-edge slab.

5. A foundation used in a crawl space where the distance is too large for a single span.

6. Permanent wood foundation.

7. All weather wood foundation.

8. Waterborne preservative salts.

9. Supports a portion of the load of the building.

10. Formerly called an I-beam.

11. Equals 1,000 pounds.

12. A horizontal structural element which supports the load over openings such as windows or doors.

13. The combination of cement, sand, aggregate, and water.

14. Contains lime, silica, alumina, iron components, and gypsum.

15. Stone or gravel.

16. Used to smooth a concrete surface.

17. A foot long board with a handle attached to one of the flat sides.

18. A concrete finishing tool used in a circular motion to further harden the surface and develop a very smooth finish.

19. Used in large areas of concrete to control cracking.

20. Used to cut grooves in freshly placed concrete.

1. _____

2. _____

3. _____

4. _____

5. _____

6. _____

7. _____

8. _____

9. _____

10. _____

11. _____

12. _____

13. _____

14. _____

15. _____

16. _____

17. _____

18. _____

19. _____

20. _____

1.

DIRECTIONS:
Draw a typical foundation wall section for a thickened—edge slab which includes the following elements:
> Scale: 3/4"=1'-0"
> Foundation 10" thick and 48" from top of slab to bottom of foundation (no footing).   Thickness and depth should conform to code.
> Welded wire fabric in foundation and slab.
> Slab 4" thick on 1" RF insulation and 4" compacted sand.
> Wall on foundation of 8" concrete block with 3/4" RF insulation outside extending 24" below the grade.   Use wood siding over insulation to 2" above the grade.   Flash exposed insulation with aluminum.
> Label and dimension.   Add scale.

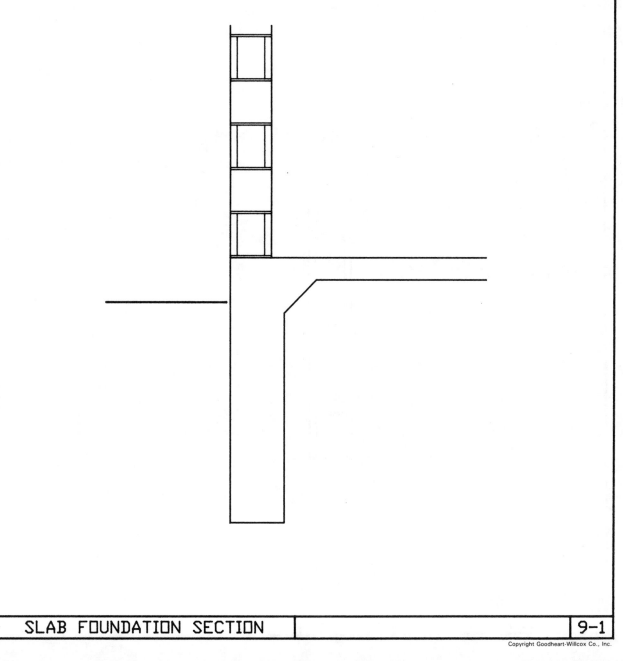

SLAB FOUNDATION SECTION		9-1

2.

DIRECTIONS:
Draw a typical foundation wall section for a frame structure with siding which has a crawl space. Include the following elements in your drawing:
> Scale: 3/4"=1'-0"
> Continuous footing 8"x 16" with 2-1/2" re-rods and 4" perforated drain tile in pea gravel.
> 8" concrete block foundation wall (6 courses high or code) with 1/2" parge coat for moisture protection. Grade 8" below top of foundation and crawl space from top of footing to bottom of joists.
> 2"x 8" treated sill plate with 1/2"x 16" anchor bolts and sill sealer.
> 2"x 10" floor joist with 3/4" T&G P.W. glued and nailed.
> Frame wall with 3/4" RF insulation to top of foundation with horizontal siding, 3 1/2" batt insulation, and 1/2" drywall.
> Label and dimension.   Add scale.

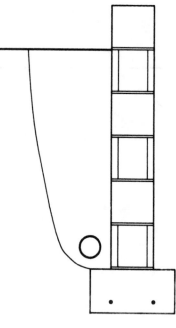

FOUNDATION WITH CRAWL SPACE		9-2

3.

DIRECTIONS:
Draw a typical foundation/basement wall section for a brick veneer on frame residential structure.   Include the following elements in your drawing:
 > Scale: 3/4"=1'-0"
 > Continuous footing 12"x 24" with 2-1/2" re-rods and 4" perforated drain tile in pea gravel.
 > 12" thick basement wall with 4" brick ledge and dampproofing.   Basement floor to ceiling should be 7'-10" to 8'-0".
 > 4" basement floor slab with welded wire fabric and 4" compacted sand with vapor barrier.
 > 2"x 8" treated sill plate with sill sealer and 1/2"x 8" anchor bolts.
 > Floor system is 14" wood floor trusses to span 24'-0" with 3/4" T&G P.W. panels glued and nailed.   See Reference Section in text.
 > First floor frame wall has 3/4" RF insulation, 3 1/2" batt insulation, and 1/2" drywall inside.   Veneer is common brick with 1" air space, wall ties, and flashing.
 > Label and dimension.   Add scale.

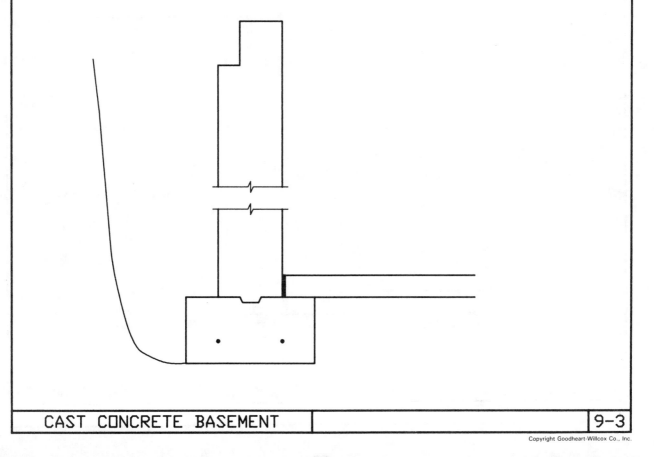

CAST CONCRETE BASEMENT

9-3

4.

DIRECTIONS:
Draw a typical foundation/basement wall section for a residential structure
which requires a wood foundation. Include the following elements:
> Scale: 3/4"=1'-0"
> Base for foundation is 8" of crushed stone or gravel.
> Foundation/basement wall is 2"x 6" frame with 2"x 10" footing plate
  and 3/4" P.W. sheathing covered with polyethylene film. All wood
  materials are specially treated for this application.
> Include protection strip at grade, double top plate, and 1"x 4" screed.
> Basement floor is 4" thick with welded wire fabric and moisture barrier.
  Include drain tiles where ground water is a problem.
> First floor system is 2"x 10" joists with 3/4" T&G P.W. glued and nailed.
> Exterior wall is 2"x 4" stud, 3/4" RF insulation, siding, and 1/2" drywall.
> Label and dimension. Add scale.

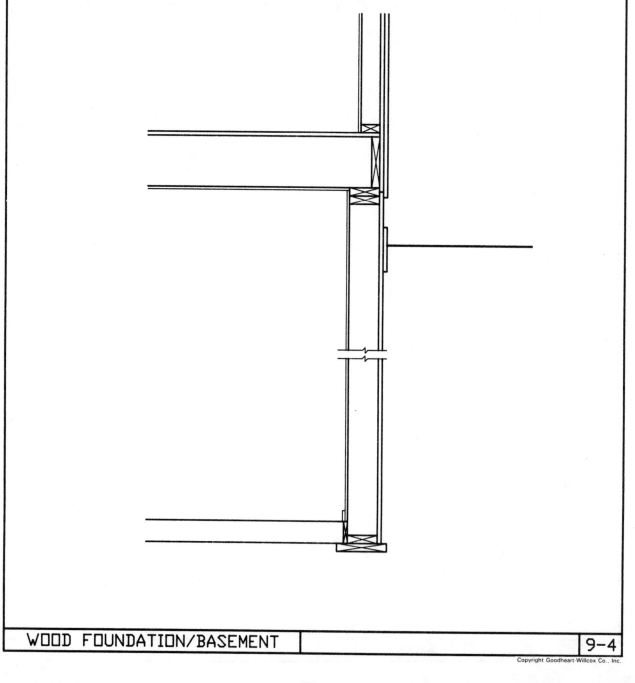

WOOD FOUNDATION/BASEMENT | | 9-4

Chapter 10

THE FOUNDATION PLAN

Text Pages 183-192

Name _____   Course _____

Date _____   Score _____

PART I: SHORT ANSWER/LISTING: Provide brief answers to the following questions.

1. From what three sources of information is the foundation plan drawn?

    A. _____

    B. _____

    C. _____

2. Name five things a foundation plan usually includes.

    A. _____

    B. _____

    C. _____

    D. _____

    E. _____

    ALSO: _____

    _____

    _____

    _____

    _____

    _____

3. Why should you examine the floor plan before drawing the foundation walls on a foundation plan?

    _____

    _____

4. What is the first step in drawing a foundation or a basement plan?

    _____

5. The basement plan contains characteristics of two plans. Name the two plans.

    A. _____

    B. _____

6. Identify the material symbols used on foundation plans.

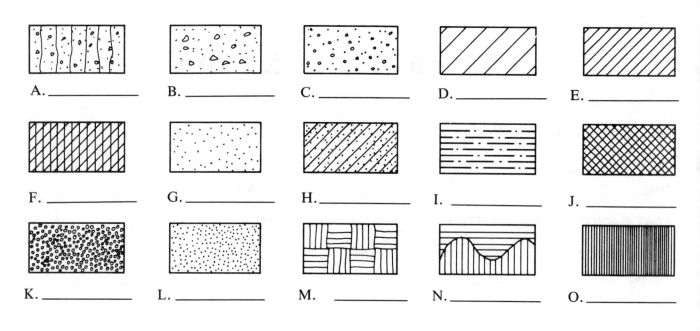

A. _____   B. _____   C. _____   D. _____   E. _____

F. _____   G. _____   H. _____   I. _____   J. _____

K. _____   L. _____   M. _____   N. _____   O. _____

7. Why is it good practice to use the preliminary floor plan as an underlay for drawing the foundation plan?
   _____

8. A beam generally is represented by which of the following symbols? Circle the symbol.

   A. ————————————————

   B. ——— — — ——— — — —

   C. ——— — ——— — ———

   D. None of the above.

9. Are piers dimensioned to the center or to the edge?
   _____

10. How does a basement/foundation plan differ from a foundation plan?
   _____
   _____
   _____
   _____

11. What is the final step to be completed when drawing a foundation plan or basement plan?
   _____
   _____

12. Is it necessary to show electrical switches, outlets, and fixtures on a basement plan?
   _____

Name _____

PART II: COMPLETION: Complete each sentence with the proper response. Place your answer on the blank in the right column.

1. A _____ house is a good example of a house style that requires both a foundation plan and a basement plan.

1. _____

2. The foundation plan shows the location and size of footings, piers, _____, foundation walls, and supporting beams.

2. _____

3. The foundation plan is prepared primarily for the excavator, _____, and cement workers.

3. _____

4. Houses in cold climates usually have _____ (basements/slab foundations).

4. _____

5. The foundation plan is usually drawn after the _____ plan and elevations have been roughed out.

5. _____

6. The scale most commonly used in residential drawings is _____.

6. _____

7. The _____ line symbol is used for drawing the footings for foundation walls.

7. _____

8. Interior frame walls should be dimensioned to the _____ (edge/center) of the wall on a basement/foundation plan.

8. _____

9. Openings in a masonry wall are dimensioned to the (edge/center) _____ of the opening.

9. _____

10. Study the elevation and plot plan to determine if retaining walls, stepped _____, or other grade considerations are needed.

10. _____

11. Considering the cost per square foot, a basement costs much less than the _____ floor.

11. _____

PART III: MULTIPLE CHOICE: Select the best answer and place its letter in the blank at right.

1. Which one of the following steps is included in drawing a foundation plan, but not a basement plan?
   A. Locate and draw the beam and supports or bearing wall partition.
   B. Locate the supporting beam if one is required and draw the beam using a thick center line symbol.
   C. Design the room layout and darken in the lines.
   D. Show electrical switches, outlets, and fixtures.

1. _____

2. Mr. Smith and Mr. Jones are each building a house from the same floor plan. Mr. Smith is using a stud wall with siding and Mr. Jones is using brick veneer. Which of the following statements applies to Mr. Smith and Mr. Jones?
   A. Mr. Jones's foundation plan will be 8 in. longer and wider than Mr. Smith's because a brick veneer house needs a 4 in. ledge on all four sides.
   B. The size of the foundations will be exactly the same.
   C. Mr. Smith's foundation plan will be 4 in. longer and wider than Mr. Jones's because a stud wall requires a 4 in. ledge on the length and width.
   D. None of the above statements apply.

2. _____

3. Prior to drawing the foundation plan, you should: 3. _____
   A. Study available information to make a decision about the size of the footings and foundation walls.
   B. Determine the frost penetration depth for the area where the dwelling will be built.
   C. Check with local building codes to be sure that the requirements are being met.
   D. All of the above.

PART IV: MATCHING: Match the correct term with its description listed below. Place the corresponding letter on the blank at right.

  A. Dwarf walls   D. Material symbols
  B. Concrete block symbol   E. Soil bearing test
  C. Foundation details   F. Windows or doors

1. Verifies the load bearing capacity of the soil.   1. _____

2. Describes the foundation structure.   2. _____

3. Used on drawings to represent various building materials.   3. _____

4. Low walls constructed to retain an embankment or excavation.   4. _____

5. Openings in the foundation wall.   5. _____

6. Used to shade concrete block foundation walls.   6. _____

1.

DIRECTIONS:
Use the floor plan of the Garden House below to construct a
thickened—edge slab foundation in the space provided.   Scale is
1/4"=1'—0".   Include the following elements in your drawing:
 > Thickness of foundation wall (8") and slab floor (4")
 > Anchor bolts (1/2" x 8") at least every 4 feet along perimeter
 > Cutting plane through one foundation wall. Draw the section
   and dimension it. Foundation depth should be at least 24" or
   frost depth for your area.

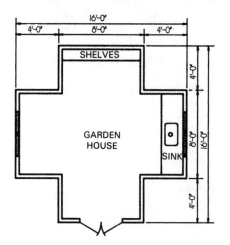

FLOOR PLAN
SCALE: 1/8" = 1'–0"

FOUNDATION PLAN		10–1

2.

ASSIGNMENT 10–2

Factors to be considered in the evaluation of this assignment include: form and style of your work, accuracy of the solution, elements identified properly, and accepted construction technology represented.

DIRECTIONS:
Study Chapter 10 in your text before starting this assignment. You will need a sheet of "C" size (18" x 24") paper for this assignment. Using the floor plan provided below, construct a basement/foundation plan at 1/4"=1'-0" scale which includes the following features:
> Show footings for the foundation walls and pier.
> Use either 12" concrete block, 8" concrete block with pilasters, or 10" cast concrete foundation walls.
> Include stairs and all interior walls in the basement (You decide on the arrangement and use of space.)
> Show all openings in the foundation walls and provide several basement windows and walkout to a patio to the rear of the house.
> Indicate floor joist direction, spacing, and size
> Provide a floor drain and sump near the washer
> Locate the water storage tank, hot water heater, washer, dryer, furnace, electrical distribution panel in the basement
> Add material symbols, dimensions, scale, and title block
> Show a cutting plane line to indicate a typical wall section detail

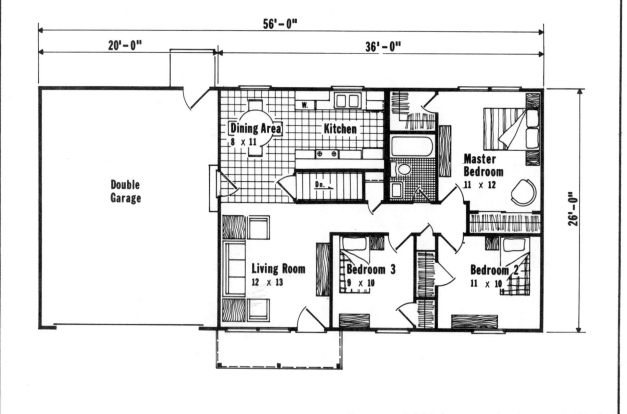

Chapter 11

SILL AND FLOOR CONSTRUCTION

Text Pages 193-208

Name _____   Course _____

Date _____   Score _____

PART I: SHORT ANSWER/LISTING: Provide brief answers to the following questions.

1. Which type of floor framing is commonly used in residential construction?

   _____

2. Name the structural members that are used in both platform and balloon framing.

   A. _____

   B. _____

   C. _____

3. List three reasons why platform framing is popular.

   A. _____

   B. _____

   C. _____

   ALSO: _____

   _____

4. When using platform framing to construct a floor, what is the starting point?

   _____

5. What members provide support for the flooring?

   _____

6. Double joist framing is required to accommodate large openings in the floor. Give two examples of typical openings.

   A. _____

   B. _____

7. Name two disadvantages of balloon framing.

   A. _____

   B. _____

8. What feature of balloon framing makes it unique?

   _____

9. List the two types of sill construction used in balloon framing.

   A. _____

   B. _____

10. Why is it a good practice to use balloon framing in two-story houses with stucco or brick veneer?

_____

11. Name the four factors that determine the joist sizes chosen for a particular area of the structure.

    A. _____

    B. _____

    C. _____

    D. _____

12. Using the chart in the text, determine the allowable span for a 2 x 12 joist when the following conditions are present: grade is #2 Dense, spacing is 16 in. o.c., specie is Southern Yellow Pine, and the load is 30 lbs./sq. ft.

    _____

13. Name two reasons why panel products are often used as subfloor materials.

    A. _____

    B. _____

14. Subflooring panels 1/2 in. or 5/8 in. thick are used when the joists are placed 16 in. o.c. List the types of panel products which may be used.

    A. _____

    B. _____

    C. _____

    D. _____

15. Name two techniques used in residential construction to provide the required support for floors with heavy loads.

    A. _____

    B. _____

16. In post and beam construction, 2 inch decking is commonly used. What is the maximum allowable span generally allowed between beams?

    _____

    _____

17. Two types of foundations are possible for post and beam construction. Name both.

    A. _____

    B. _____

18. What size beam is needed in the following situation? (Refer to the chart in the text.) The designer has specified a glued laminated roof beam to span 24'-0"; the dead load is expected to be 8 lbs./sq. ft.; the live load is estimated to be 20 lbs./sq. ft.; and the beam spacing is 10 ft.

    _____

    _____

Name _____

19. Label the drawings of the various beams used in post and beam construction.

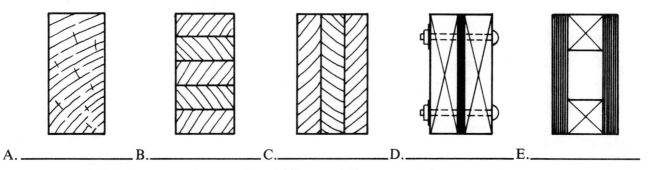

A._____ B._____ C._____ D._____ E._____

20. Why is the spacing of floor joists either 12, 16, or 24 in. o.c.?

_____

_____

21. Name two types of wood from which joists are usually made.

A. _____

B. _____

ALSO: _____

PART II: COMPLETION: Complete each sentence with the proper response. Place your answer on the blank in the right column.

1. In the _____ (transverse/longitudinal) system of beam placement in post and beam construction, the beams are placed at right angles to the roof slope.

1. _____

2. Curtain _____ construction allows wide expanses of glass without the need for headers.

2. _____

3. Cross bridging is used to stiffen the _____ and spread the load over a broader area in typical floor joist construction.

3. _____

4. In platform framing, a method called _____ sill construction is used.

4. _____

5. In T-sill construction (balloon framing), a _____ is placed inside the stud perimeter.

5. _____

6. The actual (dry) size of a 2 x 10 floor joist is _____.

6. _____

7. The framing member that is nailed to the ends of the floor joists is called a _____.

7. _____

8. When a floor area is to be cantilevered 2 ft. beyond a foundation wall, the joists should extend inside _____ ft. for adequate support.

8. _____

9. In T-sill construction, the studs are nailed to the sill plate and the _____.

9. _____

10. Advantages of balloon framing include little shrinkage and _____ (horizontal/vertical) stability.

10. _____

11. A nominal 1 x 6 board is what size when dry. (Refer to chart in book.)

11. _____

12. A floor which uses girders or _____ requires fewer support members.

12. _____

13. Load bearing walls may be made from concrete block, cast concrete, or _____ framing.

13. _____

14. Use solid blocking between the joists when the space between the joists is used as a _____ (hot/cold) air duct.

14. _____

15. Floor trusses are made of _____-graded lumber to minimize the amount of material used.

15. _____

16. Engineered wood floor trusses are commonly made from _____ or 2 x 6 lumber.

16. _____

17. Subfloor panels require _____ along all edges.

17. _____

18. In some areas of the country, the subfloor and _____ are combined into a single thickness.

18. _____

19. Subfloor panels should have some space between them to allow for _____.

19. _____

20. In post and beam construction, wide overhangs may be provided by lengthening the large _____.

20. _____

21. Roof and floor decking planks generally range in thickness from 2 to _____ in.

21. _____

22. Insulation for roof planking is placed between the _____ and roof material.

22. _____

PART III: MULTIPLE CHOICE: Select the best answer and place its letter in the blank at right.

1. Actual dimensions of sills used in residential construction are:
   A. 1 1/2 x 5 1/2 in.
   B. 2 x 6 in.
   C. 2 1/2 x 6 1/2 in.
   D. 3 x 7 in.

1. _____

2. Which of the following statements is true of solid sill construction?
   A. Studs are nailed to the sill plate and the header.
   B. Headers are not required.
   C. A firestop is unnecessary.
   D. All of the above.

2. _____

3. In residential construction, floor joists are usually spaced _____ in. o.c.
   A. 12.
   B. 14.
   C. 16.
   D. 24.

3. _____

4. Beams used to reduce the span of joists may be made from which of the following materials?
   A. Metal S-beam.
   B. Solid timber.
   C. Built-up from dimension lumber.
   D. All of the above.

4. _____

5. Engineered wood floor trusses are commonly spaced _____ in. o.c.
   A. 12.
   B. 18.
   C. 24.
   D. 30.

5. _____

Name _____

6. An advantage of gluing and nailing subfloor panels is:
   A. Labor costs are eliminated.
   B. The panels become stronger.
   C. A squeak-free structure results.
   D. All of the above.

6. _____

7. Gluing and nailing 5/8 in. subfloor panels to 2 x 8 joists increases stiffness by approximately _____ percent.
   A. 25.
   B. 50.
   C. 75.
   D. 100.

7. _____

8. The concrete base for tile or stone supported by wood floor joists should:
   A. Be reinforced with wire mesh.
   B. Have a layer of building felt under the concrete.
   C. Use a special type of concrete.
   D. All of the above.

8. _____

9. In post and beam construction, most of the weight is carried by the:
   A. Beams.
   B. Headers.
   C. Posts.
   D. Curtain wall.

9. _____

10. In post and beam construction, the size of the footings will be determined by:
    A. The width of the building.
    B. The soil bearing capacity.
    C. The type of curtain wall used.
    D. All of the above.

10. _____

PART IV: MATCHING: Match the correct term with its description listed below. Place the corresponding letter on the blank at right.

A. A special type of concrete
B. Built-in camber
C. Cantilevered joists
D. Engineered wood floor trusses
E. National Forest Products Association
F. Metal plates
G. Post and beam construction
H. Transverse method

1. Provides long, clear spans in a light-weight assembly.

1. _____

2. Assures that the chords of the floor trusses will be level when loaded.

2. _____

3. Used when a portion of the floor extends outside the foundation wall.

3. _____

4. Supplies specifications and test results of various woods and wood products.

4. _____

5. Provides a base for ceramic tile, stone, and slate floors.

5. _____

6. Provides greater spans and more flexibility in design.

6. _____

7. A system used in post and beam construction when the beams follow the roof slope and decking runs parallel to the roof ridge.

7. _____

8. Used to connect large beam segments.

8. _____

1.

DIRECTIONS:
Using guidelines and proper form, label and dimension the basement wall
section below using the following information:
> Footing is 12" x 24" with two 1/2" re-rods and drain tile in pea gravel
> Basement floor is 4" thick with 4" sand base and 3/8" expansion joint
> Basement wall is 12" concrete block with 1/2" parge coat outside
> Distance from top of footing to grade (224.2' El.) is 8'-8"
> Floor to underside of 24" trusses is 8'-2"
> Anchor bolts are 1/2" x 16" spaced 8'-0" apart
> Flooring material (1st floor) is 3/4" T&G P.W.
> Stud wall is covered with 3/4" RF insulation and panel siding.

SCALE: 1/2" = 1'-0"

WALL SECTION PARTS		11-1

2.

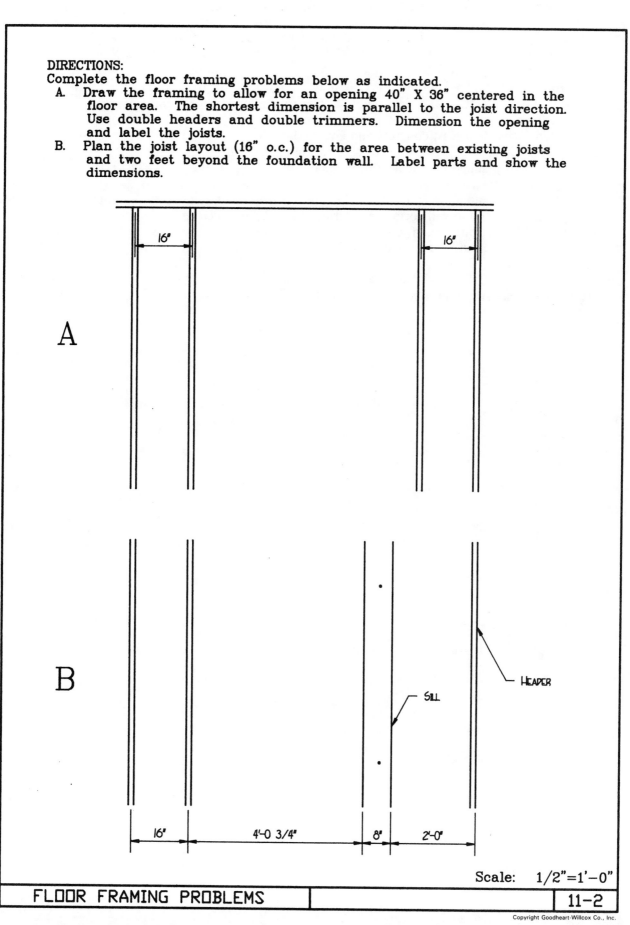

DIRECTIONS:
Complete the floor framing problems below as indicated.
A. Draw the framing to allow for an opening 40" X 36" centered in the floor area. The shortest dimension is parallel to the joist direction. Use double headers and double trimmers. Dimension the opening and label the joists.
B. Plan the joist layout (16" o.c.) for the area between existing joists and two feet beyond the foundation wall. Label parts and show the dimensions.

A

16"   16"

B

HEADER

SILL

16"   4'-0 3/4"   8"   2'-0"

Scale: 1/2"=1'-0"

FLOOR FRAMING PROBLEMS   11-2

3. **Floor Framing Plan.** This assignment will be evaluated based on the following factors: quality of work, use of proper construction techniques, use of appropriate size building materials for spans and economy, and overall communication provided.

   Directions. You are to draw a floor framing plan and a typical section for the house shown in Fig.10-13 in your text. The scale should be 1/4" = 1'-0". Use "C" size paper and center the drawing on this sheet. Include the following elements in your drawing:

   - Use typical #2 Douglas Fir floor framing materials (2 x 8, 2 x 10, 2 x 12) for sills and floor joists and standard 4 x 8 ft. by 3/4 in. tongue-and-groove plywood for floor material.
   - Use platform framing and box sill construction.
   - The basement is 10 in. cast concrete and covers the space under the living area of the house except the garage. The garage has a 4 in. thick floating slab floor.
   - A steel beam is planned for the length of the house to support the joists. The total floor load is 50 lbs./sq. ft.
   - Floor framing should allow space for 3/4 in. rigid foam insulation sheathing on top of the foundation wall. Wood siding will form the exterior skin of the structure.
   - Draw a typical section of the foundation wall between the garage and utility storage showing floor levels and construction. The garage floor should be 4 in. above the grade line. Use 1/2" = 1'-0" scale for the section.
   - The sandstone hearth is to be supported on the floor.
   - Add dimensions and notes necessary to build the floor framing.

Chapter 12

WALL AND CEILING CONSTRUCTION

Text Pages 209-222

Name _____   Course _____

Date _____   Score _____

PART I: MATCHING: Match the correct term with its description listed below. Place the corresponding letter on the blank at right.

A. Ashlar stonework
B. Ceiling joists
C. Common brick
D. Corner bracing
E. Cripples
F. Door schedule
G. Fire cut

H. Flashing
I. Rubble stonework
J. Sole plate
K. Subfloor
L. Trimmers
M. Veneer

1. Framing member used in residential frame wall construction.   1. _____

2. Provides a work surface for the construction of the frame walls.   2. _____

3. Short studs used above and below wall openings.   3. _____

4. Studs used in wall openings to support the header.   4. _____

5. Provides additional corner support in frame wall construction.   5. _____

6. Provides specific information about each door included in the plan.   6. _____

7. Placed across the width of the structure after the top plates have been added.   7. _____

8. An angular cut at the end of a joist to prevent the wall from falling in the event of a fire.   8. _____

9. Composed of dressed, cut, or squared stones.   9. _____

10. Composed of irregular-shaped field stones.   10. _____

11. Facing material used in wall construction.   11. _____

12. Prevents moisture from entering solid masonry or brick veneer walls.   12. _____

13. May have a lip on one or more edges.   13. _____

PART II: MULTIPLE CHOICE: Select the best answer and place its letter in the blank at right.

1. Which of the following species are generally used in wall framing lumber?   1. _____
   A. Southern yellow pine.
   B. Redwood.
   C. Oak.
   D. All of the above.

2. Frame wall construction begins with the:
   A. Header.
   B. Sole plate.
   C. Top plate.
   D. Studs.

2. _____

3. Exterior wall corners provide:
   A. Space for the wall to be built in small sections.
   B. Adequate wind bracing.
   C. Sufficient support for the building.
   D. All of the above.

3. _____

4. A nailing base for interior wall materials may be provided by:
   A. A 2 x 6 fastened to cross blocking.
   B. Placing 1/2 in. plywood sheathing next to the studs.
   C. Applying rigid foam insulation to the wall section.
   D. All of the above.

4. _____

5. Header size refers to:
   A. The overall size of the header.
   B. The size of the material used.
   C. The size of the rough opening plus the size of the spacer.
   D. None of the above.

5. _____

6. Trussed headers are more functional for:
   A. Frame walls without corner bracing.
   B. Areas subject to high winds.
   C. Openings wider than 8'-0".
   D. All of the above.

6. _____

7. Special framing is needed for:
   A. Extra bathtub support.
   B. Wall openings for heating ducts.
   C. Wall backing for a water closet.
   D. All of the above.

7. _____

8. Which of the following statements is true of masonry veneer?
   A. Moisture does not collect between the veneer and the frame wall.
   B. The veneer does not support the weight of the wall.
   C. The most common thickness used is 1 in.
   D. None of the above.

8. _____

9. A building material which has sharp corners and lines and is very uniform in size is:
   A. Face brick.
   B. Common brick.
   C. Cobweb stone.
   D. Random rubble.

9. _____

PART III: COMPLETION: Complete each sentence with the proper response. Place your answer on the blank in the right column.

1. The trend in residential frame wall construction is toward more _____ and less on-site construction.

1. _____

2. The most common lumber grade is _____ grade.

2. _____

3. The sole plate functions as an anchor for the wall and a _____ for interior and exterior wall sheathing.

3. _____

Name _____

4. A space of 8'-1 1/2" from the bottom of the ceiling joists to the top of the subfloor allows a finished wall height of approximately _____ ft.

4. _____

5. The advantage of using solid blocking is a _____ (shorter/longer) construction time.

5. _____

6. The distance is usually the same from the top of each window and door to the _____.

6. _____

7. All wall openings need a _____ or lintel above the opening to provide support for the weight above.

7. _____

8. To prevent the ceiling joists from interfering with the roof slope, the upper corner of the joist is cut to match the _____ of the roof.

8. _____

9. Framing around a ceiling opening for a disappearing stairway requires the use of _____ headers.

9. _____

10. To provide support for a bow window, cantilevered _____ should be used.

10. _____

11. Corrugated metal wall ties may be placed in mortar joints 16 in. apart vertically and _____ in. apart horizontally. These bond the masonry wall to the frame wall or bond two thicknesses of masonry together.

11. _____

12. One inch of dead air space should be left between masonry veneer and the _____ wall.

12. _____

13. Termite _____ are placed at the base of solid masonry or brick veneers to prevent the entrance of termites.

13. _____

14. The length, width, and thickness of one commonly used firebrick is _____ (nominal size).

14. _____

PART IV: SHORT ANSWER/LISTING: Provide brief answers to the following questions.

1. List the three types of residential wall construction.

A. _____

B. _____

C. _____

2. Name the three types of bracing commonly used in frame wall construction.

A. _____

B. _____

C. _____

3. Why would the exterior frame wall be placed 1/2 to 3/4 in. in from the outside edge of the foundation wall?

_____

_____

4. Is greater shrinkage more likely to occur in solid blocking construction or cripple construction?

_____

5. In frame wall construction, the header is usually longer than the rough opening. Explain why.

_____

_____

6. How does ceiling joist construction differ from floor joist construction?

_____

_____

_____

7. List the advantages and disadvantages of concrete block walls.

_____

_____

_____

_____

8. Advantages of a brick or stone veneer wall over a solid masonry wall are:

A. _____

B. _____

C. _____

9. Identify the brick bonds shown below.

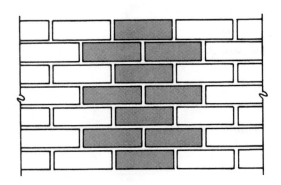

A. _____

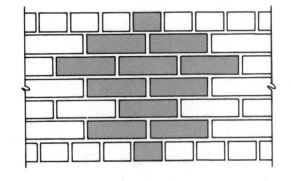

B. _____

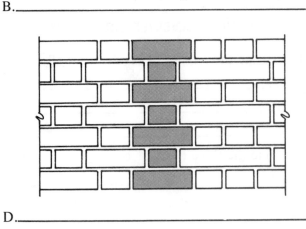

C. _____

D. _____

1.

DIRECTIONS:
Complete the wall framing in each of the problems below applying the specific requirements noted.
A.   Frame a rough opening which is 52" wide by 40" high.   Use a solid (2" x 12") header.   Label all framing members and dimension R.O. and height from floor to top of the opening.
B.   In these two problems, complete the plan view framing for a corner formed with three full studs (left) and a wall intersecting at a stud (right).

A

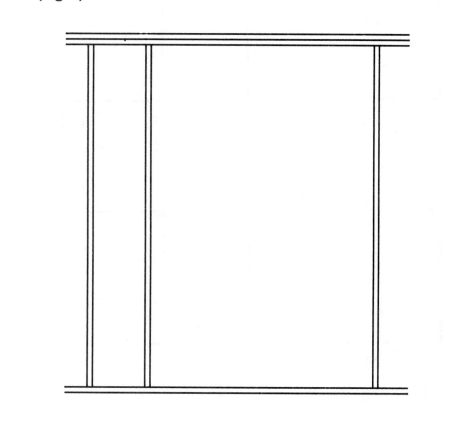

B

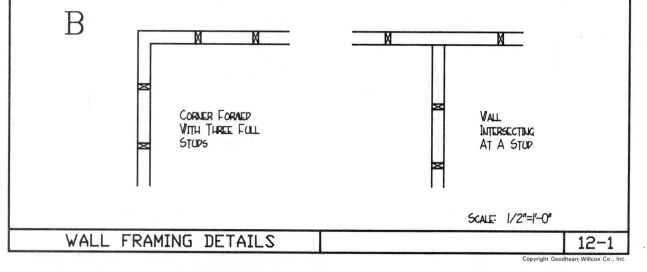

CORNER FORMED WITH THREE FULL STUDS

WALL INTERSECTING AT A STUD

SCALE: 1/2"=1'-0"

WALL FRAMING DETAILS		12-1

2.

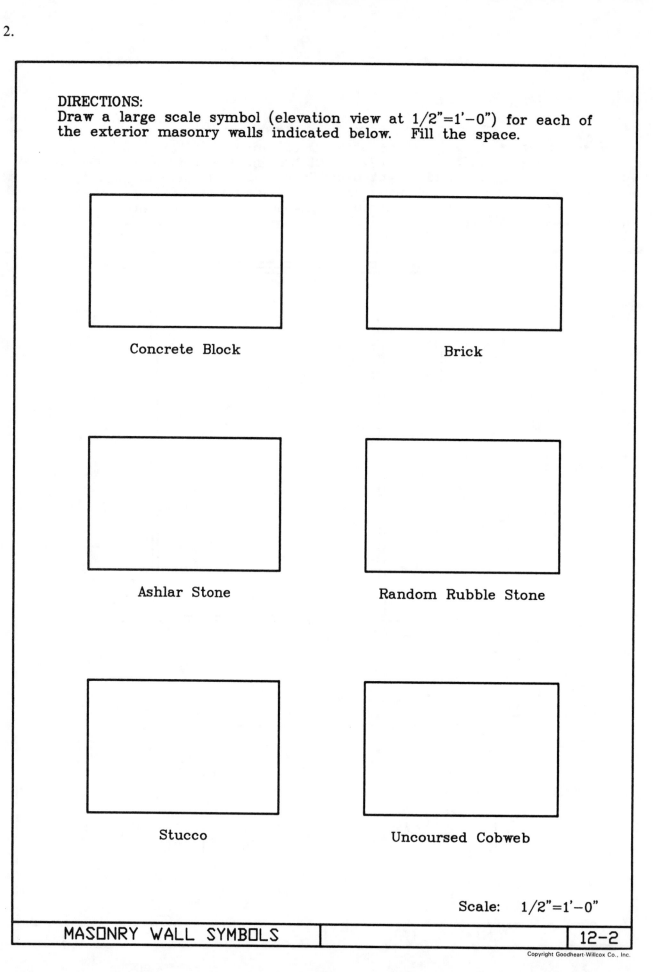

DIRECTIONS:
Draw a large scale symbol (elevation view at 1/2"=1'-0") for each of the exterior masonry walls indicated below. Fill the space.

Concrete Block

Brick

Ashlar Stone

Random Rubble Stone

Stucco

Uncoursed Cobweb

Scale: 1/2"=1'-0"

MASONRY WALL SYMBOLS

12-2

Chapter 13

DOORS AND WINDOWS

Text Pages 223-252

Name _____   Course _____

Date_____   Score _____

PART I: MULTIPLE CHOICE: Select the best answer and place its letter in the blank at right.

1. Types of interior doors include:
   A. Sliding.
   B. Double-action.
   C. Pocket.
   D. All of the above.

1. _____

2. Metal bi-fold doors are usually _____ thick and are commonly used as closet doors.
   A. 1 in.
   B. 1 1/8 in.
   C. 1 1/4 in.
   D. 1 1/2 in.

2. _____

3. Sliding or bi-pass doors are:
   A. Used frequently for large openings.
   B. Not subject to warping.
   C. Limited to two doors for each opening.
   D. All of the above.

3. _____

4. Double-action doors may be:
   A. Used for large openings.
   B. Hinged to swing through an arc of 180 degrees.
   C. Made of metal and usually 1 in. thick.
   D. All of the above.

4. _____

5. Accordion doors:
   A. Require little space.
   B. Are produced in a large variety of designs.
   C. May use individual hinged panels.
   D. All of the above.

5. _____

6. Exterior glass doors are:
   A. Declining in use.
   B. Frequently used between kitchens and dining rooms.
   C. Usually have wood or aluminum frames.
   D. None of the above.

6. _____

7. Doorjambs used in residential construction are:
   A. Usually made of bronze.
   B. Composed of two side jambs and a head jamb across the top.
   C. 1 3/4 in. thick for exterior doors and 1 in. thick for interior doors.
   D. All of the above.

7. _____

8. Which of these statements should you follow when planning the windows for a dwelling?
   A. To gain the maximum amount of light possible, place primary windows on the west.
   B. Four small windows will yield less contrast than one large window.
   C. Glass area which is 20 percent of the floor area should provide adequate natural light.
   D. The best distribution of light is achieved by placing the windows on one wall as opposed to two walls.

8. _____

9. To provide ample ventilation in a home:
   A. The openings should be at least 10 percent of the floor area.
   B. Windows should be placed to receive prevailing breezes.
   C. Plan the location of windows for the best movement of air across a room.
   D. All of the above.

9. _____

10. Windows of basically the same type have:
    A. Different specifications from each manufacturer to each manufacturer.
    B. Uniform specifications from manufacturer to manufacturer.
    C. Specifications which are not important to the designer or contractor.
    D. None of the above.

10. _____

11. The rough framed space in the wall needed to install the window is the:
    A. Glass size.
    B. Basic unit.
    C. Rough opening.
    D. Sash opening.

11. _____

12. Casement windows have side hinged sashes that swing out and may be opened or closed by:
    A. Handles on the sash.
    B. Push bars on the frame.
    C. Cranks.
    D. All of the above.

12. _____

13. Which of the following lines should be used to show the hinge positions on a hinged window?
    A. Dashed line.
    B. Object line.
    C. Short break line.
    D. Section line.

13. _____

14. Which of the following statements best represents hopper windows?
    A. Hopper windows rarely interfere with room arrangement.
    B. Hopper windows are more efficient when placed low on the wall because they direct air upward.
    C. Hopper windows are available in a wide range of sizes.
    D. Hopper windows are difficult to operate and maintain.

14. _____

15. Picture windows may:
    A. Open to provide ventilation.
    B. Require custom-made screens.
    C. Be large fixed glass units used with other window types.
    D. None of the above.

15. _____

Name _____

16. Which of the window styles listed would most likely be found in a traditional style home?
    A. Casement
    B. Horizontal sliding
    C. Jalousie
    D. Bay

16. _____

17. The side units in a bay window are normally placed _____ degrees to the exterior wall.
    A. 90.
    B. 60.
    C. 45.
    D. None of the above.

17. _____

18. Bow window units normally use _____ casement units to form the arc.
    A. 3 to 6.
    B. 4 to 7.
    C. 5 to 8.
    D. Any of the above.

18. _____

19. Which of the following is a characteristic of clerestory windows?
    A. They can produce striking architectural effects.
    B. They are often installed in the roof of a dwelling.
    C. They are typically fixed windows.
    D. None of the above.

19. _____

PART II: COMPLETION: Complete each sentence with the proper response. Place your answer on the blank in the right column.

1. Interior flush doors are normally covered with 1/8 in. mahogany or _____ plywood and are smooth on both sides.

1. _____

2. Pocket doors are a variation of the sliding door and are often used between _____ and dining rooms.

2. _____

3. Accordion doors are available in wood, _____, and plastics. They are often used for large openings when other doors are unacceptable.

3. _____

4. The top half of a(n) _____ door may operate separately from the bottom half.

4. _____

5. Exterior flush doors are commonly 1 3/4 in. thick and _____ high.

5. _____

6. Exterior panel doors are produced in white pine, _____, fir, and various other woods.

6. _____

7. To provide for an automatic garage door opener, allow extra headroom to mount the _____ drive when the door is open.

7. _____

8. The information listed in the door schedule is obtained from _____ literature.

8. _____

9. In frame construction, the space between the jamb and rough framing is covered with trim called _____.

9. _____

10. A _____ is placed at the bottom of the door opening between the two side jambs. It drains water away from the door.

    10. _____

11. Construction details of windows and doors are normally drawn in _____ through the head jamb, the side jamb, and the sill.

    11. _____

12. Extremely bright areas and dark corners are eliminated by proper design and _____ of windows.

    12. _____

13. A shallow penetration of light over a broad area can be achieved by using short, _____ windows.

    13. _____

14. A thin, deep penetration of light over a broad area can be achieved by using tall, _____ windows.

    14. _____

15. Windows placed _____ (high/low) on the wall result in a higher degree of light penetration into the room.

    15. _____

16. Areas of large glass will make a room appear _____ (smaller/larger).

    16. _____

17. Three common materials used in the manufacture of window frames are wood, _____, and plastics.

    17. _____

18. Window sashes are held in place by _____ devices or are counter balanced.

    18. _____

19. The overall dimensions of the window unit is the _____ unit size.

    19. _____

20. A series of narrow horizontal glass slats are the components of a _____ window.

    20. _____

21. Circle top windows may be used as _____ (single/double) units or joined with other window styles.

    21. _____

22. Special _____ windows may be custom made in various shapes and sizes from window manufacturers.

    22. _____

23. Casement windows are usually placed _____ degrees to the exterior wall in a box bay window.

    23. _____

24. Most skylights are _____ in shape to fit between roof trusses, while others can be made to accommodate most any design situation.

    24. _____

PART III: SHORT ANSWER/LISTING: Provide brief answers to the following questions.

1. What materials are commonly used in the panels of panel doors?

    A. _____

    B. _____

    C. _____

2. List advantages and disadvantages of pocket doors.

_____

_____

_____

_____

Name _____

3. French doors have panels which are always glass. Where are French doors often used?

_____

_____

4. What are the basic differences between interior and exterior doors?

_____

_____

_____

_____

5. Name the two types of garage doors used in residential construction.

A. _____

B. _____

6. Where would a door schedule be found in a set of drawings?

_____

_____

7. What is the purpose of a doorjamb?

_____

8. Why are rough openings framed with extra space in the length and width for interior doors?

_____

_____

9. What materials are most commonly used in the construction of window and door sills?

A. _____

B. _____

C. _____

D. _____

10. List three factors you should consider when planning the location of a window to take advantage of a pleasing view.

A. _____

_____

B. _____

_____

C. _____

_____

11. When selecting windows, first consider the interior requirements. What considerations should be given as to window selection to produce continuity in the exterior design?

_____

_____

12. What is meant by the sash opening?

_____

_____

13. When would it be wise to draw a section of the support mullion?

_____

14. List four variations of circle top windows commonly used in residential construction.

A. _____

B. _____

C. _____

D. _____

15. List the specific information commonly found on a window schedule.

A. _____

B. _____

C. _____

D. _____

E. _____

PART IV: MATCHING: Match the correct term with its description listed below. Place the corresponding letter on the blank at right.

A. Awning
B. Brick mold
C. Drip cap
D. Double-hung
E. Fixed
F. Glass size

G. Glider
H. Mullions
I. Muntins
J. Prehung doors
K. Rails
L. Stiles

1. Vertical members of a panel door.   1. _____

2. Horizontal members of a panel door.   2. _____

3. Units consisting of the jamb and door hung ready for installation.   3 _____

4. A strip used in frame construction to shed water over a door or window.   4. _____

5. Used in a masonry wall to cover the space between the jamb and the rough framing.   5. _____

6. Windows with two sashes that slide up and down in grooves.   6. _____

7. Thin vertical or horizontal bars which divide the glass area into smaller sections.   7. _____

8. Vertical or horizontal components which divide window units.   8. _____

9. Comparable to the inside sash dimensions.   9. _____

10. Also known as horizontal sliding windows.   10. _____

11. Top-hinged windows that swing out at an angle.   11. _____

12. Random shapes, circle top, and picture windows are examples of this window type.   12. _____

1.

DIRECTIONS:
Draw a Plan View symbol for each of the door types specified below.

Flush or Panel Door   Bi-Fold Doors

Dutch Door   Accordion Door

Pocket Door   Sliding (Bi-Pass) Doors

Double-Action Door   French Doors

Exterior Panel Door   Glass Sliding Door

Garage Door

Scale: 1/4"=1'-0"

PLAN VIEW DOOR SYMBOLS		13-1

2.

DIRECTIONS:
Draw a Plan View symbol for each of the window types specified below.

Double Hung Window

Awning Window

Casement Window (2 Sash)

Fixed Window

Horizontal Sliding Window

Hopper Window

Double Hung 45° Bay Window

Five Unit Casement Bow Window

Scale: 1/4"=1'-0"

PLAN VIEW WINDOW SYMBOLS

13-2

3.

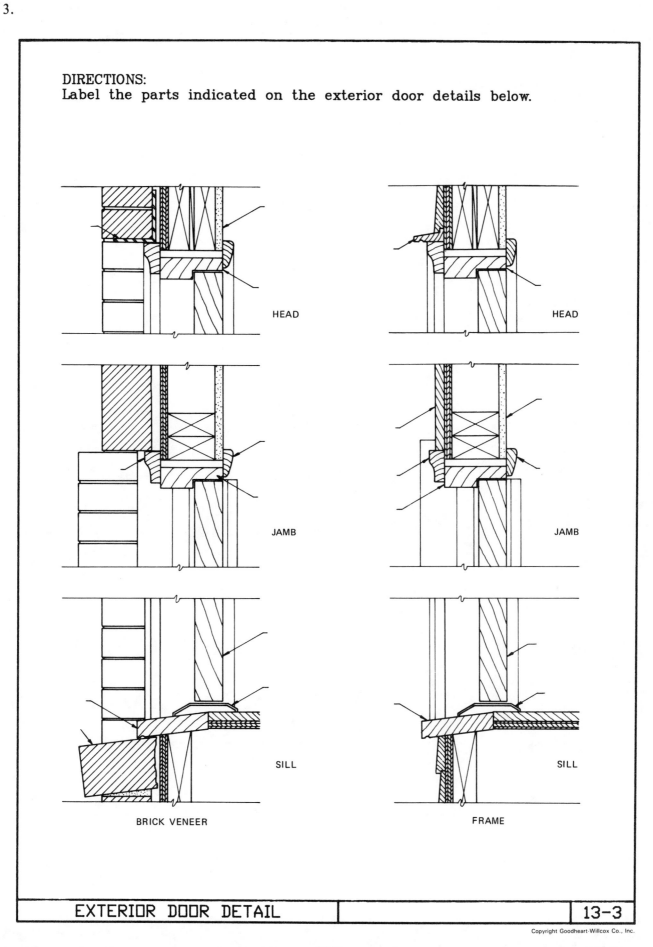

DIRECTIONS:
Label the parts indicated on the exterior door details below.

HEAD

HEAD

JAMB

JAMB

SILL

SILL

BRICK VENEER

FRAME

EXTERIOR DOOR DETAIL

13-3

4. Continue to collect pictures to add to your notebook. Include various types of doors and windows. Label each picture with the type of door or window it represents.

Chapter 14

STAIRS

Text Pages 253-264

Name _____   Course _____

Date _____   Score _____

PART I: MATCHING: Match the correct term with its description listed below. Place the corresponding letter on the blank at right.

A. Balusters
B. Circular
C. L
D. Landing
E. Newel
F. Nosing
G. Open
H. Plain stringer
I. Rise
J. Riser

K. Run
L. Stairway
M. Stairwell
N. Straight run
O. Stringer
P. Total rise
Q. Total run
R. Tread
S. U
T. Winder

1. A series of steps connecting two or more levels of a structure.   1. _____

2. Stairs which require a long open space.   2. _____

3. A type of stairs with one landing.   3. _____

4. Stairs with two flights of steps parallel.   4. _____

5. Stairs with "pie-shaped" steps at the point of the landing.   5. _____

6. The basic shape of these stairs stems from an irregular curve or arc.   6. _____

7. Vertical components that support the handrail on open stairs.   7. _____

8. Floor area at the top, bottom, or along the flight of stairs.   8. _____

9. The primary posts of the handrail.   9. _____

10. The rounded tread overhang which extends past the face of the riser.   10. _____

11. Stairs without walls on one or both sides.   11. _____

12. A stringer notched or cut to fit the shape of the steps.   12. _____

13. Vertical distance from the surface of one tread to the surface of the next tread.   13. _____

14. Vertical face of a step.   14. _____

15. Distance from the face of one riser to the face of the next riser.   15. _____

16. Opening in which a set of stairs are constructed.   16. _____

17. A structural member which supports the treads and risers.   17. _____

(Continued)

18. The total vertical height of the stairs.

18. _____

19. The total horizontal length of the stairs.

19. _____

20. The horizontal member of each step.

20. _____

PART II: COMPLETION: Complete each sentence with the proper response. Place your answer on the blank in the right column.

1. Simple ascent or descent and _____ should be important considerations in designing stairs.

1. _____

2. Service stairs are usually made from _____ lumber, constructed on the site, and are steeper than main stairs.

2. _____

3. Wide U stairs have a well between the two flights. In _____ U stairs, the space is small or nonexistent.

3. _____

4. In homes where little space is available, _____ stairs may be a solution.

4. _____

5. _____ stairs are the most complicated to build and require exceptional quality of work.

5. _____

6. A stringer is sometimes called the _____.

6. _____

7. The main stairway should be at least _____ wide.

7. _____

8. When constructing plain stringers, nail the treads and risers directly to the _____.

8. _____

9. Glue and _____ hold the treads and risers in place permanently on a plain stringer stairs.

9. _____

10. Common housed stringer treads are 1 1/4 in. _____ (fir/oak) in 10 1/2 and 11 1/2 in. widths.

10. _____

11. The most popular tread width for housed stringers is _____ in.

11. _____

PART III: SHORT ANSWER/LISTING: Provide brief answers to the following questions.

1. What is the term used to describe a set of L stairs that has a landing near the top or bottom?

_____

2. In a set of winder stairs, how is the width of the "pie-shaped" steps determined?

_____

_____

3. List the three factors to consider when designing a set of stairs.

A. _____

B. _____

C. _____

4. In a set of stairs requiring more than two stringers, where should the third stringer be placed?

_____

_____

5. List advantages and disadvantages of plain stringer stair construction.

_____

_____

_____

Name _____

6. What method is commonly used to hold the treads and risers in housed stairs?

_____

_____

_____

7. What is the ideal range of riser height?

_____

8. List the four rules to follow when determining the rise-run ratio.

A. _____

_____

B. _____

_____

C. _____

_____

D. _____

_____

9. Why is there always one less tread than there are risers?

_____

10. Label the drawings of the general types of stairs below.

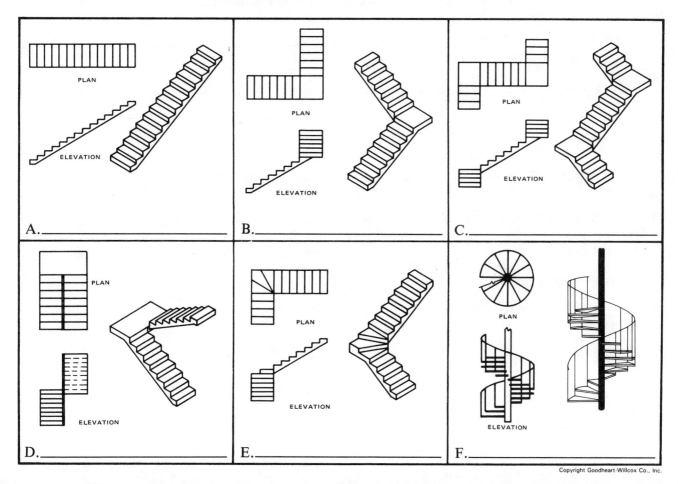

A. _____ B. _____ C. _____

D. _____ E. _____ F. _____

11. Locate and label the newel, handrail, and baluster on the stairway drawing below.

A. _____

B. _____

C. _____

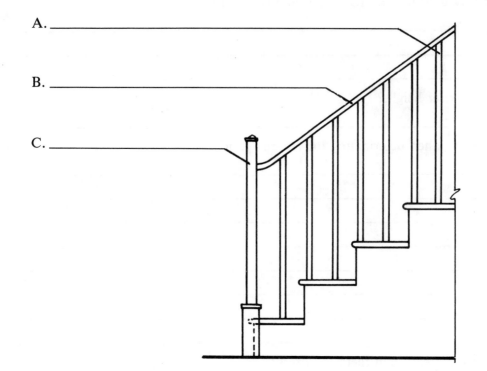

12. Calculate the following design elements for a set of stairs for a two-story home. The total rise is 72 in., with a standard tread of 11 1/2 in. A 1 in. nosing is required and the stairs should have an acceptable slope of 30 to 35 degrees. Calculate the following: total run, number of risers, riser height, number of treads, and run of a step.

Total Run = _____

Number of Risers = _____

Riser Height = _____

Number of Treads = _____

Run of a Step = _____

PART IV: MULTIPLE CHOICE: Select the best answer and place its letter in the blank at right.

1. Indicate the house style most likely to use stairs.   1. _____
   A. Garrison.
   B. Salt box.
   C. Southern colonial.
   D. All of the above.

2. The type of stairs used most in residential construction is: 2. _____
   A. L stairs.
   B. Straight run.
   C. Spiral.
   D. Winder.

3. Circular stairs have _____ shaped steps.   3. _____
   A. Triangular.
   B. Pie-shaped.
   C. Trapezoid.
   D. Winder.

Name _____

4. Enclosed stairs are also known as:
   A. Closed stairs.
   B. Housed stairs.
   C. Box stairs.
   D. All of the above.

4. _____

5. Plain stringers are constructed for:
   A. Uncarpeted main stairs.
   B. Service stairs.
   C. Circular stairs.
   D. All of the above.

5. _____

6. Housed stringers are:
   A. Constructed from finished lumber.
   B. Usually purchased precut or preassembled.
   C. Sometimes made from 1 x 12 or 2 x 12 lumber.
   D. All of the above.

6. _____

7. The actual size of an oak tread used in housed stringer construction is _____ thick.
   A. 3/4 in.
   B. 1 in.
   C. 1 1/16 in.
   D. 1 1/4 in.

7. _____

8. All stairs should have at least one handrail. The recommended handrail height is:
   A. 30 in. along the incline and 34 in. at the landing.
   B. 32 in. along the incline and 36 in. at the landing.
   C. 34 in. along the incline and 38 in. at the landing.
   D. None of the above.

8. _____

9. Minimum stairway headroom is:
   A. 6'-0".
   B. 6'-6".
   C. 7'-0".
   D. 7'-5".

9. _____

1.

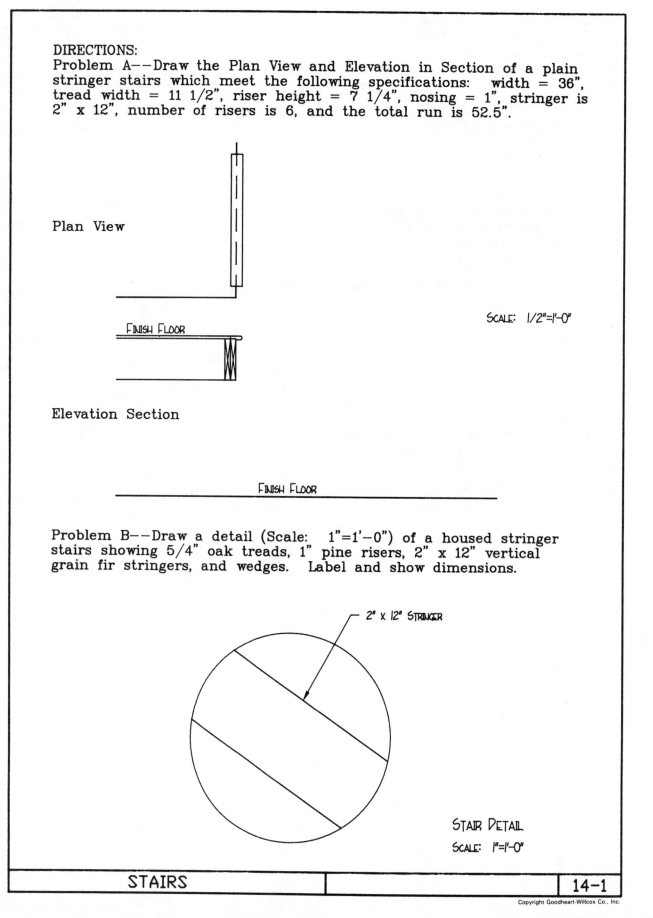

DIRECTIONS:
Problem A––Draw the Plan View and Elevation in Section of a plain stringer stairs which meet the following specifications: width = 36", tread width = 11 1/2", riser height = 7 1/4", nosing = 1", stringer is 2" x 12", number of risers is 6, and the total run is 52.5".

Plan View

SCALE: 1/2"=1'-0"

FINISH FLOOR

Elevation Section

FINISH FLOOR

Problem B––Draw a detail (Scale: 1"=1'-0") of a housed stringer stairs showing 5/4" oak treads, 1" pine risers, 2" x 12" vertical grain fir stringers, and wedges.   Label and show dimensions.

2" x 12" STRINGER

STAIR DETAIL
SCALE: 1"=1'-0"

| STAIRS | | 14-1 |

Name _____

2. **Stair Details.** This assignment will be evaluated based on the following factors: quality of work, design parameters met, accurately and completely communicated design, and directions followed.

   Directions. Your task is to design a set of enclosed straight run main stairs. Show both a plan view and elevation in section. The stairs are between the first and second floors of a residence. The scale is to be 1" = 1'-0". Include these elements in your design:
   - Finshed floor-to-finished floor distance (total rise) is 9' - 1/2". (2 x 12 joists, 1/2 in. drywall, and 3/4 in. finished floor).
   - Minimum headroom is 6'-6".
   - Width of stairs (outside to outside of stringers) is 36 in.
   - Stairs use housed stringer with wedges and glue.
   - Treads are 5/4 in. oak, risers are white pine, and stringers are 2 x 12 oak.
   - Use standard 11 1/2 in. wide treads — allow a 1 in. nosing.
   - Angle of the stairs must be between 30 and 37 degrees.
   - Indicate stairwell dimensions with a minimum headroom of 6'-6".
   - Show handrail of your design on the elevation section drawing.
   - Show all dimensions and necessary notes.
   - Prepare a Stair Data chart which shows:

Total Rise:	Angle of stairs:
Total Run:	Stairwell opening:
Rise of a step:	Nosing:
Run of a step:	Handrail height:
Width of the stair:	

   Be sure the views project, and include all material symbols, scale, and title block.

3. Collect pictures of various stair designs and manufacturers' literature to add to your notebook. This information will be useful for future design applications.

Architecture Workbook

Chapter 15

FIREPLACES AND CHIMNEYS

Text Pages 265-282

Name _____   Course _____

Date_____   Score _____

PART I: COMPLETION: Complete each sentence with the proper response. Place your answer on the blank in the right column.

1. A fireplace is often a _____ point of a room.   1. _____

2. Fireplaces may either be gas fired or _____ burning.   2. _____

3. The hearth should be made from _____ materials such as ceramic tile, stone, or slate.   3. _____

4. If the fireplace is giving off only a small amount of heat, then the fire chamber is probably too _____ (shallow/deep).   4. _____

5. A fireplace which smokes is likely to be the result of a fire chamber which is too _____ (shallow/deep).   5. _____

6. Ashes are removed from the ash chamber through the _____.   6. _____

7. The back and the sides of a prefabricated steel heat-circulating fireplace are made with a double _____ passageway where the air is heated.   7. _____

8. The damper opens to the back of the fireplace _____.   8. _____

9. The location of the _____ governs the height of the smoke shelf.   9. _____

10. The flue starts at the top of the smoke chamber and proceeds to the top of the _____.   10. _____

11. A _____ is required for each fireplace.   11. _____

12. For maximum _____, the flue should be located directly above the center of the fireplace.   12. _____

13. When selecting a flue for a fireplace, it is better to choose one which is too _____ (small/large) rather than too _____ (small/large).   13. _____

14. Greater efficiency is achieved from a _____ (warm/cold) chimney.   14. _____

15. The chimney does not support any part of the house; thus it is a _____ structure.   15. _____

16. The recommended clearance for framing members around a chimney is _____ in.   16. _____

17. The space between the chimney and the framing should be filled with _____ material.

17. _____

18. A chimney placed at the peak or ridge line of a roof _____ (increases/decreases) the chance of water problems.

18. _____

19. Wide chimneys or extremely low roof slopes usually require a _____ along the chimney.

19. _____

20. Single-face fireplaces normally operate _____ (efficiently/inefficiently) and are the least complicated to construct of all the fireplace types.

20. _____

21. The three-face fireplace is also referred to as a _____ fireplace.

21. _____

22. Before installing prefabricated metal fireplaces, consult the local _____ codes.

22. _____

23. _____ (Radiant/Circulating) stoves provide more even heat.

23. _____

24. Medium efficiency stoves have less air leakage into the stove, have better combustion, and are _____ to 50 percent efficient.

24. _____

25. The length of a standard 12 x 12 in. clay flue liner is _____ ft.

25. _____

PART II: MULTIPLE CHOICE: Select the best answer and place its letter in the blank at right.

1. The hearth should extend _____ in front of the fireplace.
   A. 12 in.
   B. 14 in.
   C. 16 in.
   D. 18 in.

1. _____

2. The fire chamber should be _____ thick.
   A. 8 in.
   B. 9 in.
   C. 10 in.
   D. 12 in.

2. _____

3. Prefabricated steel heat-circulating fireplaces are:
   A. Somewhat efficient.
   B. Very efficient.
   C. Inefficient.
   D. None of the above.

3. _____

4. Fireplace dampers:
   A. Prevent down drafts of cold air when the fireplace is not being used.
   B. Are made of cast iron or steel.
   C. Should be located 6 or 8 in. above the top of the fireplace opening.
   D. All of the above.

4. _____

5. The shape of the smoke chamber is:
   A. Basically square.
   B. An elongated rectangle.
   C. Basically a pyramid with the backside usually vertical.
   D. None of the above.

5. _____

Name _____

6. The lining of the flue is usually made from:
   A. Clay.
   B. Concrete block.
   C. Firebrick.
   D. Poured concrete.

6. _____

7. _____ of brick should be placed on all sides of the flue with a lining.
   A. 8 in.
   B. 6 in.
   C. 4 in.
   D. 2 in.

7. _____

8. At least _____ of brick should be placed on all sides of the flue when it does not have a lining.
   A. 8 in.
   B. 6 in.
   C. 4 in.
   D. 2 in.

8. _____

9. Assume that you have designed a fireplace for a new home. The opening measures 32 x 48 in. What size of flue would be large enough to provide the proper draft? (Refer to chart in the text for sizes available).
   A. 12 x 16.
   B. 16 x 16.
   C. 16 x 20.
   D. 20 x 20.

9. _____

10. Building codes usually require that a flue be at least _____ above the highest point of the roof to prevent sparks flying out of the flue and setting the roof on fire.
    A. 2 ft.
    B. 3 ft.
    C. 4 ft.
    D. 5 ft.

10. _____

11. Lintels used to support the masonry above fireplace openings are:
    A. Wood beams.
    B. Cast concrete.
    C. Lintel blocks.
    D. Angle steel.

11. _____

12. The two-face (adjacent) fireplace:
    A. Usually functions more efficiently than other fireplace types.
    B. Opens on the front and either left or right sides.
    C. Is not subject to drafts.
    D. All of the above.

12. _____

13. Prefabricated steel heat-circulating fireplaces may require:
    A. Framing enclosures.
    B. Masonry enclosures.
    C. A and B.
    D. Fruitwood logs.

13. _____

14. High efficiency stoves which are over 50 percent efficient, use
_____ to increase output.
    A. Chimneys.
    B. Bellows.
    C. Heat exchange devices.
    D. All of the above.

14. _____

15. The actual size of a 12 x 12 in. clay flue liner is:
    A. 11 1/2 x 11 1/2 in.
    B. 11 3/4 x 11 3/4 in.
    C. 12 1/4 x 12 1/4 in.
    D. 12 1/2 x 12 1/2 in.

15. _____

PART III: SHORT ANSWER/LISTING: Provide brief answers to the following questions.

1. Name the five different types of fireplaces.

    A. _____

    B. _____

    C. _____

    D. _____

    E. _____

2. What materials are normally used for the inner hearth?

    _____

3. What is the purpose of fire clay and where might it be used?

    _____

    _____

4. Why is the design of the fire chamber important?

    _____

    _____

5. List the six major parts of a prefabricated steel heat-circulating fireplace.

    A. _____

    B. _____

    C. _____

    D. _____

    E. _____

    F. _____

6. Explain how a prefabricated steel heat-circulating fireplace gains its additional efficiency.

    _____

    _____

    _____

7. What is the function of the smoke shelf?

    _____

    _____

Name _____

8. What materials are commonly used in the construction of the smoke chamber?

_____

_____

9. What is the rule of thumb to follow when selecting a flue for a fireplace opening?

_____

_____

10. List two circumstances which would require an increased size of the flue?

A. _____

B. _____

11. May a chimney have more than one flue?

_____

12. List four appliances or features of a home which require their own flue.

A. _____

B. _____

C. _____

D. _____

13. List two framing members used to provide support in the opening through which a chimney passes.

A. _____

B. _____

14. When chimneys are placed along a single slope of the roof, water can back up and seep under the shingles and produce leaks. What steps can be taken to prevent this?

_____

_____

_____

15. Why would fireplace inserts be used?

_____

_____

16. List the two combustion materials used by stoves.

_____

17. How do radiant stoves and circulating stoves differ?

_____

_____

_____

18. Which of the two types of stoves—radiant or circulating—has a lower surface temperature?

_____

19. List three examples of low-efficiency stoves.

    A. _____

    B. _____

    C. _____

20. When installing a stove in front of a fireplace opening, what should be done to reflect the heat back into the room?

    _____

21. What effect will extending the height of a chimney have on the draft?

    _____

22. What is the recommended opening height for a 36 in. wide single face fireplace?

    _____

PART IV: MATCHING: Match the correct term with its description listed below. Place the corresponding letter on the blank at right.

A. Ash chamber
B. Damper
C. Ash dump
D. Fire clay
E. Flue
F. Hearth
G. Lintel
H. Saddle

I. Single-face
J. Smoke chamber
K. Smoke shelf
L. Stove
M. Three-face
N. Two-face (adjacent)
O. Two-face (opposite)

1. Protects the floor from sparks.

1. _____

2. Fire-resistant mortar.

2. _____

3. Opening in the fireplace floor with a metal trap door.

3. _____

4. Holds ashes after they are removed from the fire chamber.

4. _____

5. Regulates the rate of burning.

5. _____

6. Prevents down rushing cold air from forcing smoke into the room.

6. _____

7. The space directly above the smoke shelf and damper.

7. _____

8. Supplies a smoke path from the fireplace.

8. _____

9. Designed to shed water away from the chimney.

9. _____

10. Supports the masonry above a fireplace opening.

10. _____

11. Most popular type of fireplace.

11. _____

12. A fireplace that is open on both front and back sides.

12. _____

13. Also known as a projecting corner fireplace.

13. _____

14. A fireplace which is open on three sides.

14. _____

15. A good choice for localized heat source.

15. _____

1.

DIRECTIONS:
Study the pictorial section of a fireplace and chimney below and identify each of the materials, parts, etc. indicated by the leaders. Use these specific notes:

> Ash pit
> Ash dump
> Clean—out door
> Damper
> Double header
> Face brick
> Fire brick
> Floor joist

> Smoke chamber
> Smoke shelf
> Steel lintel
> Stone hearth
> 4" Reinforced concrete inner hearth
> Minimum thickness of walls of fire chamber is 8"
> Flue lining

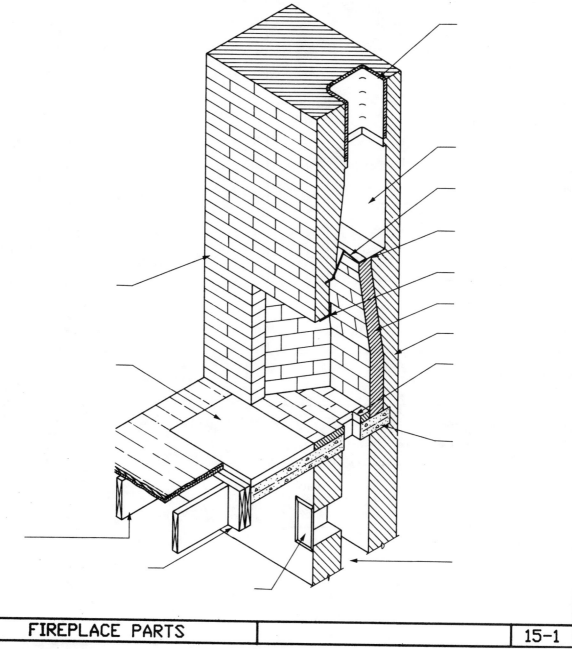

| FIREPLACE PARTS | | 15-1 |

2.

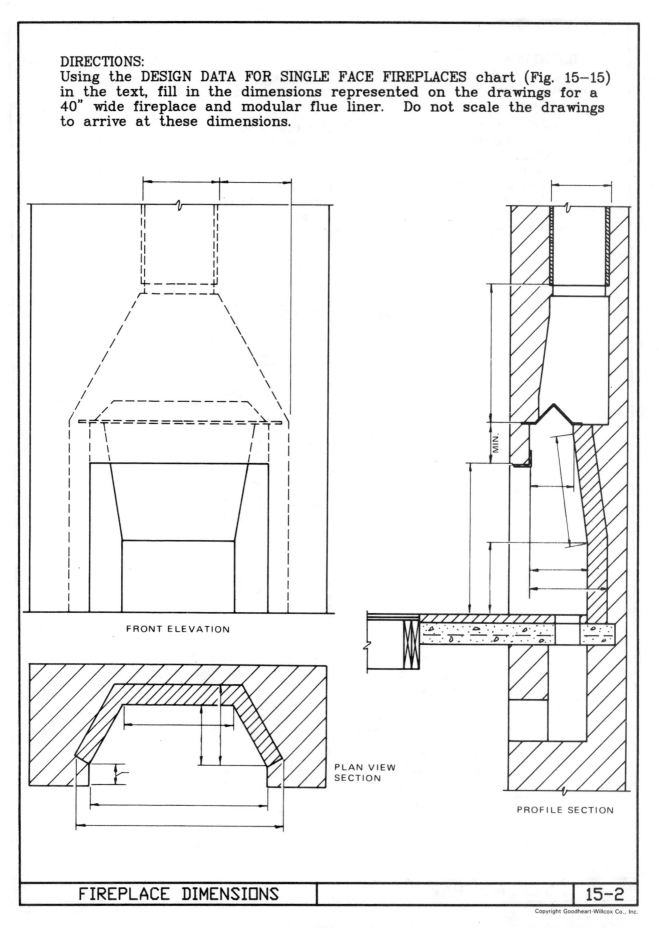

DIRECTIONS:
Using the DESIGN DATA FOR SINGLE FACE FIREPLACES chart (Fig. 15–15) in the text, fill in the dimensions represented on the drawings for a 40" wide fireplace and modular flue liner. Do not scale the drawings to arrive at these dimensions.

FRONT ELEVATION

PLAN VIEW
SECTION

MIN.

PROFILE SECTION

FIREPLACE DIMENSIONS | 15-2

Name _____

3. **Fireplace Details.** This assignment will be evaluated based on the following factors: quality of work, design parameters met, accurately and completely communicated design, and directions followed. **Directions.** You are to design a single-face masonry fireplace. Show the design using a plan view section and front elevation. Also provide a profile section from the footing to the top of the chimney. The scale is to be 1/2" = 1'-0". Use a sheet of "C" size paper. Include the following elements in your design.
   - The fireplace is for a ranch style house which has a 24" crawl space. A 12 x 12 in. ash cleanout is located in the crawl space.
   - The masonry chimney is 28 in. x 60 in. x the necessary height. Facing is brick. Chimney structure is concrete block.
   - Fireplace opening is 36 in. wide with an 18 x 60 in. sandstone outer hearth.
   - A 2 x 3 in. angle steel support should be used above the fireplace opening for brick ledge.
   - Flue damper is cast iron (see text for dimensions).
   - The inner and outer hearth should be supported on a 4 in. reinforced concrete slab.
   - Fire pit should be lined on all sides with firebrick (2 1/2 x 5 x 9 in.) and provide a 5 x 9 in. ash dump.
   - Use 12 in. modular terra-cotta flue tile.
   - Height of the chimney is planned for a structure with a 5:12 pitch roof and a total rise of 6'-0" at the peak. The chimney passes through the ridge.
   - Top of the chimney is between 2 and 3 ft. above the highest point of the roof and has a 4 in. concrete cap.
   - Show roof flashing where appropriate.
   - All dimensions should conform to design data presented in the text.
   - Views should project.

4. Collect pictures of the various styles and types of fireplaces and stoves. Try to find examples of each of the styles of fireplaces discussed in the text and label them.

Chapter 16

THE FLOOR PLAN

Text Pages 283-300

Name _____   Course _____

Date_____   Score _____

PART I: SHORT ANSWER/LISTING: Provide brief answers to the following questions.

1. List features that generally are shown on the floor plan.

    A. _____

    B. _____

    C. _____

    D. _____

    E. _____

    F. _____

    G. _____

    H. _____

    I. _____

2. You should use standard symbols representing various sizes of cabinets, appliances, and permanent fixtures on the floor plan. What information do you need, and where do you find it?

    _____

    _____

    _____

    _____

3. What stairway information should be included on the floor plan?

    A. _____

    B. _____

    C. _____

    D. _____

    E. _____

4. What fireplace/chimney information should be included on the floor plan?

    A. _____

    B. _____

    C. _____

    D. _____

    E. _____

5. Is it necessary to indicate the size of the various rooms on the floor plan? If so, where should the information be included?

_____

_____

_____

6. Dimension lines should be placed away from the drawing to prevent crowding. How far out should they be placed?

_____

7. Where should the scale be located on the drawing?

_____

8. Where should the number of each sheet be placed?

_____

_____

9. One method of numbering sheets in a set of drawings is to indicate the sheet number and total sheets. For example, the first sheet is 1 of 4, the second sheet 2 of 4, etc. What advantage(s) are there to this method?

_____

_____

10. Before starting the steps to draw the floor plan, what preliminary work should be done?

_____

_____

11. What is the first step in drawing a floor plan?

_____

12. Should the type of windows planned be indicated on the floor plan?

_____

13. If the house will have stairs, what preliminary work should be done before the stairs can be drawn?

_____

_____

14. When should dimensions, notes, and room names be added to the floor plan?

_____

_____

_____

15. What information should be included in the title block?

A. _____

B. _____

C. _____

D. _____

E. _____

F. _____

Name _____

16. Why are expansion plans advisable?

A. _____

_____

_____

B. _____

_____

17. Does the overall length dimension of a house include the siding?

_____

18. What is the actual thickness of an exterior stud wall composed of the following materials: 1/2 in. drywall, 2 x 4 studs, 3/4 in. rigid foam insulation, and 1/2 in. plywood siding?

_____

PART II: MULTIPLE CHOICE: Select the best answer and place its letter in the blank at right.

1. The floor plan is normally started:
   A. First.
   B. Last.
   C. After the elevations.
   D. After the electrical plan.

   1. _____

2. The floor plan is actually a(n):
   A. Top view.
   B. Elevation view.
   C. Section view.
   D. None of the above.

   2. _____

3. Frequently, interior stud walls with drywall on both sides are drawn _____ thick.
   A. 4 or 8 in.
   B. 5 in.
   C. 6 in.
   D. 8, 10, or 12 in.

   3. _____

4. The _____ opening should be shown for windows.
   A. Rough.
   B. Sash.
   C. Finished.
   D. None of the above.

   4. _____

5. The _____ door width should be used for doors.
   A. Actual.
   B. Rough.
   C. Finished.
   D. None of the above.

   5. _____

6. What line symbol is used to show an archway or plain opening on a floor plan?
   A. Object line.
   B. Cutting plane line.
   C. Hidden line.
   D. Center line.

   6. _____

7. Information on patios and swimming pools that is included on the floor plan can include:
   A. Location.
   B. Size.
   C. Materials.
   D. All of the above.

7. _____

8. The name of the room should be placed near the center of the room. It should be lettered _____ in. larger than the near-by lettering.
   A. 1/16 in.
   B. 1/8 in.
   C. 3/16 in.
   D. 1/4 in.

8. _____

9. In architectural drawing, dimension lines are continuous lines with the figure placed:
   A. At the end of the line.
   B. Above the line.
   C. Under the line.
   D. At the beginning of the line.

9. _____

10. Recommended spacing between dimension lines is:
    A. 1/4 or 3/8 in.
    B. 3/8 or 1/2 in.
    C. 1/2 or 5/8 in.
    D. None of the above.

10. _____

11. Which of the following methods of showing a dimension is proper?
    A. 18".
    B. 1'-6".
    C. All of the above.
    D. None of the above.

11. _____

12. The preferred method of dimensioning interior walls is to the:
    A. Inside of the wall.
    B. Outside of the wall.
    C. Center.
    D. All of the above.

12. _____

13. Overall width and length of primary walls should be multiples of _____ to comply with building material sizes.
    A. 4 ft.
    B. 6 ft.
    C. 8 ft.
    D. 10 ft.

13. _____

14. The scale commonly used for residential floor plans is:
    A. Half size.
    B. 1" = 1'-0".
    C. 1/2" = 1'0".
    D. 1/4" = 1'-0".

14. _____

Name _____

15. After the exterior walls have been completed, draw the:
    A. Windows and doors.
    B. Interior walls.
    C. Stairs.
    D. Title block and scale.

15. _____

16. The interior and exterior walls may be darkened in after:
    A. The doors, windows, stairs, and fireplaces have been drawn.
    B. The kitchen cabinets, appliances, and bathroom fixtures are drawn.
    C. Checking the drawing for accuracy.
    D. Construction is underway.

16. _____

17. Outside features such as patios, walks, or decks should be drawn:
    A. Before the exterior walls are drawn.
    B. After the house has been built.
    C. Before the kitchen cabinets, appliances, and bathroom fixtures have been drawn.
    D. After all interior features have been drawn.

17. _____

18. Base cabinets for kitchens are drawn _____ in. deep while wall cabinets are _____ in. deep.
    A. 24 and 12.
    B. 12 and 24.
    C. 16 and 10.
    D. 36 and 24.

18. _____

19. The material symbols should be added:
    A. When the design elements that use these materials are drawn.
    B. Only if the contractor wants them drawn.
    C. At any time.
    D. When the drawing is almost complete.

19. _____

20. Object lines, hidden lines, center lines, etc. should be:
    A. Blue and the same width.
    B. Erased.
    C. Black and vary in width.
    D. None of the above.

20. _____

21. The type of line used on a drawing to indicate ceiling beams is a(n):
    A. Section line.
    B. Object line.
    C. Center line.
    D. Hidden line.

21. _____

PART III: MATCHING: Match the correct term or symbol with its description listed below. Place the corresponding letter on the blank at right.

A. Dimensions

B. Floor Plan   I.

C. Hidden Line

D. Solid or Object   J.

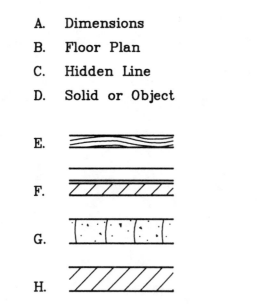

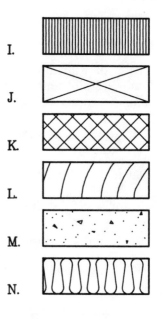

1. The heart of a set of construction drawings.   1. _____

2. Frame wall symbol.   2. _____

3. Concrete block wall symbol.   3. _____

4. Solid brick wall symbol.   4. _____

5. Brick veneer and frame wall symbol.   5. _____

6. A symbol used to signify an archway.   6. _____

7. Aluminum flashing symbol.   7. _____

8. RF insulation symbol.   8. _____

9. Symbol that indicates batt insulation.   9. _____

10. Cast concrete symbol.   10. _____

11. Symbol which represents finish board.   11. _____

12. Symbol that represents dimension lumber.   12. _____

13. Shows the size of a feature or its location on a floor plan.   13. _____

14. Lines used for base cabinets.   14. _____

PART IV: COMPLETION: Complete each sentence with the proper response. Place your answer on the blank in the right column.

1. In addition to the features normally found on a floor plan, you may also place electrical, heating/cooling, or _____ information on a less complicated floor plan.   1. _____

2. Brick exterior walls are generally _____ in. thick.   2. _____

3. To assure that the wall thicknesses are accurate on your drawing, set your _____ to the correct dimension and use them to measure each time rather than using a scale.   3. _____

The Floor Plan

Name _____

4. A _____ line should be drawn through the middle of the opening for windows shown on the floor plan.

    4. _____

5. Exterior doors and some _____ should show sills.

    5. _____

6. The door _____ indicates which way the the door will open.

    6. _____

7. Material _____ should be used on drawings to indicate construction materials.

    7. _____

8. Dimensions should always be _____ (parallel/perpendicular) to the dimension line.

    8. _____

9. Leaders should be a maximum of _____ in.

    9. _____

10. Dimension solid masonry walls to the _____ of the wall.

    10. _____

11. Dimension brick veneer walls to the _____ of the stud wall.

    11. _____

12. Include the overall dimensions for the length and _____ of the building.

    12. _____

13. Use _____ lines to lay out the exterior walls.

    13. _____

14. Find the _____ line of the opening first and then locate the windows and doors in a frame wall.

    14. _____

15. If the house is to have a fireplace, draw the _____ using exact dimensions.

    15. _____

16. The size and _____ of the fireplace must be indicated on the floor plan.

    16. _____

17. Wall cabinets should be drawn with _____ (solid/hidden) lines.

    17. _____

18. Dimensions for _____ (interior/exterior) wall elements should be identified along the wall where they are placed.

    18. _____

19. Guidelines should be left on the drawing, but _____ lines should be removed.

    19. _____

20. After the drawing is complete, examine the entire drawing for _____ and completeness.

    20. _____

21. Openings in a concrete or masonry wall are generally dimensioned to the _____ (edge/center) of the opening.

    21. _____

22. In a frame wall, a door or window is dimensioned to _____ (edge/center) of the rough opening.

    22. _____

PART V: PROBLEMS/ACTIVITIES

1.

DIRECTIONS:
Complete the Plan View of the following symbols which are used on typical residential floor plans:

BRICK VENEER ON FRAME

SOLID BRICK WALL

CONCRETE BLOCK WALL

CAST CONCRETE WALL

ARCHWAY OR PLAIN OPENING

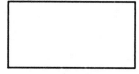

TERRA COTTA TILE
Section

TERRAZZO
Section

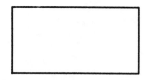

SLATE
Section

RUBBLE STONE
Section

Scale: 1/4"=1'-0"

FLOOR PLAN SYMBOLS		16-1

2.

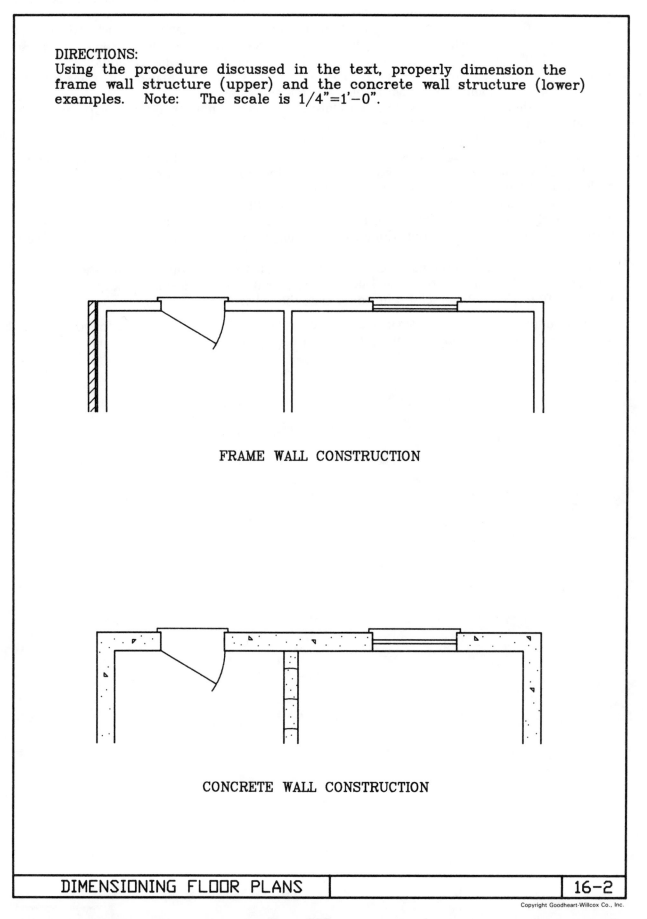

DIRECTIONS:
Using the procedure discussed in the text, properly dimension the frame wall structure (upper) and the concrete wall structure (lower) examples.   Note: The scale is 1/4"=1'−0".

FRAME WALL CONSTRUCTION

CONCRETE WALL CONSTRUCTION

DIMENSIONING FLOOR PLANS   16−2

3. **Floor Plan:** This assignment will be evaluated based on the following factors: quality of work, use of proper symbols, use of proper size symbols, use of proper size features, good planning, proper dimensions, and overall communication provided.

   Directions: Study chapters 12, 13, and 16. You are to draw a floor plan for a ranch style house (no basement or second floor). Follow the procedure for drawing a floor plan described in the text. Scale is 1/4" = 1'-0". Use "C" size paper. The design should meet the following criteria:
   - Outside dimensions of the house are to be 34'-0" x 64'-0". (The house may deviate some from these dimensions to accommodate room layout, a porch and garage.)
   - The house should contain the following rooms: living room, dining area, three bedrooms, kitchen, family room, two baths, and single-car garage.
   - Include ample closet space with shelves and rods.
   - Exterior doors should be 3'-0" wide and interior doors should be 2'-10" except for baths (2'-6" or 2'-8"). Closets may vary depending on the type of door used or closet design.
   - Use standard size appliances, fixtures, and windows.
   - Label rooms and show approximate room sizes below the name.
   - Completely dimension the floor plan using the procedures described in the text.
   - Identify every window and door with a letter or number so that a window and door schedule could be developed.
   - Your house may use any standard exterior material that you wish. Interior walls should use 2 x 4 studs with 1/2 in. drywall on either side. Wet walls may have 2 x 6 studs if desired.
   - Garage floor should be at least 4 in. lower than the house floor.

4. Collect examples of floor plans from magazines, newspapers, and builder's literature for your notebook. Make notes of features you particularly like about each plan.

Chapter 17

ROOF DESIGNS

Text Pages 301-318

Name _____   Course _____

Date_____   Score _____

PART I: MULTIPLE CHOICE: Select the best answer and place its letter in the blank at right.

1. Which of the following characteristics is typical of a gable roof?   1. _____
   A. Easy to build.
   B. Sheds water well.
   C. Provides for ventilation.
   D. All of the above.

2. A roof type more suited to houses in warm, dry climates than   2. _____
   in cold, wet climates is a(n) _____ roof.
   A. Flat.
   B. Hip.
   C. Shed.
   D. A-frame.

3. Which of the following is a feature of common rafters?   3. _____
   A. Common rafters run parallel to the top wall plate.
   B. Common rafters run parallel to the ridge of the roof.
   C. Common rafters extend from the plate or beyond to the
      ridge of the roof.
   D. All of the above.

4. Which of the following is a roofing material that is light in   4. _____
   weight?
   A. Slate.
   B. Asphalt shingles.
   C. Clay tile.
   D. All of the above.

5. The width of a narrow box cornice is normally between: 5. _____
   A. 4 and 8 in.
   B. 5 and 10 in.
   C. 6 and 12 in.
   D. 7 and 14 in.

6. In a(n) _____ cornice, the rafter does not protrude beyond   6. _____
   the wall.
   A. Close.
   B. Open.
   C. Narrow box.
   D. Wide box without lookouts.

7. Which of the following is a feature of lightweight wood roof trusses?
   A. Most lightweight roof trusses can span distances of 50 to 60 ft.
   B. Generally, 2 x 4 lumber is used in lightweight wood roof trusses.
   C. In most instances, lightweight wood roof trusses are more expensive than traditional roof frame construction.
   D. None of the above.

7. _____

8. The recommended total area of ventilator openings in the attic space should be a minimum 1/300th of the ceiling area. How much ventilator area should be planned for a house with a ceiling area of 1800 sq. ft.?
   A. At least 6 sq. ft.
   B. At least 9 sq. ft.
   C. At least 3 sq. ft.
   D. None of the above.

8. _____

9. Flashing should be used:
   A. Where any feature pierces the roof.
   B. Where a roof attaches to a second floor wall.
   C. Next to the chimney.
   D. All of the above.

9. _____

10. You can use 6 or 8 in. individual boards as sheathing. For rafters spaced 16 or 24 in. o.c., the boards should be at least _____ thick.
    A. 1/4 in.
    B. 1/2 in.
    C. 3/4 in.
    D. 1 in.

10. _____

11. Two requirements of roofing materials are to waterproof the roof and provide many years of service. The most popular type is:
    A. Asphalt.
    B. Wood.
    C. Copper.
    D. Clay.

11. _____

12. When the roof pitch is 12:12 and the span is 24 ft., how high is the roof ridge above the top plate?
    A. 4 ft.
    B. 8 ft.
    C. 12 ft.
    D. 24 ft.

12. _____

Name _____

MATCHING: Match the correct term with its description listed below. Place the corresponding letter on the blank at right.

A. A-frame
B. Butterfly
C. Clear span
D. Cornice
E. Drip edge
F. Flashing
G. Flat
H. Gable
I. Gambrel
J. Gusset
K. Gutters

L. Hip
M. Mansard
N. Pitch
O. Rafters
P. Rake
Q. Rise
R. Roof trusses
S. Run
T. Sheathing
U. Shed

1. A type of roof that is very popular.   1. _____

2. A popular roof style, but it does not have as many advantages as the gable.   2. _____

3. A "built-up" or membrane roof covering is needed for this type of roof.   3. _____

4. This type of roof is similar to a flat roof, but has more pitch.   4. _____

5. A roof type of French design.   5. _____

6. Dutch colonial homes are suited to this type of roof.   6. _____

7. A roof type that provides ample light and ventilation.   7. _____

8. This roof type forms both the walls plus the roof.   8. _____

9. Roof framing structural element.   9. _____

10. Also referred to as slope.   10. _____

11. Horizontal distance from the inside of one stud wall to the inside of the opposite stud wall.   11. _____

12. The vertical distance from the top of the wall plate to the underside of the rafters at the ridge.   12. _____

13. Half of the clear span.   13. _____

14. Roof overhang at the eaves line that links the sidewalls and roof.   14. _____

15. Also known as gable end.   15. _____

16. A form composed of triangular shapes.   16. _____

17. Wood or metal fasteners used in trusses.   17. _____

18. Galvanized sheet metal, aluminum, or copper applied to a roof to prevent water from entering.   18. _____

19. Metal edging used to eliminate water from the gable and eaves.   19. _____

20. Provides a path to remove water from the roof.   20. _____

21. Supports the roofing material.   21. _____

PART III: SHORT ANSWER/LISTING: Provide brief answers to the following questions.

1. How is a built-up roof made?

   _____

   _____

2. Rafters are cut to the desired measurements by finding four cuts. Name the four cuts.

   A. _____

   B. _____

   C. _____

   D. _____

3. Rafter size is determined by three factors. Name the three factors.

   A. _____

   B. _____

   C. _____

4. When would rafters become ceiling joists?

   _____

   _____

5. List three designs where the open cornice may be used.

   A. _____

   B. _____

   C. _____

6. When is a wide box cornice without lookouts typically used?

   _____

7. Where is the soffit material nailed in the wide box cornice without lookouts?

   _____

8. Wide overhangs are more expensive to build than a close rake; however, wide overhangs do produce two advantages. Name the two advantages.

   A. _____

   B. _____

9. The house style often dictates the type of roof or cornice required. What type of cornice is best suited for a Colonial or Cape Cod?

   _____

10. Before ordering wood trusses for a specific structure, what four factors should be known?

   A. _____

   B. _____

   C. _____

   D. _____

Name _____

11. In some buildings, the bottom chord of the roof trusses extends past the exterior wall. List two advantages which result from this feature.

A. _____

B. _____

12. Air movement results when the temperature of the outside air is different from that of the attic. This movement of air lowers the temperature inside. Ventilators should be installed in the attic to assist air movement. What are two ways to ventilate the attic space?

A. _____

B. _____

13. Plywood is generally used for roof sheathing; however, other materials are sometimes used. List three other materials commonly used for roof sheathing.

A. _____

B. _____

C. _____

PART IV: COMPLETION: Complete each sentence with the proper response. Place your answer on the blank in the right column.

1. A roof type that is the least expensive to construct is the _____.

1. _____

2. The shed roof may require a built-up roof unless the pitch of the roof is over _____.

2. _____

3. The type of roof used a great deal on barns is the _____.

3. _____

4. Two roof styles which are contemporary in design and produced in prefabricated units are folded plate and _____.

4. _____

5. It is good practice to use one of the standard roof _____ or slopes when designing a roof.

5. _____

6. Light roofing material weighs less than _____ pounds per sq. ft.

6. _____

7. The cornice forms on two sides of a _____ roof.

7. _____

8. In _____ cornices, rafter ends are exposed and generally tapered or curved to eliminate bulk.

8. _____

9. The soffit board is nailed to the underside of the rafter in a _____ box cornice.

9. _____

10. Added support members, or _____, are generally needed in a wide box cornice with lookouts to attach the soffit.

10. _____

11. Wide box cornices without lookouts have _____ soffits.

11. _____

12. The span of a gable roof past the end wall of the dwelling is the _____, or gable end.

12. _____

13. The W-Type truss, the _____ truss, or the Scissors truss are generally used in residential construction.

13. _____

14. Two results of a well-ventilated attic are less _____ build-up to cause damage to the underside of the sheathing and a cooler house in the summer.

14. _____

15. The width of the valley flashing is dependent upon the slope of the roof. A roof slope of 5:12 requires flashing at least _____ in. wide.

15. _____

16. Gutters are commonly made from galvanized sheet metal, aluminum, copper, and vinyl. One popular style of aluminum or vinyl gutter is the _____.

16. _____

17. Plywood sheathing should be placed with the face grain _____ (parallel/perpendicular) to the rafters.

17. _____

18. A moisture barrier is required between the sheathing and the shingles. Generally, building paper of 15 lb. saturated _____ provides this barrier.

18. _____

19. _____ is required where any feature (chimney, section of a wall, skylight, etc.) pierces the roof.

19. _____

20. The area of the roof which includes the fascia and overhang is called the _____.

20. _____

1.

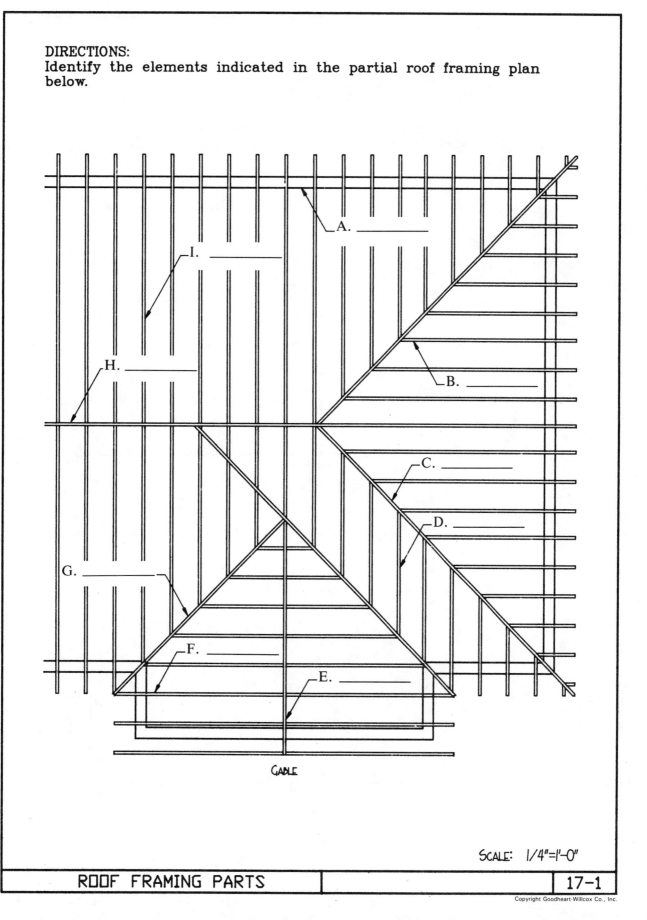

DIRECTIONS:
Identify the elements indicated in the partial roof framing plan below.

A. _____

I. _____

B. _____

H. _____

C. _____

D. _____

G. _____

F. _____

E. _____

GABLE

SCALE: 1/4"=1'-0"

ROOF FRAMING PARTS		17-1

2.

DIRECTIONS:
A. Construct the ceiling joist (2" x 6") and rafter (2" x 4") layout for a cottage which has a clear span of 19'-3 1/2", a roof slope of 6:12, and an 18" overhang. Dimension the rise and run and show the roof slope triangle.
B. Instead of ceiling joists and rafters, show the roof structure using roof trusses ("W" or "Kingpost"). Dimension as above.

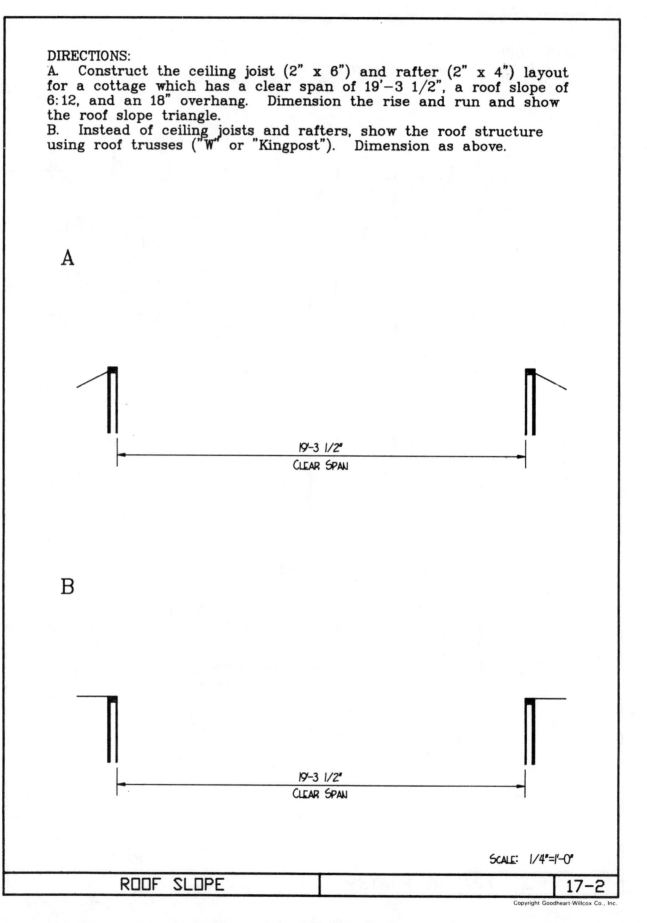

A

19'-3 1/2"
CLEAR SPAN

B

19'-3 1/2"
CLEAR SPAN

SCALE: 1/4"=1'-0"

| ROOF SLOPE | | 17-2 |

3.

DIRECTIONS:

Draw a large scale (1"=1'–0") section through a wide box cornice with lookouts. Incorporate the following dimensions, materials, etc. in your drawing:

> 2" x 4" stud wall with 3/4" RF insulation and horizontal siding on the outside and 1/2" DW inside
> 24" overhang (outside of insulation to end of rafters) with ventilation
> 2" x 6" rafters and 2" X 8" ceiling joists
> 1/2" plywood roof sheathing, redwood fascia board, and asphalt shingles.

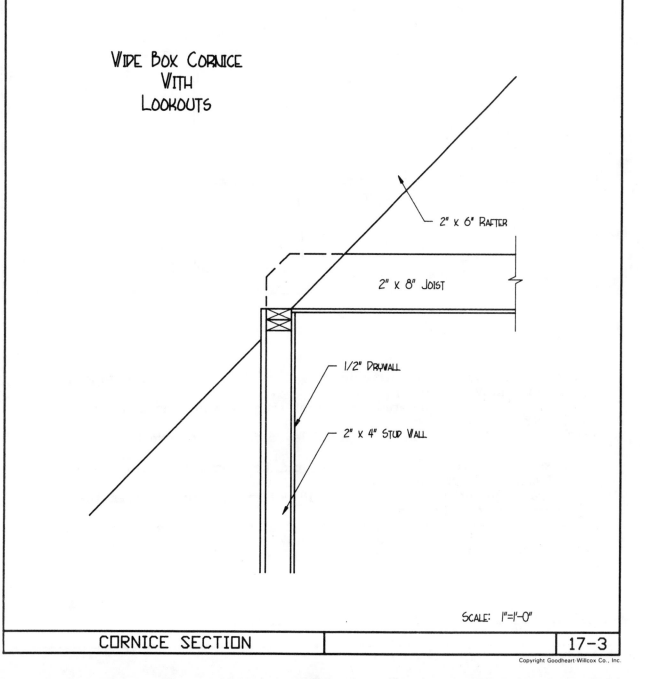

WIDE BOX CORNICE
WITH
LOOKOUTS

2" x 6" RAFTER

2" x 8" JOIST

1/2" DRYWALL

2" x 4" STUD WALL

SCALE: 1"=1'-0"

CORNICE SECTION | 17-3

4.

ASSIGNMENT 17-4
Factors to be considered in the evaluation of this assignment include:
Quality of your work, application of appropriate construction
techniques, use of appropriate size building materials for spans and
economy, and overall communication provided.

DIRECTIONS:
Study Chapter 17 in your text before attempting this drawing. You
are to draw a roof framing plan for an L-shaped ranch home which
has the following exterior dimensions:

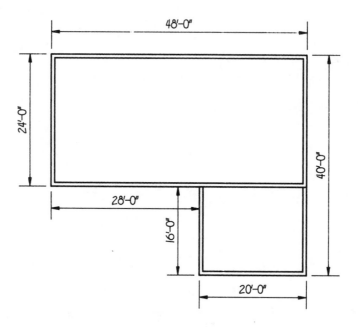

Use "C" size paper and a scale of 1/4"=1'-0". Include the following
elements in your design:
> Use 2" x 4" engineered wood roof trusses which have a pitch of
  5:12 and spaced 24" O.C.
> Plan the roof framing for a gable roof with 24" overhangs on
  all sides.
> Bottom chord of the trusses should be horizontal from fascia to
  fascia to allow for 12" insulation in the attic.
> Frame an opening for a 16" x 16" chimney which pierces the
  roof between two trusses.
> Draw a large scale detail of a typical roof truss to be used to
  span the 20 ft. wide section. Show dimensions.
> Include a note that bracing should be as per code and sheathing
  is 1/2" CDX plywood.

| ROOF FRAMING PLAN | | 17-4 |

Name _____

5. Collect photos of houses with interesting roof designs for your notebook. Note the style and materials used.

Chapter 18

ELEVATIONS

Text Pages 319-330

Name _____   Course _____

Date_____   Score _____

PART I: COMPLETION: Complete each sentence with the proper response. Place your answer on the blank in the right column.

1. The term "elevation" usually refers to the exterior elevations. Interior elevations are generally referred to as _____.

   1. _____

2. Two methods of elevation identification are acceptable. The first method uses front, rear, right side, and left side. The second method uses north, south, east, and west. The _____ (first/second) method is more widely used.

   2. _____

3. The grade line is a very important feature of any exterior elevation. All parts of the structure below this line are shown as _____ lines.

   3. _____

4. The floor area of an attached garage should be at least _____ in. lower than the interior floor.

   4. _____

5. The line symbol used to show the location of the finished floor and ceiling on an elevation is usually a _____ line.

   5. _____

6. An exterior elevation is generated from two drawings — the floor plan and _____ drawing.

   6. _____

7. The fractional pitch or slope triangle may be used to illustrate the roof pitch. However, the _____ is the preferred method.

   7. _____

8. Notes typically found on an elevation drawing include grade information, exterior wall material notes, roof covering material details, fascia material, and _____ material.

   8. _____

9. The usual scale of a residential exterior elevation is _____.

   9. _____

10. The exterior walls are drawn on the elevation using the _____ plan as a guide.

    10. _____

11. The _____ lines of walls, windows and doors, etc. are drawn in after the vertical heights have been drawn.

    11. _____

12. An excellent reference for information on features such as trim, window muntins, window wells, gable ventilators, and railings is _____.

    12. _____

13. After examining the elevation drawing carefully for completeness and accuracy, the title block and _____ are added.

    13. _____

PART II: SHORT ANSWER/LISTING: Provide brief answers to the following questions.

1. An elevation is usually drawn for each side of the dwelling. What purpose do these elevations serve?

   A. _____

   _____

   B. _____

   _____

2. There are a number of features which should be indicated on an elevation. The primary feature is identification of the side of the house. Name four other features.

   A. _____

   B. _____

   C. _____

   D. _____

   ALSO: _____

   _____

3. Two methods of measuring floor to ceiling height are: finished floor-to-finished ceiling distance, and the construction dimension. Explain both methods and indicate the one carpenters prefer.

   _____

   _____

   _____

   _____

   _____

   _____

   _____

   _____

4. Most building codes specify that the top of the foundation wall be at least 8 in. above the grade. Why is this requirement important?

   _____

5. The placement of windows on an elevation is obtained from the floor plan. How is the vertical height determined?

   _____

   _____

   _____

6. On an elevation, gable ends are drawn to indicate the height of the roof. If the dwelling has more than one roof height, which is drawn first (highest/lowest)?

   _____

Name _____

7. The following steps should be used to draw a gable end. Place them in the proper order by labeling them A through E.

_____ Lay out the desired slope from the top inside corner of the plate.

_____ Measure the amount of desired overhang, include the thickness of the roof sheathing.

_____ Repeat the procedure for the other side of the roof.

_____ Locate the top of the upper wall plate and center line of the proposed ridge location.

_____ Measure the width of the rafter perpendicular to the bottom edge and draw the top edge parallel to the bottom edge of the rafter.

8. Vertical dimensions are generally placed on the elevation drawing. List four vertical dimensions which should be included.

A. _____

B. _____

C. _____

D. _____

ALSO: _____

_____

9. The first lines to appear on the elevation drawing are vertical heights of the grade, footings, doors and windows, eaves, and roof. What type of lines are used in this step?

_____

10. At what point should the dimensions, notes, and symbols be added to the elevation?

_____

_____

_____

PART III: MULTIPLE CHOICE: Select the best answer and place its letter in the blank at right.

1. The current grade line for each outside wall may be obtained from the:
   A. Site or floor plan.
   B. Plot or site plan.
   C. Floor or plot plan.
   D. Foundation plan.

1. _____

2. Ceiling heights of basements should be at least 6'-2" high, while 8'-0" is preferred. Garages must have a ceiling height of at least:
   A. 8'-0".
   B. 8'-6".
   C. 9'-0".
   D. 9'-6".

2. _____

3. _____ lines are used on the elevation to indicate visible wall corners.
   A. Hidden.
   B. Construction.
   C. Object.
   D. Guide.

3. _____

4. Window details should be shown on the elevation. The swing, plus the _____, should be shown on hinged windows.
   A. Brick mold or window trim.
   B. Glass elevation symbol.
   C. Identification symbols for windows and doors.
   D. All of the above.

4. _____

5. A number of symbols are normally shown on an elevation. As a rule, the front elevation shows more than the other elevations. From the list of symbols below, which symbol is ALWAYS placed on an elevation drawing?
   A. Exterior wall covering symbol.
   B. Roof pitch symbol.
   C. Window swing symbol.
   D. Cutting plane symbol.

5. _____

6. The roof elements and wall height are important features of the elevation drawing. The _____ supplies the measurements for these two features.
   A. Floor plan.
   B. Section drawing.
   C. Foundation plan.
   D. Plot plan.

6. _____

7. Any changes to be made in the elevation should be done:
   A. After the dimensions, notes, and symbols have been added.
   B. At any time.
   C. Before the features have been darkened.
   D. After the vertical and horizontal lines have been drawn and the features have been darkened.

7. _____

1.

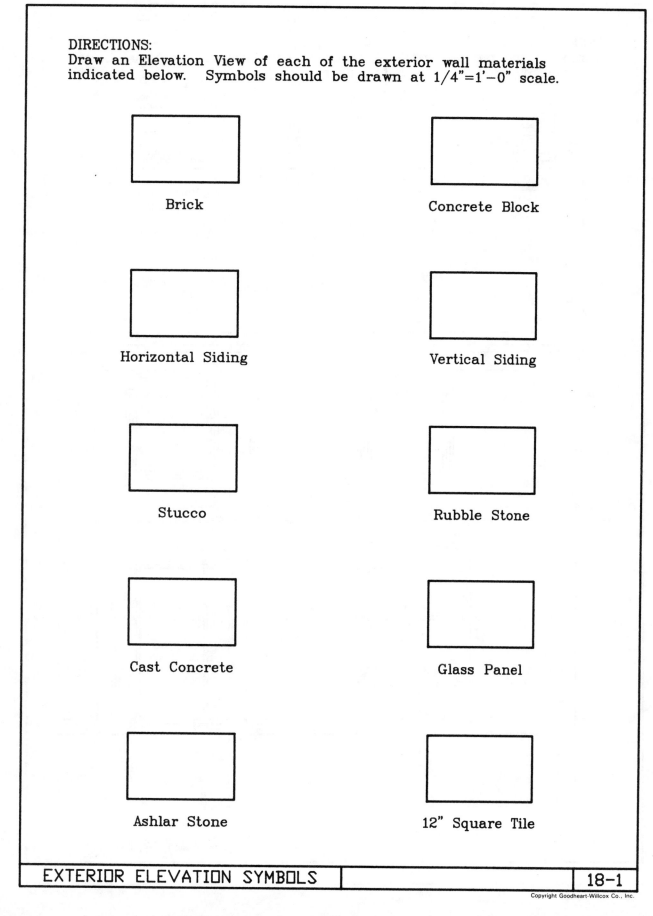

DIRECTIONS:
Draw an Elevation View of each of the exterior wall materials indicated below. Symbols should be drawn at 1/4"=1'-0" scale.

Brick

Concrete Block

Horizontal Siding

Vertical Siding

Stucco

Rubble Stone

Cast Concrete

Glass Panel

Ashlar Stone

12" Square Tile

EXTERIOR ELEVATION SYMBOLS   18-1

2.

DIRECTIONS:
Complete the partial Front Elevation of the two—story colonial below. See Figures 18—1 and 18—2 for ideas.

SCALE: 1/4"=1'-0"

COLONIAL HOUSE ELEVATION | 18-2

3.

DIRECTIONS:
Draw a complete Front Elevation for the Garden House shown below using the following information: Thickened—edge slab 24" deep, floor to ceiling height of 8'—0", 6'—10" to top of windows and doors, 12" overhang with bottom of soffit level with finished ceiling (truss construction), floor 4" above the grade, 12:12 roof slope, asphalt shingles, 6" fascia, vertical siding (rough sawn 12" boards with 1" channel, four—panel doors.   Follow the procedure described in Chapter 18 in the text.

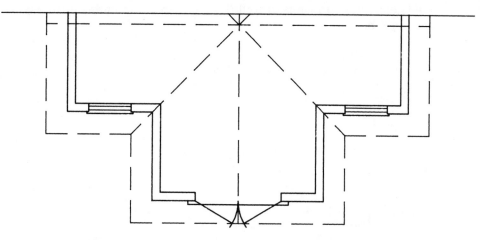

GRADE

SCALE: 1/4"=1'—0"

GARDEN HOUSE ELEVATION   18—3

4. **Front Elevation:** This assignment will be evaluated based on the following factors: quality of work, use of proper symbols, good dimensioning, an accurate solution, and overall communication provided.
   Directions: Study Chapter 18 in your text before attempting this drawing. You are to draw the Front Elevation for the ranch style home that you designed for assignment 16-3. Follow the procedure for drawing an exterior elevation presented in the text. Be sure your solution includes the following:
   - Scale of the drawing is 1/4" = 1'-0".
   - Use "C" size paper.
   - Standard ceiling height of 8'-0".
   - Typical crawl space of at least 18 in. and footing below the average maximum frost penetration depth for your area.
   - At least a 5:12 roof pitch with asphalt shingles.
   - Grade line, floor level, and ceiling levels shown using the proper symbols.
   - Proper exterior symbols and recommended height dimensions. (6'-10" to the top of windows).
   - Flashing, gable vents, etc. as required for your house.

5. Select several quality elevation drawings of well-designed homes from magazines or the newspaper. Include these in your notebook.

Chapter 19

RESIDENTIAL ELECTRICAL

Text Pages 331-342

Name _____   Course _____

Date_____   Score _____

PART I: MULTIPLE CHOICE: Select the best answer and place its letter in the blank at right.

1. To install 240 volt overhead service to a residence, plan to have _____ wires between the service drop and service head.
    A. 1.
    B. 2.
    C. 3.
    D. 4.

1. _____

2. Recommended wire size for branch lighting circuits is:
    A. 6.
    B. 8.
    C. 10.
    D. 12.

2. _____

3. Overcurrent protection devices commonly used in residential construction today are:
    A. Fuses.
    B. Circuit breakers.
    C. Volts.
    D. Amperes.

3. _____

4. Lighting circuits provide electricity for _____ volt devices such as lamps, radios, and televisions.
    A. 120.
    B. 140.
    C. 240.
    D. None of the above.

4. _____

5. Special appliance circuits normally require No. 12 wire with a 20 amp. circuit breaker or fuse. Each circuit can supply _____ watts.
    A. 120.
    B. 240.
    C. 2400.
    D. All of the above.

5. _____

6. An individual appliance circuit should be used:
    A. For an appliance which uses a large amount of electricity.
    B. For any 120 volt permanently connected appliance rated over 1,400 watts.
    C. For any 120 volt permanently connected appliance with an automatically starting electric motor.
    D. All of the above.

6. _____

7. Convenience outlets are typically placed 12 or 18 in. above the
   floor and are spaced approximately _____ apart.
   A. 4 ft.
   B. 8 ft.
   C. 12 ft.
   D. 16 ft.

7. _____

8. Devices that open the circuit when a leakage of electrical cur-
   rent to the ground is detected are:
   A. Circuit breakers.
   B. Fuses.
   C. Ground-fault interrupters.
   D. All of the above.

8. _____

9. A three-way switch is switched from _____ locations.
   A. 1.
   B. 2.
   C. 3.
   D. 4.

9. _____

10. The wires used in the relays in low voltage switching carry
    _____ volts.
    A. 24.
    B. 14.
    C. 12.
    D. None of the above.

10. _____

PART II: SHORT ANSWER/LISTING: Provide brief answers to the following questions.

1. Recommended service entrance voltage is 240 volts. How many voltages are typically available from
   the 240 volt service?

   _____

2. If too small of wire is used in the electrical system, electricity is wasted and resistance is increased. What
   other situation may occur?

   _____

3. What mechanism is used to terminate current to the house?

   _____

4. A primary reason for using branch circuits in residential construction is to allow smaller fuses or circuit
   breakers and smaller wires to keep costs at a minimum and to provide ease of handling. Name two
   advantages of using branch circuits.

   A. _____

   _____

   B. _____

   _____

Name _____

5. List three appliances or equipment items in the home that require individual appliance circuits.

A. _____

B. _____

C. _____

6. Calculate the recommended number of lighting circuits required for a house which is 40' x 56'. Allow one lighting circuit for each 400 sq. ft.

_____

_____

7. To determine the size of electrical service entrance, the size of the house, lighting, and appliances should be considered. Also, consider the type and number of branch circuits. Calculate the amperage of the service required for a house measuring 40' x 50'. (Use the minimum code requirement of 3 watts per sq. ft. to calculate the lighting circuits.) Allow a minimum of two special appliance circuits for the kitchen and one special appliance circuit in the shop. Some of the appliances to consider include: electric range (with oven), refrigerator, washer, dryer (electric), dishwasher, garbage disposal, furnace, and water heater (2000 watts). Refer to chart in the text for additional appliance electrical requirements.

8. How are electrical boxes used in an electrical system?

_____

_____

9. Name at least two areas of the home where three-way switches are convenient.

A. _____

B. _____

ALSO: _____

10. What two services do security systems provide?

    A. _____

    B. _____

11. What system would permit the control of all lights in the house from one location?

    _____

PART III: COMPLETION: Complete each sentence with the proper response. Place your answer on the blank in the right column.

1. A _____ head should be used when the service entrance equipment is placed along the eaves line.

   1. _____

2. Generally, electrical cable installed in conduit can handle a _____ (larger/smaller) amperage than electrical cable in open air installation.

   2. _____

3. The National Electrical Code recommends that a minimum of 100 amp. service be supplied to all residences. However, a designer may request as much as _____ amp. service to allow for future requirements.

   3. _____

4. A workshop would require special _____ circuits above the workbench for hand drills, electric screwdrivers, or soldering irons.

   4. _____

5. No. 12 copper wire and _____ amp. overcurrent protection is commonly used for most branch circuits in homes built today.

   5. _____

6. Some appliances require 120 volt circuits, while others require _____ volt circuits. Always check the rating of the appliance to determine which circuit is needed.

   6. _____

7. Convenience outlets that are _____ should be placed on each exterior wall for work or play activities.

   7. _____

8. Switches are placed _____ in. above the floor.

   8. _____

9. Locate switches in the bathroom out of reach of the shower or _____.

   9. _____

10. A type of switch which permits the light to be adjusted to the desired brightness is a _____ switch.

    10. _____

Name _____

PART IV: MATCHING: Match the correct term with its description listed below. Place the corresponding letter on the blank at right.

A. Ampere
B. Circuit
C. Circuit breaker
D. Conductor
E. Convenience outlet
F. Fuse
G. Lighting outlet
H. Low voltage switching

I. Ohm
J. Receptacle
K. Service drop
L. Service entrance
M. Service panel
N. Voltage
O. Watt

1. Also known as convenience outlet.

1. _____

2. The path of electricity that flows from the source to one or more outlets and then back to the source.

2. _____

3. One amp. under one volt of pressure.

3. _____

4. Unit of current used to measure the amount of electricity flowing through a conductor per unit of time.

4. _____

5. A safety device which opens an electric circuit if overloaded.

5. _____

6. The force which causes current to move through a wire.

6. _____

7. The unit of measured resistance.

7. _____

8. A relay which opens and closes the circuit in the event of an overload.

8. _____

9. Conductors and fittings which bring electricity to the dwelling.

9. _____

10. The main distribution box that receives the electricity and distributes it to various parts of the house.

10. _____

11. Material that allows the flow of electricity.

11. _____

12. Service conductors from the power lines to the point of attachment to the structure.

12. _____

13. An outlet designed to provide use of a lighting fixture.

13. _____

14. A device connected to a circuit to permit electricity to be drawn off for appliances or lighting.

14. _____

15. Also called remote control wiring.

15. _____

1.

DIRECTIONS:
Label each of the electrical circuits below as to wire size, voltage, and amperage (fuse protection). See the completed example for format.

Lighting Circuit
14 Wire, 120 Volts, 15 Amps.

Special Appliance Circuit
_____

Refrigerator
_____

Automatic Washer
_____

Dishwasher
_____

Garbage Disposer
_____

Gas Furnace
_____

Electric Water Heater
_____

Electric Range/Oven
_____

12,000 Btu Window Air Conditioner
_____

RESIDENTIAL ELECTRICAL CIRCUITS | | 19-1

2.

DIRECTIONS:
Plan the location of switches and outlets for each of the situations below.

A. Ceiling outlet fixture with single pole switch.

B. Ceiling outlet fixture switched from two locations.

C. Room with switched ceiling outlet fixture and duplex outlets approximately 6 feet apart along the walls.

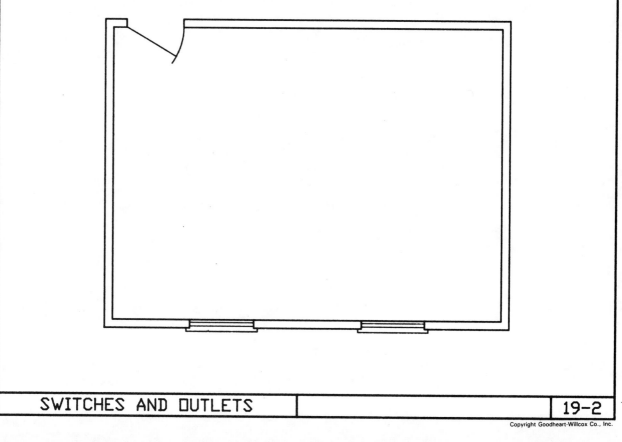

SWITCHES AND OUTLETS

19-2

3. Prepare a list of standard electrical hardware items used in a residence. Examples are switches, outlets, #12 wire, conduit, electrical boxes, etc. Go to your local building supply store and list the price of each item. Add this data to your notebook.

Chapter 20

THE ELECTRICAL PLAN

Text Pages 343-348

Name _____   Course _____

Date_____   Score _____

PART I: SHORT ANSWER/LISTING: Provide brief answers to the following questions.

1. What is the purpose of an electrical plan?

   _____

   _____

2. List at least five items commonly shown on an electrical plan.

   A. _____

   B. _____

   C. _____

   D. _____

   E. _____

   ALSO: _____

   _____

3. A home may require several different types of switches. What type of switch is generally the least expensive and most popular?

   _____

4. Before drawing the electrical plan, think about furniture arrangements of the individual rooms. Most rooms function better with a switched outlet. How does a switched outlet differ from a regular outlet?

   _____

   _____

5. A home may have several different types of lighting or lighting fixtures. Examples are ceiling fixtures, fluorescent tubes above a suspended ceiling, and recessed lighting fixtures. Name at least one area where each of the three types mentioned above are used.

   _____

   _____

   _____

   _____

6. Where should the voltage and amperage be shown on the electrical plan?

   _____

7. Identify the electrical symbols indicated on the partial electrical plan.

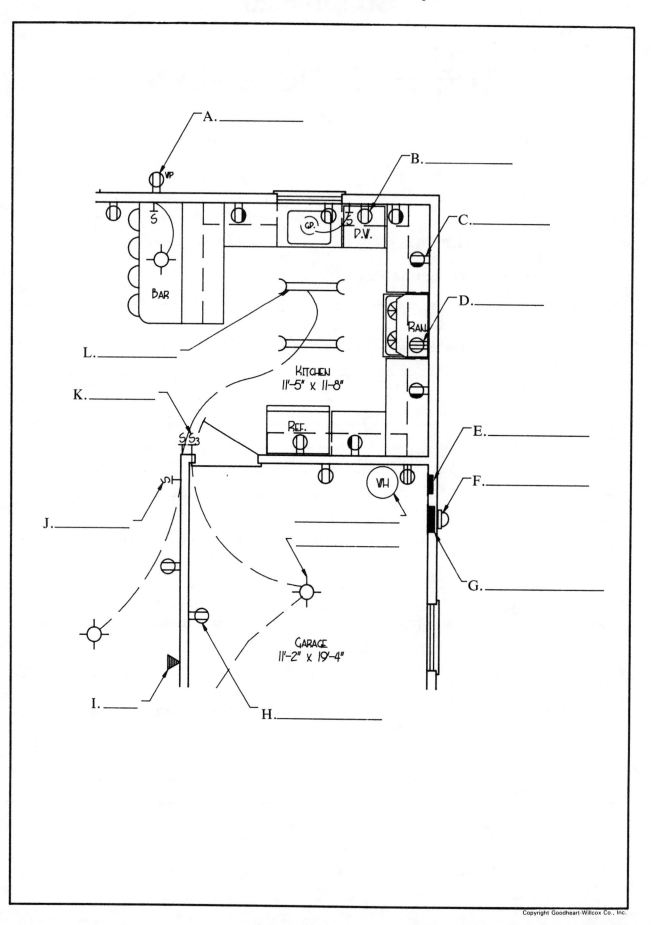

A. _____

B. _____

C. _____

D. _____

E. _____

F. _____

G. _____

H. _____

I. _____

J. _____

K. _____

L. _____

KITCHEN
11'-5" x 11-8"

GARAGE
11'-2" x 19-4"

BAR

D.V.

RAN

REF.

VH

Name _____

PART II: COMPLETION: Complete each sentence with the proper response. Place your answer on the blank in the right column.

1. The electrical plan is a _____ view drawing in section.

    1. _____

2. Locate service entrance equipment as close as possible to the place where the wires connect to the dwelling, as mandated by the _____.

    2. _____

3. Traffic _____ should be considered when locating switches to control lighting fixtures and convenience outlets.

    3. _____

4. Most convenience outlets have _____ receptacles.

    4. _____

5. The two different types of lighting fixtures commonly used in the home are incandescent and _____.

    5. _____

6. The number of _____, special appliance, and individual appliance circuits should be indicated on the electrical plan.

    6. _____

PART III: MULTIPLE CHOICE: Select the best answer and place its letter in the blank at right.

1. The electrical plan is normally traced from the:
   A. Elevations.
   B. Floor plan.
   C. Plot plan.
   D. None of the above.

    1. _____

2. It is better to locate the service entrance near the area which uses the greatest amount of electricity, because:
   A. It is less expensive and more efficient.
   B. It is a requirement of the utility company.
   C. None of the above.
   D. All of the above.

    2. _____

3. On the electrical plan, a _____ connects the switch to the fixture, outlet, or appliance it operates.
   A. Border line symbol drawn freehand.
   B. Construction line symbol drawn with a straightedge.
   C. Hidden line symbol or center line symbol drawn with an irregular curve.
   D. All of the above.

    3. _____

4. Lighting fixtures used to provide lighting for outside areas such as walks, patios, and drives should be:
   A. Recessed fixtures.
   B. Fluorescent fixtures.
   C. Interior fixtures.
   D. Exterior fixtures.

    4. _____

5. The specifications for each lighting fixture is usually listed on the:
   A. Lighting fixture schedule.
   B. Floor plan.
   C. Elevations.
   D. None of the above.

    5. _____

1.

DIRECTIONS:
Draw each of the electrical symbols specified below as shown in the completed example.   Scale is 1/4"=1'−0".

Ceiling Outlet
Fixture

Recessed Outlet
Fixture

Fan Hanger
Outlet

Junction
Box

Duplex Receptacle
Outlet

Quadruplex
Receptacle Outlet

Split−Wired
Duplex Outlet

Special Purpose
Single Receptacle

Weatherproof
Duplex Outlet

240 Volt
Outlet

Single Pole
Switch

Three−way
Switch

Push Button

Chimes

Dimmer Switch

Thermostat

Telephone

Fluorescent Fixture

ELECTRICAL SYMBOLS		20−1

2.

DIRECTIONS:
Using the Garage Floor Plan below, prepare an Electrical Plan which includes the following features:
> Three—way switch for two ceiling outlet fixtures
> Switch for two outside lights on either side of the garage door
> Four duplex outlets on garage side walls (two each side)
> Two duplex outlets above the work bench
> Garage door opener outlet and switch.

VORK BENCH

GARAGE ELECTRICAL PLAN		20-2

3. **Electrical Plan.** Draw an electrical plan for the ranch style house you designed for Problem 3 of Chapter 16. Be sure to follow the procedures described in Chapter 20 for drawing an electrical plan. Your plan will be evaluated on the proper use of symbols, application of principles discussed in the text, functional electrical layout, and quality of work. Use "C" size paper and 1/4" = 1'-0" scale.

Chapter 21

RESIDENTIAL PLUMBING

Text Pages 349-358

Name _____   Course _____

Date_____   Score _____

PART I: MATCHING: Match the correct term with its description listed below. Place the corresponding letter on the blank at right.

A. Branch main
B. Building main
C. Cleanout
D. Hot water branch
E. House sewer
F. Percolation test

G. Main stacks.
H. Secondary stacks
I. Stack wall
J. Sump
K. Vent stack

1. Water pipe that enters the house from a water source.

1. _____

2. Connects the hot water main (from water heater) to each fixture.

2. _____

3. Stacks with water closets draining into them.

3. _____

4. Stacks which do not drain water closets.

4. _____

5. Connects the fixture to the stack in the water and waste removal system.

5. _____

6. Exterior part of the house drain.

6. _____

7. Provides using a cable to dislodge waste in the house drain.

7. _____

8. Permits air into the drainage system.

8. _____

9. Provides space for the soil and stack vent.

9. _____

10. Tile or concrete pit.

10. _____

11. Soil test to determine suitability of soil for a disposal field.

11. _____

PART II: COMPLETION: Complete each sentence with the proper response. Place your answer on the blank in the right column.

1. _____ are usually installed after a branch line is provided for hose bibbs, and before the main line is divided into the cold water and hot water lines.

1. _____

2. When large pipes must pass through a joist, the joist should be _____ to strengthen the member.

2. _____

3. The water supply to a single fixture may be closed by a _____ valve.

3. _____

4. Hot and cold water lines often run parallel to each other. Some form of insulating material should be used if they are placed closer than _____ in. to each other.

4. _____

5. Drain pipes generally are smooth inside with few sharp _____ or projections.

5. _____

6. The main and _____ stacks empty into the house drain.

6. _____

7. A septic tank and _____ field are elements of a private sewage disposal system.

7. _____

8. The number of _____ and type of appliances affect the size of the septic tank.

8. _____

9. The drain field lines are laid almost level and approximately _____ ft. below the ground surface.

9. _____

PART III: SHORT ANSWER/LISTING: Provide brief answers to the following questions.

1. List the three main parts of the residential plumbing system.

   A. _____

   B. _____

   C. _____

2. List two factors to consider when installing water pipes in cold climates.

   A. _____

   _____

   B. _____

3. The local code requirements should be checked for the type of pipes which may be used. Generally, underground water supply lines are what type?

   _____

   _____

4. What are on-demand water heaters and how may they be used effectively?

   _____

   _____

   _____

   _____

5. Is it better to plan the drainage network with several drains or one main drain?

   _____

6. How does the water system provide for gas removal?

   _____

   _____

7. Name the two functions that the septic tank performs.

   A. _____

   _____

   B. _____

   _____

8. What is the function of the disposal field?

   _____

   _____

9. Calculate the seepage area for a continuous bed in poor soil for a three-bedroom home.

   _____

Name _____

PART IV: MULTIPLE CHOICE: Select the best answer and place its letter in the blank at right.

1. Cold water branch lines:
   A. Are smaller than cold water main lines.
   B. Are larger than cold water main lines.
   C. Cannot supply more than one fixture.
   D. Connect the water main to the cold water main.

   1. _____

2. Copper tubing is commonly used for water supply systems. Main lines are usually _____ in diameter.
   A. 1/2 in.
   B. 3/4 in.
   C. 1 in.
   D. 1 1/4 in.

   2. _____

3. Air compression chambers are installed in faucets to:
   A. Shut off the water supply to the faucet.
   B. Remove gas from the branch line.
   C. Increase the water flow.
   D. Cushion the water flow and reduce pipe noise during use.

   3. _____

4. The waste removal or drainage system uses _____ to carry the waste to the sewer.
   A. Pressure.
   B. Air flow.
   C. Gravity.
   D. All of the above.

   4. _____

5. Drains should be sufficiently large inside, at least _____ in., to prevent solids from clogging up the system.
   A. 2 in.
   B. 4 in.
   C. 6 in.
   D. None of the above.

   5. _____

6. The most obvious parts of the plumbing system are the _____, which include sinks, bathtubs, and water closets.
   A. Appliances.
   B. Fixtures.
   C. All of the above.
   D. None of the above.

   6. _____

7. A lot size of at least _____ is recommended when a private sewage disposal system will be required.
   A. 1 acre.
   B. 1 1/2 acres.
   C. 2 acres.
   D. 3 acres.

   7. _____

8. The minimum size of a septic tank should be _____ gallons.
   A. 250.
   B. 500.
   C. 750.
   D. 1000.

   8. _____

9. The disposal field should be located downhill from the:
   A. Driveway.
   B. Parking lot.
   C. Water supply well.
   D. All of the above.

   9. _____

1.

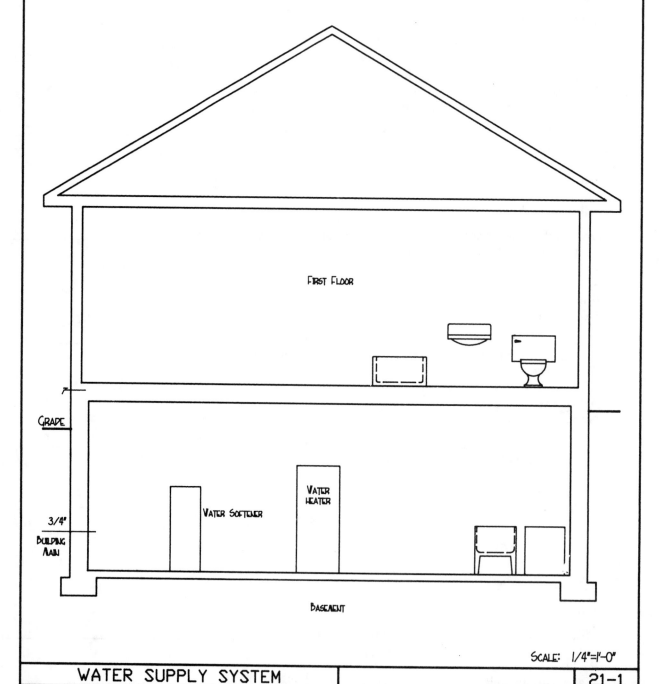

DIRECTIONS:
Using the simplified house section below, draw the schematic of a residential water supply system. Connect each fixture to the cold water and hot water mains (where appropriate). Complete the system to the building main. Label each pipe as to size and name. Include shutoff valves for each branch line and fixture. Provide a hose bib and air chamber at each faucet. See Fig. 21-1 in the text for typical layout.

FIRST FLOOR

GRADE

3/4"

BUILDING MAIN

WATER SOFTENER

WATER HEATER

BASEMENT

SCALE: 1/4"=1'-0"

WATER SUPPLY SYSTEM

21-1

2.

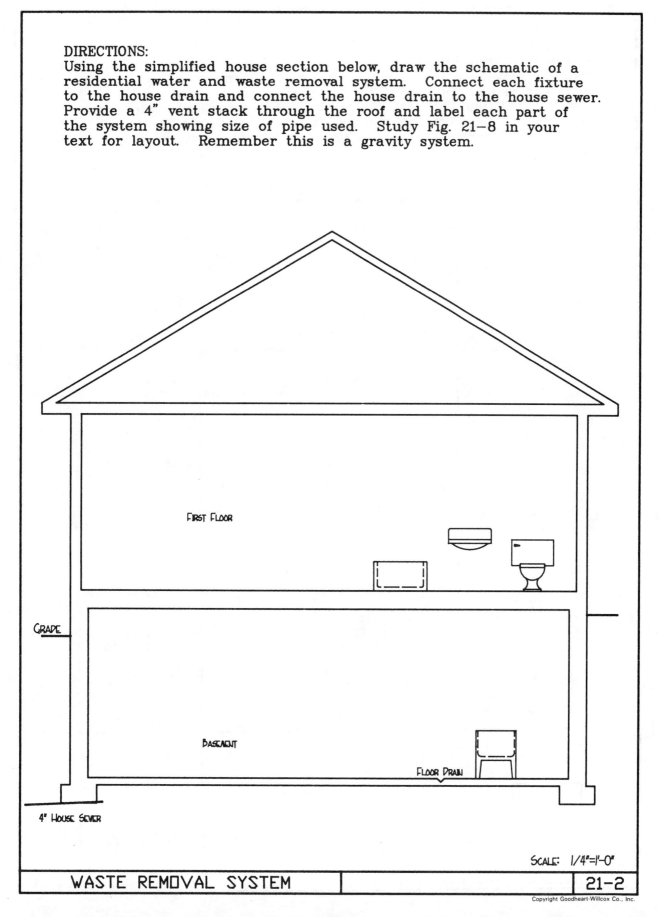

DIRECTIONS:
Using the simplified house section below, draw the schematic of a residential water and waste removal system. Connect each fixture to the house drain and connect the house drain to the house sewer. Provide a 4" vent stack through the roof and label each part of the system showing size of pipe used. Study Fig. 21—8 in your text for layout. Remember this is a gravity system.

FIRST FLOOR

GRADE

BASEMENT

FLOOR DRAIN

4" HOUSE SEWER

SCALE: 1/4"=1'-0"

WASTE REMOVAL SYSTEM

21-2

3.

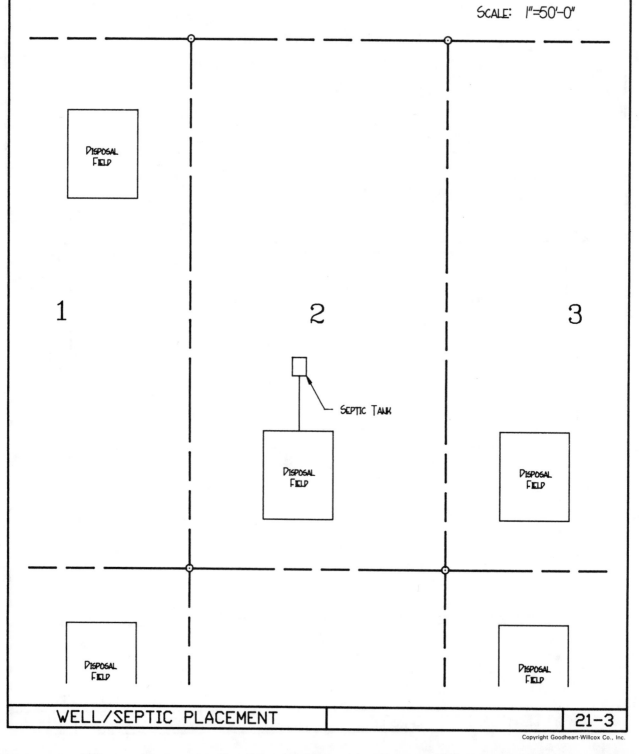

DIRECTIONS:

Suppose you purchased Lot #2 in the subdivision below and wished to install a private well for household use. The surrounding lots have wells and septic systems already and your lot has the septic tank and disposal field in place. The local code specifies a minimum distance of 150' from the disposal field and 75' from the septic tank to the well. Indicate the area on your lot where your well could be placed.

SCALE: 1"=50'-0"

DISPOSAL FIELD

1   2   3

SEPTIC TANK

DISPOSAL FIELD

DISPOSAL FIELD

DISPOSAL FIELD

DISPOSAL FIELD

WELL/SEPTIC PLACEMENT   21-3

Chapter 22

THE PLUMBING PLAN

Text Pages 359-366

Name _____   Course _____

Date _____   Score _____

PART I: COMPLETION: Complete each sentence with the proper response. Place your answer on the blank in the right column.

1. The plumbing plan illustrates the plumbing system and is a _____ view drawing.

1. _____

2. The plumbing plan should coincide with the _____ and climate control systems.

2. _____

3. The slope of waste lines, usually _____ in. per foot, should be shown on the plumbing plan.

3. _____

4. Waste lines should be drawn _____ (wider/narrower) than water supply lines.

5. Each fixture in the water supply system should have a _____ valve.

5. _____

6. Plan to use _____ (smaller/larger) pipe for long runs.

6. _____

7. Type L copper pipe is often used for interior hot and cold installations. Type K is _____ (lighter/heavier) than Type L.

7. _____

8. When drawing the plumbing plan, use _____ symbols recognized by drafters, designers, contractors, and tradeworkers.

8. _____

9. Information on exact fixtures to be used in the structure may be obtained from _____ catalogs.

9. _____

10. Every soil stack should have a _____ to provide access to the system for cleaning.

10. _____

PART II: SHORT ANSWER/LISTING: Provide brief answers to the following questions.

1. List the features commonly shown on a plumbing plan.

   A. _____

   B. _____

   C. _____

2. Minimum sizes of waste and vent lines are recommended for each fixture. Where are recommendations found?

   _____

3. Where should hose bibbs and fixtures that do not need filtered or softened water be connected?

   _____

   _____

4. How many plumbing plans will a two-story house require?

_____

5. What does the National Plumbing Code require with regard to the location of fixtures?

_____

_____

6. What does the "nominal diameter" of a pipe mean?

_____

7. A plumbing fixture schedule is a vital part of the plumbing plan. What information is usually given on the schedule?

A. _____

B. _____

C. _____

D. _____

E. _____

F. _____

8. Information is many times needed to further explain the plumbing plan. This might be installation procedures, materials, etc. Where should this information appear on the plumbing plan?

_____

_____

9. Which line symbol is typically used to outline the fixtures?

_____

10. Which of the following symbols should be used on a plumbing plan to indicate a sprinkler line?

A. —— S —— S —— S —   C. —— _ _ —— _ _ —

B. — — — — — — —.   D. —— — —— — ——

PART III: MULTIPLE CHOICE: Select the best answer and place its letter in the blank at right.

1. The plumbing plan is usually traced from the: 1. _____
   A. Site plan.
   B. Floor plan.
   C. Plot plan.
   D. Elevations.

2. The _____ should be planned first as the plumbing system   2. _____
   is usually planned around it.
   A. Hot water main.
   B. Cold water main.
   C. Waste lines.
   D. None of the above.

3. The position of the water softener, filter, and water storage   3. _____
   tank should be shown on the plumbing plan along the:
   A. Building main.
   B. Waste lines.
   C. House drain.
   D. All of the above.

Name _____

4. Plan the size of hot and cold water branch lines so that they will be large enough to supply water to the:
   A. Hose bibb.
   B. Water heater.
   C. Building main.
   D. Fixtures.

4. _____

5. Show the location of floor drains in basements and attached garages. Drains are usually connected to the:
   A. Storm sewer or dry well.
   B. Sanitary sewer system.
   C. Building main.
   D. None of the above.

5. _____

6. The Federal Housing Administration specifies that a lavatory should have at least a _____ size pipe for the water supply line.
   A. 1/2 in.
   B. 3/8 in.
   C. 3/4 in.
   D. None of the above.

6. _____

7. DWV (drain, waste, vent) copper tubing is _____ Type M.
   A. Heavier than.
   B. Much heavier than.
   C. Thinner than.
   D. The same thickness as.

7. _____

8. Use a _____ on the plumbing plan to explain uncommon symbols.
   A. Scale.
   B. Legend.
   C. Chart.
   D. All of the above.

8. _____

9. In order to plan the exact location of each fixture, study the _____ plan to determine the location of utilities (sewer, water, storm drains, and gas).
   A. Plot.
   B. Foundation.
   C. Floor.
   D. Site.

9. _____

10. Cold and hot water lines should be drawn _____ whenever possible.
    A. Perpendicular.
    B. Parallel.
    C. At right angles.
    D. None of the above.

10. _____

11. This symbol indicates a:

11. _____

   A. Coupling or sleeve.
   B. Floor drain—plan view.
   C. Gate valve.
   D. Hose bibb—plan view.

1.

DIRECTIONS:
Draw the Plan View symbol for each of the plumbing elements
specified below. The scale for these symbols is 1/4"=1'-0".

Soil Stack   Gate Valve   Coupling or Sleeve

Elbow Turned Up   Elbow Turned Down   Tee Turned Up

Meter   Hose Bib   Tee Turned Down

Cleanout   Floor Drain   Tee Horizontal

Cold Water Line   Gas Line

Hot Water Line   Sprinkler Line

Soil or Waste Line   Vent Pipe

PLUMBING SYMBOLS   22-1

2.

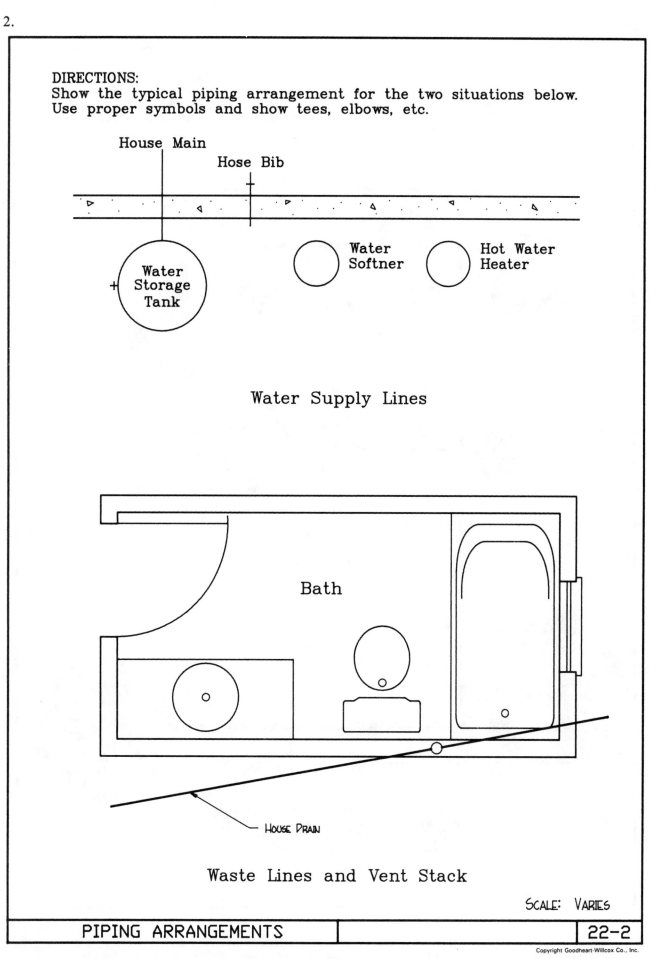

DIRECTIONS:
Show the typical piping arrangement for the two situations below.
Use proper symbols and show tees, elbows, etc.

House Main

Hose Bib

Water
Storage
Tank

Water
Softner

Hot Water
Heater

Water Supply Lines

Bath

House Drain

Waste Lines and Vent Stack

SCALE: VARIES

PIPING ARRANGEMENTS | | 22-2

Copyright Goodheart-Willcox Co., Inc.

189

3.

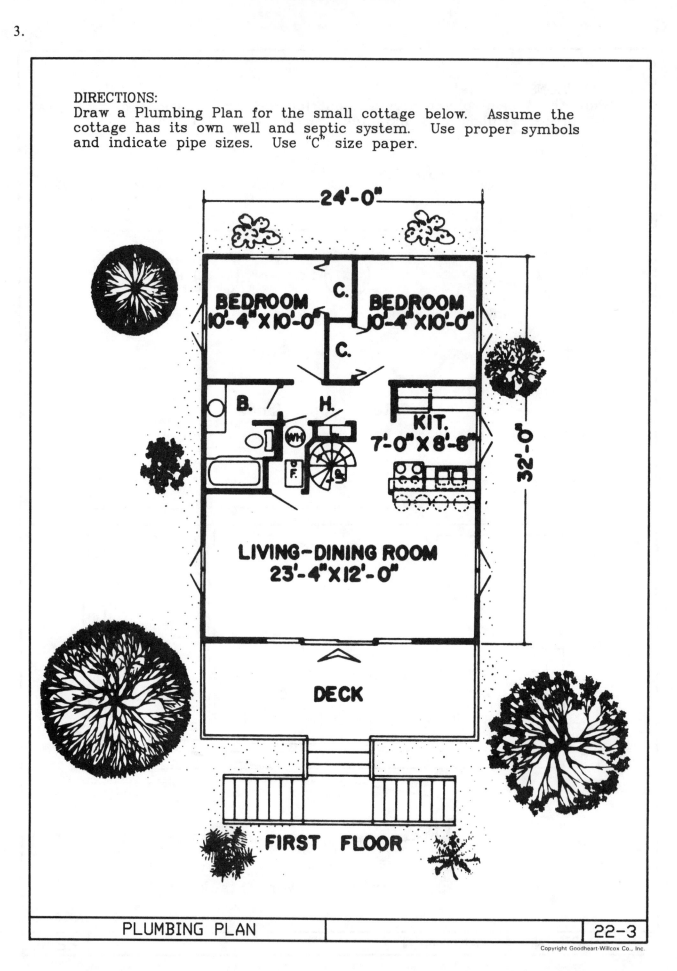

DIRECTIONS:
Draw a Plumbing Plan for the small cottage below. Assume the cottage has its own well and septic system. Use proper symbols and indicate pipe sizes. Use "C" size paper.

24'-0"

BEDROOM
10'-4" X 10'-0"

C.

BEDROOM
10'-4" X 10'-0"

C.

B.

H.

KIT.
7'-0" X 8'-8"

32'-0"

LIVING-DINING ROOM
23'-4" X 12'-0"

DECK

FIRST FLOOR

PLUMBING PLAN

22-3

Chapter 23

RESIDENTIAL CLIMATE CONTROL

Text Pages 367-386

Name _____   Course _____

Date_____   Score _____

PART I: SHORT ANSWER/LISTING: Provide brief answers to the following questions.

1. Adequate insulation is important for heating and cooling a home efficiently. Name three areas where insulation should be placed in a home with a crawl space.

   A. _____

   B. _____

   C. _____

2. Two areas of the home should be ventilated to reduce temperature and moisture. Name them.

   A. _____

   B. _____

3. What device is sometimes required to remove moisture from the air, particularly in the summer?

   _____

4. List the four types of heating systems discussed in the book.

   A. _____

   B. _____

   C. _____

   D. _____

5. List four advantages of a forced warm air system.

   A. _____

   B. _____

   C. _____

   D. _____

6. When installing a forced warm air system into a large, rambling home, what method might you consider to have an effective system?

   _____

   _____

7. Of the four types of heating systems studied in Chapter 23, which two might be a logical choice for a dwelling that has natural gas available?

   A. _____

   B. _____

8. If choosing a heating system for a house to be built in Minnesota, which heating system would not be a logical choice? Indicate why.

   _____

   _____

PART II: MULTIPLE CHOICE: Select the best answer and place its letter in the blank at right.

1. _____ insulation is often used along the foundation wall and perimeter of the floor in houses with slab foundations.
   A. Batt.
   B. Loose fill.
   C. Rigid foam.
   D. All of the above.

   1. _____

2. In residential home construction, use _____ to provide shade and block cold winter winds.
   A. Weatherstripping.
   B. Landscaping.
   C. Overhangs.
   D. None of the above.

   2. _____

3. _____ are used to increase the amount of moisture in the home during months having cold temperatures.
   A. Humidifiers.
   B. Dehumidifiers.
   C. Air cleaners.
   D. All of the above.

   3. _____

4. A(n) _____ warms the air in a furnace and moves the warmed air to various areas of the house through ducts or pipes.
   A. Electric radiant system.
   B. Forced warm air system.
   C. Hydronic system.
   D. Heat pump.

   4. _____

5. A device which automatically activates the heating or cooling system when the temperature in the house reaches a predetermined level is a:
   A. Thermostat.
   B. Cupola vent.
   C. Plenum.
   D. All of the above.

   5. _____

6. The _____ is a type of hydronic system commonly used in residential construction.
   A. Counterflow.
   B. Upflow.
   C. One-pipe.
   D. None of the above.

   6. _____

Name _____

7. One advantage of a hydronic heating system is that:
   A. The temperature of each room may be controlled individually.
   B. Adequate amounts of heat are provided quickly.
   C. Central air conditioning may be added to the system.
   D. All of the above.

7. _____

8. The disadvantage(s) of an electric radiant system include:
   A. Slow recovery after a sudden drop in temperature.
   B. No provision for humidification, air filtration, or cooling.
   C. All of the above.
   D. None of the above.

8. _____

9. A(n) _____ removes heat from outside air and sends it into the house to heat, and removes warmth from the house to cool.
   A. Forced air system.
   B. Hydronic system.
   C. Electric radiant system.
   D. Heat pump.

9. _____

PART III: COMPLETION: Complete each sentence with the proper response. Place your answer on the blank in the right column.

1. The purpose of _____ is to prevent the transfer of heat or cold from one location to another.

1. _____

2. Three important factors that affect the heating and cooling efficiency of the home are insulation, ventilation, and _____ orientation.

2. _____

3. The higher the temperature the _____ (more/less) moisture the air will hold.

3. _____

4. _____ cleaning devices remove dust and small particles from the air.

4. _____

5. A logical choice of a forced warm air furnace for a ranch style house with a crawl space and limited interior space would be a _____ type furnace.

5. _____

6. A type of hydronic system suitable for geographical areas with mild temperatures is the _____ system.

6. _____

7. _____ wiring used in electric radiant systems is placed in the ceiling, floor, or baseboards.

7. _____

8. Air cleaning and humidification are easily added to _____ pump systems.

8. _____

PART IV: MATCHING: Match the correct term with its description listed below. Place the corresponding letter on the blank at right.

A. BTU
B. Design temperature difference
C. Heat loss
D. Infiltration
E. Inside design temperature

F. Outside design temperature
G. Relative humidity
H. Resistivity
I. U factor

1. The ratio of water vapor in the atmosphere to the amount required to saturate it at the same temperature.

1. _____

2. British Thermal Unit.

2. _____

3. Ability to resist the transfer of heat or cold.

3. _____

4. The number of BTUs transmitted in one hour through 1 sq. ft. of building material for each degree of temperature difference.

4. _____

5. The amount of heat which escapes through exposed surfaces of the dwelling for average temperatures.

5. _____

6. Heat loss through spaces around windows and doors.

6. _____

7. The difference between the outside design temperature and the inside design temperature.

7. _____

8. The preferred room temperature level.

8. _____

9. The average outdoor temperature for the winter months.

9. _____

1.

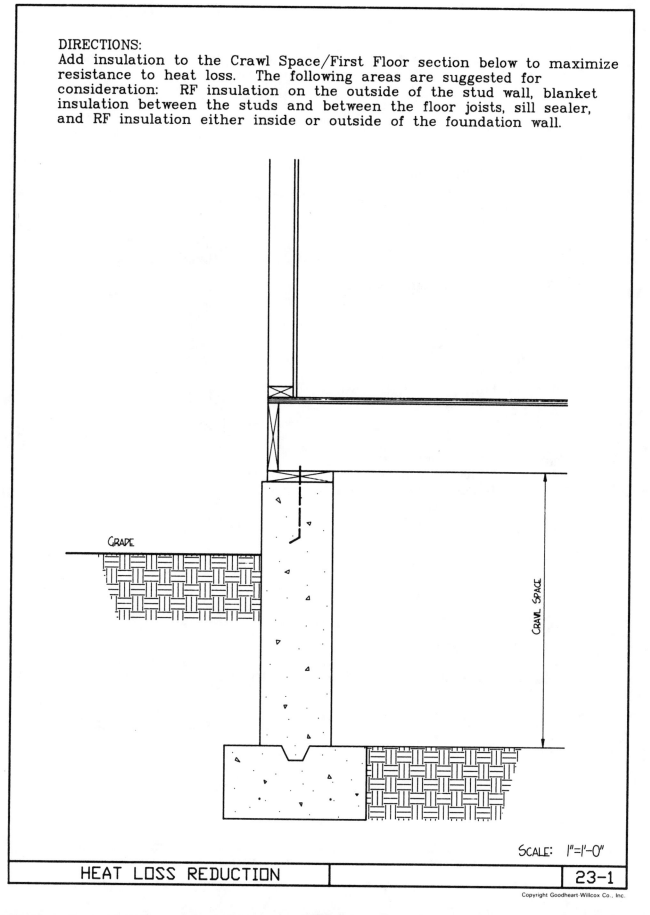

DIRECTIONS:
Add insulation to the Crawl Space/First Floor section below to maximize resistance to heat loss. The following areas are suggested for consideration: RF insulation on the outside of the stud wall, blanket insulation between the studs and between the floor joists, sill sealer, and RF insulation either inside or outside of the foundation wall.

GRADE

CRAWL SPACE

SCALE: 1"=1'-0"

HEAT LOSS REDUCTION   23-1

2.

DIRECTIONS:
Calculate the heat loss for the exterior wall below and fill in the
values as indicated. The wall has no windows or doors.

WALL AREA CALCULATION:
  Total Wall Area = 8'-0" x 12'-0" = _____ Sq. Ft.
  Window and Door Area = 0 Sq. Ft.
  Net Wall Area = _____ Sq. Ft.

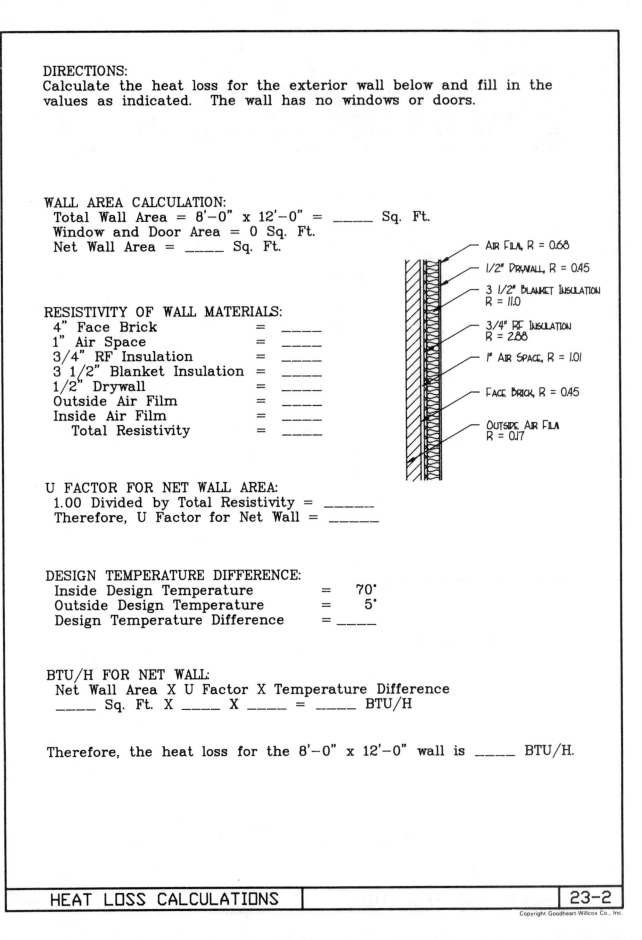

RESISTIVITY OF WALL MATERIALS:
  4" Face Brick   = _____
  1" Air Space   = _____
  3/4" RF Insulation   = _____
  3 1/2" Blanket Insulation = _____
  1/2" Drywall   = _____
  Outside Air Film   = _____
  Inside Air Film   = _____
    Total Resistivity   = _____

U FACTOR FOR NET WALL AREA:
  1.00 Divided by Total Resistivity = _____
  Therefore, U Factor for Net Wall = _____

DESIGN TEMPERATURE DIFFERENCE:
  Inside Design Temperature   =   70°
  Outside Design Temperature   =   5°
  Design Temperature Difference   = _____

BTU/H FOR NET WALL:
  Net Wall Area X U Factor X Temperature Difference
  _____ Sq. Ft. X _____ X _____ = _____ BTU/H

Therefore, the heat loss for the 8'-0" x 12'-0" wall is _____ BTU/H.

HEAT LOSS CALCULATIONS   23-2

Chapter 24

CLIMATE CONTROL PLAN

Text Pages 387-394

Name _____   Course _____

Date _____   Score _____

PART I: MULTIPLE CHOICE: Select the best answer and place its letter in the blank at right.

1. The climate control plan is traced from the:
   A. Plot plan.
   B. Foundation plan.
   C. Floor plan.
   D. Site plan.

   1. _____

2. A climate control plan should show information such as:
   A. Electrical outlets and switches.
   B. Location of thermostats and registers or baseboard convectors.
   C. The hot water branch lines to each fixture.
   D. All of the above.

   2. _____

3. The perimeter system of outlets:
   A. Concentrates heating or cooling along outside walls.
   B. Concentrates heating or cooling along interior walls.
   C. Does not use registers or baseboard units.
   D. All of the above.

   3. _____

4. Larger round pipes, usually 8 in. in diameter, are typically used in systems which heat as well as cool because:
   A. Warm air moves slower than cool air.
   B. Warm air moves at the same speed as cool air.
   C. Cool air moves slower than warm air.
   D. None of the above.

   4. _____

5. The sectional area of the supply duct should equal:
   A. The total area of the round register pipes.
   B. The size of the extended plenum.
   C. All of the above.
   D. None of the above.

   5. _____

6. The heat loss for each room should be calculated for a hydronic system to determine:
   A. Whether an extended plenum or radial system should be used.
   B. The size of the baseboard unit or convector cabinet.
   C. The size of pipe to use.
   D. All of the above.

   6. _____

7. A thermostat should be located:
   A. On an outside wall near a window.
   B. In the kitchen near the cooking center.
   C. On an inside wall away from any lamps or heat-producing equipment.
   D. All of the above.

   7. _____

8. Many decisions have to be made before the climate control plan
   can be drawn. Some include:
   A. The type and size of heating and cooling system to be used.
   B. The location of all the equipment required for the system.
   C. All of the above.
   D. None of the above.

8. _____

PART II: COMPLETION: Complete each sentence with the proper response. Place your answer on the blank in the right column.

1. The _____ control plan is a plan view drawing in section.

1. _____

2. Ducts distribute large amounts of air for heating or cooling,
   while _____ distribute hot water or steam for heating.

2. _____

3. An area or room larger than 180 sq. ft. should have at least
   two _____ for heating and cooling.

3. _____

4. The _____ system uses rectangular ducts for the main
   supply and round pipes connecting to each register.

4. _____

5. The duct size required to accommodate eight pipes used for
   heating and cooling would be _____.

5. _____

6. For the most efficient heat, _____ should be located below
   windows.

6. _____

7. Specifications that show items, such as equipment or registers,
   to be used in the system may be shown on _____.

7. _____

8. The return air ducts for a forced air system should be drawn
   using a _____ line symbol.

8. _____

9. The scale used for drawing the climate control plan is
   _____.

9. _____

PART III: SHORT ANSWER/LISTING: Provide brief answers to the following questions.

1. List features typically shown on the climate control plan.

   A. _____

   B. _____

   C. _____

   _____

2. How are ducts and pipes indicated on the climate control plan?

   _____

3. How many inlets does a split-level house using a forced warm air heating system need?

   _____

4. Which duct system is more popular—the radial system or the extended plenum system?

   _____

5. What size of main is required for a 175,000 BTU hydronic system?

   _____

6. A forced warm air system with one furnace requires how many thermostats?

   _____

7. What determines the size of basement heating equipment?

   _____

PART IV: PROBLEMS/ACTIVITIES

1.

DIRECTIONS:
Draw the climate control symbols indicated below. The scale is 1/4"=1'–0".

Warm Air Supply

Cold Air Return

Second Floor Supply

Second Floor Return

12" x 18" Duct/Flow

Duct Change in Size

Thermostat

Humidistat

Radiator

Convector

Register

Ceiling Duct Outlet

Scale: 1/4'=1'–0"

CLIMATE CONTROL SYMBOLS		24-1

2.

DIRECTIONS:
Design a simple heating duct system for the small house below which illustrates the desired distribution of warm air and provides for cold air return. You may assume the extended warm air plenum to be 8" x 14" with ducts 6" in diameter. Remember to provide for cold air return. Study Fig. 24—7 in the text.
Draw the plan on "B" size paper at a scale of 1/4"=1'—0".

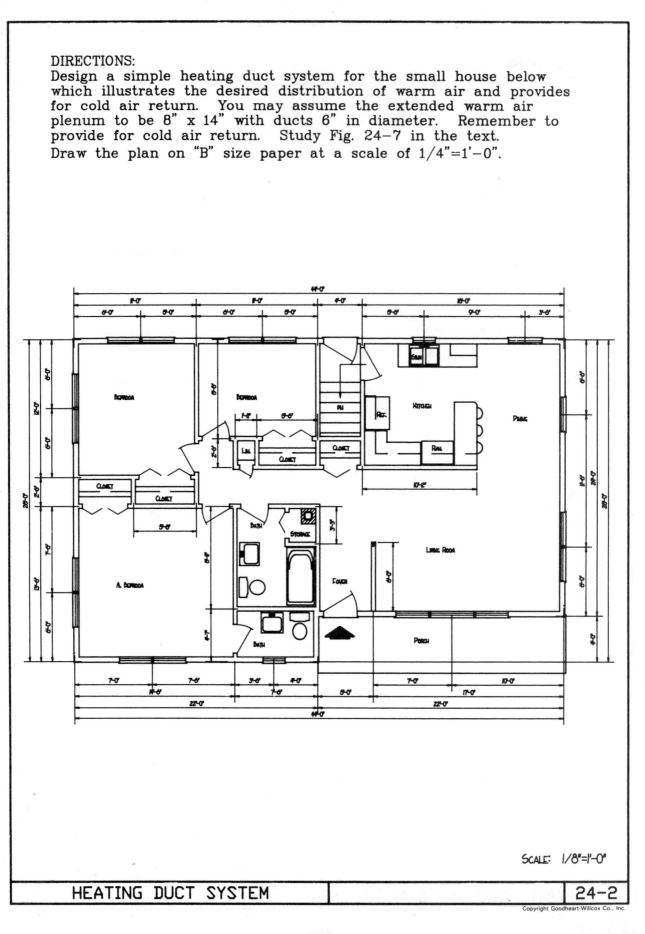

SCALE: 1/8"=1'-0"

| HEATING DUCT SYSTEM | | 24-2 |

Chapter 25

SOLAR SPACE HEATING

Text Pages 395-404

Name _____   Course _____

Date_____   Score _____

PART I: COMPLETION: Complete each sentence with the proper response. Place your answer on the blank in the right column.

1. Fans and pumps are not used in _____ (active/passive) solar space heating systems.

    1. _____

2. Massive structures used by _____ gain systems to store excess heat are thick masonry walls, floors, and furnishings.

    2. _____

3. Masonry walls store heat more efficiently if the insulation is placed on the _____ (inside/outside) of the wall.

    3. _____

4. Energy is collected and stored outside the living space in a(n) _____ gain system.

    4. _____

5. Pumps, fans, and other devices to distribute heat are required in the _____ solar heating system.

    5. _____

6. The _____ should provide as much surface area to the sun as possible to absorb maximum heating. This is critical to the operation of the solar heating system.

    6. _____

7. A stone-filled box or crawl space area is often used for _____. It should be well insulated.

    7. _____

8. Warm _____ solar systems use solar collectors with tubes attached to the absorber plate, or cavities in the absorber plate.

    8. _____

9. Heat collected in a warm water system is distributed to the living space by a _____.

    9. _____

PART II: SHORT ANSWER/LISTING: Provide brief answers to the following questions.

1. Name the two basic systems used in solar space heating.

    A. _____

    B. _____

2. What type of glazing is most frequently used in direct gain systems? It allows large amounts of sunlight to enter the interior space.

    _____

3. Why are large thermal masses necessary in a direct gain system?

_____

_____

_____

4. What are the advantages and/or disadvantages of a drum wall?

_____

_____

_____

_____

5. List five requirements of a solar greenhouse in order to be efficient in a cold climate.

A. _____

B. _____

C. _____

D. _____

_____

E. _____

6. What features should be present in a good-quality solar collector?

A. _____

_____

B. _____

_____

7. Generally, what is the most efficient tilt and orientation for a solar collector?

_____

_____

8. How is heat from the storage area distributed to the living area in a warm air system?

_____

_____

9. Name two concerns to address when considering a warm water solar system.

A. _____

_____

_____

B. _____

_____

_____

PART III: MULTIPLE CHOICE: Select the best answer and place its letter in the blank at right.

1. A direct gain system: 1. _____
   A. Is a popular type of active solar system.
   B. Uses pumps and fans to move the heat.
   C. Is a type of passive solar system.
   D. None of the above.

Name _____

2. Indirect gain systems:
   A. Use a group of solar collectors to collect heat.
   B. Use a large thermal mass located between the sun and living space to store heat.
   C. Are the most popular type of solar heating systems.
   D. All of the above.

2. _____

3. The vents in the Trombe wall should be closed at night during the heating season to prevent:
   A. Reverse thermosiphoning.
   B. Thermosiphoning.
   C. All of the above.
   D. None of the above.

3. _____

4. Advantage(s) of the isolated gain system include:
   A. Little interior space need be exposed to the sun.
   B. Little interior space is required for heat collection devices.
   C. Heat collected is easier to control.
   D. All of the above.

4. _____

5. A bank of collectors, a heat storage box with stones, and blowers are required in the:
   A. Warm water system.
   B. Warm air solar system.
   C. Direct gain system.
   D. Indirect gain system.

5. _____

6. The most common material for warm air absorber plates is:
   A. Copper.
   B. Aluminum.
   C. Steel.
   D. Cast iron.

6. _____

7. As a rule, the size of the heat storage for active solar systems should be:
   A. Sufficiently large to store enough heat for three days of cloudy weather.
   B. One-half the size of the collector area.
   C. Twice the size of the collector area.
   D. As large as possible.

7. _____

8. The heated water necessary in the warm water system is usually stored in a(n):
   A. Large tank placed in the utility room.
   B. Indoor swimming pool.
   C. Large insulated tank usually located in the basement or crawl space.
   D. None of the above.

8. _____

9. Warm water solar systems heat the air in the living space by:
   A. Absorber plates with copper tubes attached.
   B. Liquid-to-air heat exchangers such as baseboard convectors.
   C. Solar collectors.
   D. All of the above.

9. _____

PART IV: MATCHING: Match the correct term with its description listed below. Place the corresponding letter on the blank at right.

A. Conduction
B. Convection
C. Flat plate collectors
D. Glauber's salt
E. Radiation

F. Solar radiation
G. Sun space
H. Thermosiphoning
I. Trombe wall
J. Water storage wall

1. The sun's energy. 1. _____

2. Transfer of heat by moving fluids, such as liquids or gases. 2. _____

3. The flow of heat through an object by the movement of heat from one molecule to another. 3. _____

4. Waves of infrared or invisible light which move heat through space. 4. _____

5. A massive wall colored dark on the outside to absorb heat from the sun. 5. _____

6. The result of a fluid expanding and rising. 6. _____

7. A wall made of water-filled containers capable of storing heat. 7. _____

8. A phase change material which changes from a solid to a liquid as it heats up. 8. _____

9. A solar greenhouse. 9. _____

10. A type of absorber plate. 10. _____

1.

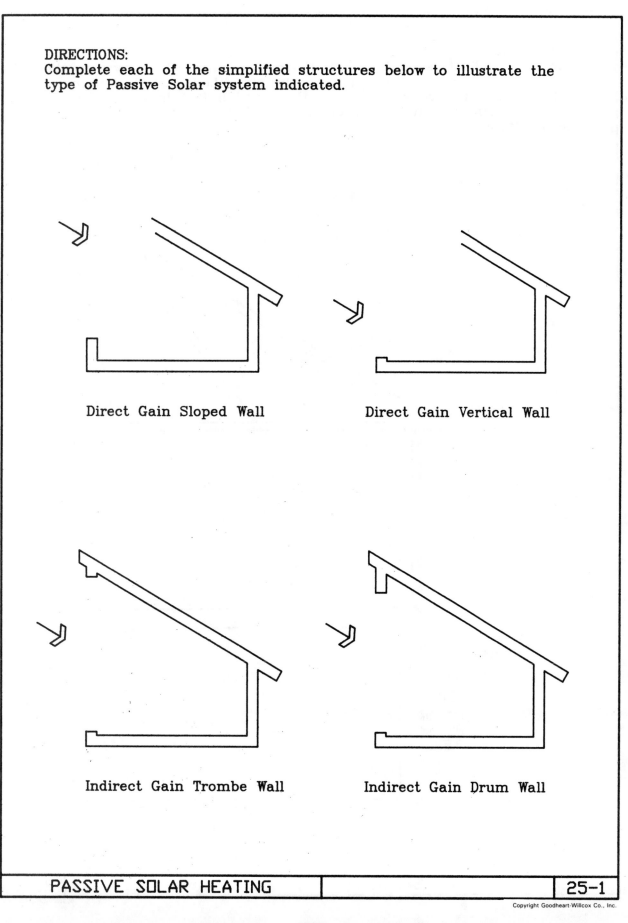

DIRECTIONS:
Complete each of the simplified structures below to illustrate the type of Passive Solar system indicated.

Direct Gain Sloped Wall

Direct Gain Vertical Wall

Indirect Gain Trombe Wall

Indirect Gain Drum Wall

PASSIVE SOLAR HEATING

25-1

Copyright Goodheart-Willcox Co., Inc.

2.

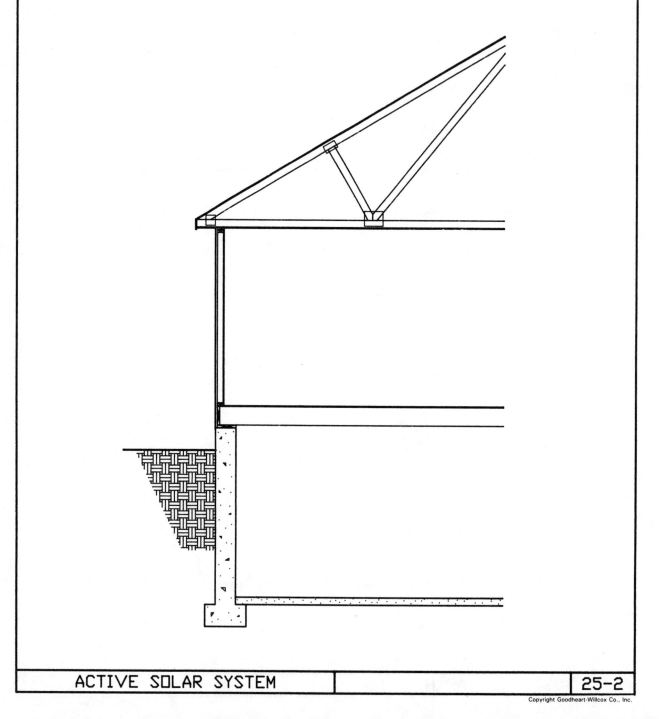

DIRECTIONS:
Add solar collectors on the roof, thermal storage with blower in the basement, and connecting ducts to the simplified partial structure below.   Show the collectors as 6" thick and 8 feet long, the ducts as 6" in diameter, and the storage as 4' x 8'.   See Fig. 25—11 for design layout.

ACTIVE SOLAR SYSTEM   25-2

Chapter 26

EARTH SHELTERED DWELLINGS

Text Pages 405-412

Name _____   Course _____

Date_____   Score _____

PART I: SHORT ANSWER/LISTING: Provide brief answers to the following questions.

1. List four factors to consider when selecting a site for an earth sheltered dwelling.

    A. _____

    B. _____

    C. _____

    D. _____

2. From which direction do summer breezes come in northern climates?

    _____

3. Why is soil type and groundwater so critical when locating a site for an earth sheltered dwelling?

    _____

    _____

    _____

4. Backfill against an earth sheltered dwelling should be sand or gravel. Why is expansive clay not a viable choice?

    _____

    _____

5. Name two factors that affect the energy conservation of an earth shelter.

    A. _____

    B. _____

6. The two structural systems generally used in earth sheltered dwellings to support the heavy roof loads are conventional flat roof systems and unconventional systems. Describe each.

    _____

    _____

    _____

    _____

    _____

    _____

    _____

7. If a suitable site can be found, what are the positive aspects of choosing an earth sheltered house having a slope design?

_____

_____

_____

PART II: MULTIPLE CHOICE: Select the best answer and place its letter in the blank at right.

1. Orientation to the sun is an important factor in placing earth sheltered dwellings because:
   A. North facing orientations are better suited for northern climates.
   B. South facing orientations are more effective in warm climates.
   C. Solar energy may be used to heat the interior space.
   D. All of the above.

   1. _____

2. Site selection for an earth sheltered dwelling is very important. _____ sites permit greater design possibilities.
   A. Sloping.
   B. Flat.
   C. All of the above.
   D. None of the above.

   2. _____

3. Soil characteristics affecting the design of the structure include:
   A. Soil color and depth of the topsoil.
   B. Bearing capacity and tendency to expand when wet.
   C. All of the above.
   D. None of the above.

   3. _____

4. Soils that have the optimum bearing capacity and should be used under the foundation of an earth sheltered dwelling are:
   A. Fine-grained soils.
   B. Rock two to three inches in diameter.
   C. Expansive clay.
   D. Compacted sand or gravel.

   4. _____

5. Generally, an earth sheltered structure which will conserve the greatest amount of energy:
   A. Has a small surface area exposed.
   B. Has a large surface area exposed.
   C. Is long across the front and narrow on the sides.
   D. Has two levels.

   5. _____

6. The advantage(s) of choosing an earth sheltered dwelling over a conventional dwelling is:
   A. A longer life span.
   B. Less maintenance.
   C. Lower energy needs.
   D. All of the above.

   6. _____

7. The living areas are located around a central courtyard in the atrium design. This design is:
   A. Probably better suited for warm climates.
   B. Convenient for efficient traffic circulation in cold climates.
   C. A compact plan.
   D. Suitable for south-facing windows.

   7. _____

Name _____

8. An advantage of selecting an earth sheltered house is: 8. _____
   A. Most contractors are generally quite knowledgeable about
      their construction requirements.
   B. Their high resistance to fire damage.
   C. They are adaptable to any neighborhood setting.
   D. Code requirements present no problems.

PART III: COMPLETION: Complete each sentence with the proper response. Place your answer on the blank in the right column.

1. An earth sheltered dwelling built in Michigan would be more   1. _____
   efficient if windows and doors were placed on the _____
   (north/south) side of the structure to prevent heat loss from
   the cold winter winds.

2. To provide shade in warm seasons and permit sun penetration   2. _____
   in cool seasons, plant _____ (evergreen/deciduous) trees.

3. Soil on the roof of the structure should be _____ (fine-   3. _____
   grained/coarse-grained) to support vegetation and not be subject
   to frost heave.

4. Sites with _____ (good/poor) drainage provide the best   4. _____
   conditions to support an earth sheltered home.

5. Energy conservation is usually highly efficient when a   5. _____
   _____ (small/large) area of the structure has an earth
   cover.

6. The _____ design has windows and doors on one side of   6. _____
   the dwelling.

7. The _____ design permits windows and doors at certain   7. _____
   points around the structure.

1.

DIRECTIONS:
Draw a simplified Section View of a single level residential structure
of the slope design for the site indicated below by the dotted line.
(See Fig. 26–10 in the text.)   The plan should incorporate the
following: 8 ft. ceiling, 24 ft. depth (front to back), 2 ft. of soil on
top of a 1 ft. thick ceiling, glass wall on south side, and 4 ft. bubble-
type skylight near the rear of the home.   Scale is 1/8"=1'–0".

EARTH SHELTERED HOME | 26–1

2.

DIRECTIONS:
Study the Topographical Drawing of the site below and show the placement of a 24' x 60' earth sheltered home of the slope design. The location should take into consideration the direction of the sun for maximum heating, direction of winter winds and summer breezes, patterns of water runoff, and groundwater conditions. The scale of the drawing is 1/16"=1'-0".

Winter wind from NW, summer breezes from SE, and sun from S.

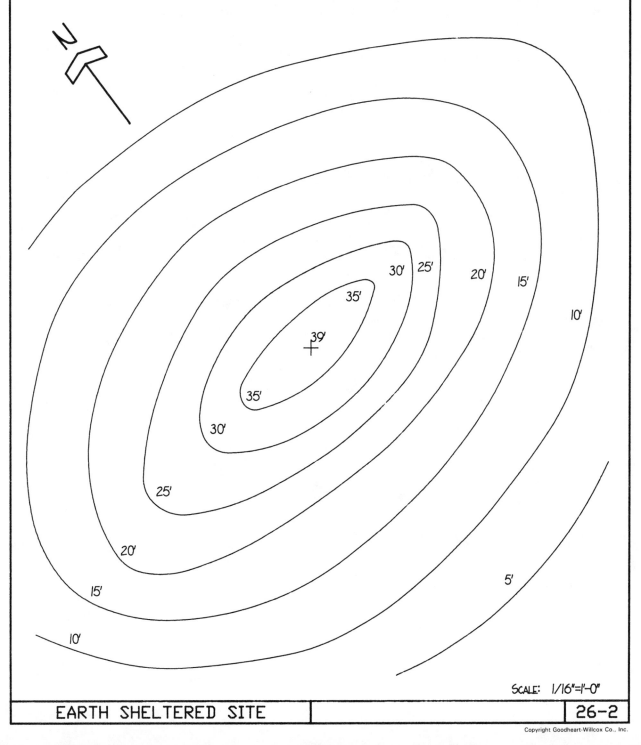

SCALE: 1/16"=1'-0"

EARTH SHELTERED SITE | 26-2

Chapter 27

DOME STRUCTURES

Text Pages 413-420

Name _____   Course _____

Date_____   Score _____

PART I: MULTIPLE CHOICE: Select the best answer and place its letter in the blank at right.

1. The geodesic dome is based on what shape?   1. _____
   A. Triangle.
   B. Rectangle.
   C. Circle.
   D. Trapezoid.

2. The dome provides an open interior space because: 2. _____
   A. Interior walls or beams would interfere with the floor plan.
   B. The structure of the dome is self supporting.
   C. Mr. Fuller did not like interior walls.
   D. The ceilings are too high for support walls.

3. Two basic domes have evolved from the original geodesic dome.   3. _____
   Both use triangles to form:
   A. Pentagons, trapezoids, and rectangles.
   B. Hexagons, pentagons, and rectangles.
   C. Hexagons, pentagons, and trapezoids.
   D. All of the above.

4. Cutting the proper _____ is critical for the pieces to join   4. _____
   together properly in a dome structure.
   A. Circles.
   B. Angles.
   C. All of the above.
   D. None of the above.

5. The foundation for a dome should be a: 5. _____
   A. Basement.
   B. Crawl space.
   C. Slab foundation.
   D. All of the above.

6. Riser walls have _____ walls on each side to completely   6. _____
   enclose the structure.
   A. Wing.
   B. Side.
   C. Top.
   D. Bottom.

PART II: COMPLETION: Complete each sentence with the proper response. Place your answer on the blank in the right column.

1. The original geodesic dome was popularized by _____ (person).

    1. _____

2. Common exterior materials for dome structures include _____ shingles and cedar shakes.

    2. _____

3. Domes may be constructed similar to conventional homes. The panels may be shipped from the factory complete and ready to bolt together, _____ at the factory and shipped in individual pieces, or built on the site using standard lumber and plywood.

    3. _____

4. Studs are spaced _____ o.c. in the 32 ft. Hexadome.

    4. _____

5. The 32 ft. dome home illustrated in the text has _____ (number) primary support walls.

    5. _____

6. A dome home is probably _____ (more/less) suitable for a lot in a suburb than a wooded site on the outskirts of town.

    6. _____

PART III: SHORT ANSWER/LISTING: Provide brief answers to the following questions.

1. Two positive aspects of dome homes are the reduced heat loss and less building material required. What is the approximate reduction in building materials per square foot of usable area?

_____

2. The true geodesic dome which Fuller developed uses a series of small triangles. Why have most dome home designers modified Fuller's design?

    A. _____

       _____

    B. _____

       _____

3. The 32 ft. Hexadome uses six panels of triangles to form a raised hexagon. How many hexagons and trapezoids are needed to complete the dome?

_____

4. What piece of equipment is required to place the dome on its foundation?

_____

5. Are riser walls necessary in a dome structure? If so, why?

_____

6. Why would a dome structure be a logical house choice in a northern climate where winter temperatures are low and winds are a concern?

_____

_____

_____

1.

DIRECTIONS:
Scale the manufacturer's drawings of the 45 ft. diameter dome home below and draw the basic shape (upper and lower levels) at a scale of 1/4"=1'-0" on "C" size paper. Modify the interior space to suit yourself, but in keeping with good design principles. Remember, headroom is reduced near the exterior walls in most locations on the upper level.

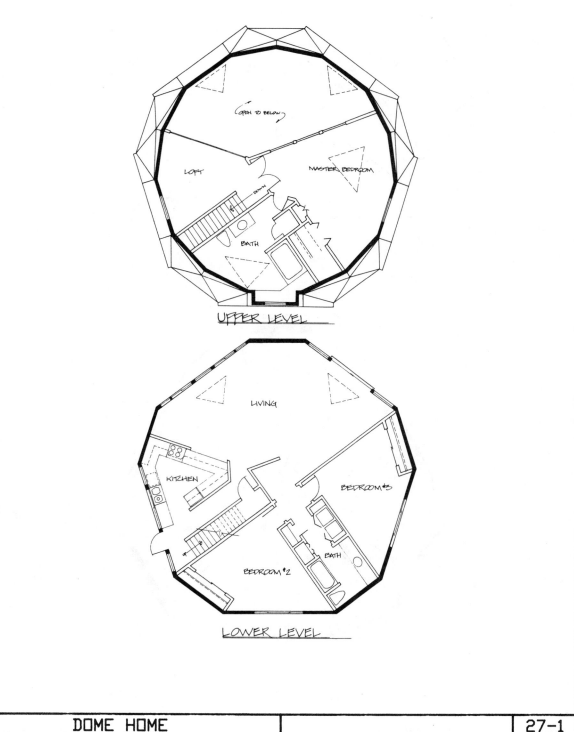

DOME HOME		27-1

2.

DIRECTIONS:
Using the dimensions below, build a 32 ft. diameter dome model at
1/2" or 1" scale. Riser walls should be approximately 2 ft. high.
Use foamcore, heavy illustration board, or thin wood paneling to form
each module. Accuracy is very important!

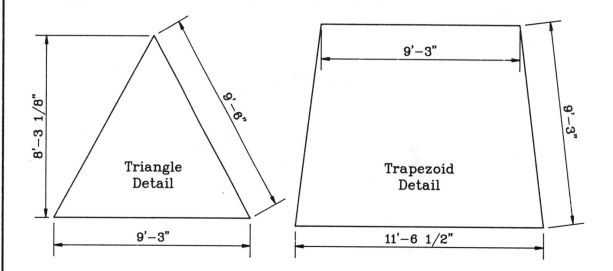

Triangle Detail — 8'-3 1/8", 9'-6", 9'-3"

Trapezoid Detail — 9'-3", 9'-3", 11'-6 1/2"

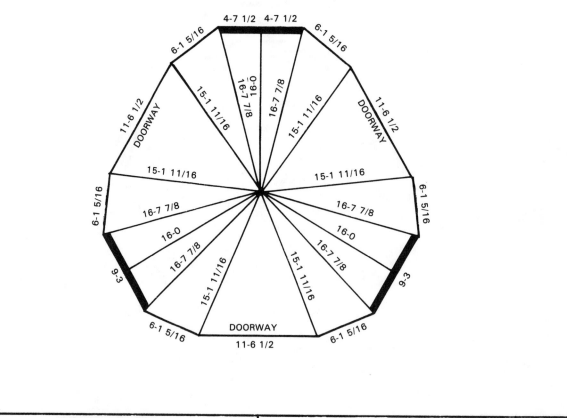

DOME MODEL		27-2

Chapter 28

MODULAR APPLICATIONS

Text Pages 421-428

Name _____   Course _____

Date_____   Score _____

PART I: COMPLETION: Complete each sentence with the proper response. Place your answer on the blank in the right column.

1. A type of construction which takes individual pieces of building materials and puts them together on the construction site is referred to as _____.

    1. _____

2. Standard size building materials are required in _____ construction.

    2. _____

3. Widths ranging from 16 to 196 in., in multiples of _____ in. are often common for modular panel components.

    3. _____

4. An arrow indicates that the dimension ends on the grid line while the _____ indicates that the dimension ends off the grid line.

    4. _____

5. Some modules are produced on a(n) _____ line.

    5. _____

6. With modular construction, an entire _____ may be selected just as you would a new automobile.

    6. _____

PART II: SHORT ANSWER/LISTING: Provide brief answers to the following questions.

1. What are the benefits gained by using modular sizes and mass production in housing?

    _____

2. Modular construction is based on the 4 in. cube, known as the standard module, which measures 4 x 4 x 4 in. Name the other two modules and their sizes typically found in modular construction.

    _____

    _____

3. For drawing and dimensioning modular houses, a designer should use a _____ to help with layout.

    _____

4. What are modular components?

    _____

    _____

5. List three advantages of prefabricated panels or panelized construction.

A. _____

B. _____

C. _____

ALSO: _____

_____

6. House modules are built on a special frame to protect them during transportation. From what material is the frame made?

_____

PART III: MULTIPLE CHOICE: Select the best answer and place its letter in the blank at right.

1. Houses that are built in the factory to the specifications of prospective owners are referred to as:
   A. Custom homes.
   B. Mobile homes.
   C. Factory-built homes.
   D. All of the above.

1. _____

2. Studs and joists are placed 16 and 24 in. o.c. to coincide with _____ modules.
   A. Standard.
   B. Minor.
   C. Major.
   D. All of the above.

2. _____

3. Details of the structure should begin and end:
   A. On the grid line.
   B. Above the grid line.
   C. Below the grid line.
   D. None of the above.

3. _____

4. Floor panels, roof panels, wall sections, or roof trusses are all examples of:
   A. Partitions.
   B. Modular components.
   C. Stock lumber.
   D. All of the above.

4. _____

5. In factory-built homes:
   A. The quality is generally not as good as in traditional construction.
   B. The quality of lumber is unimportant.
   C. Jigs and fixtures are used to cut and fit parts together.
   D. None of the above.

5. _____

6. A characteristic of factory-built houses is:
   A. The modules are usually complete with plumbing, wiring, finished floors, and doors.
   B. They require a special foundation.
   C. Little versatility of modules is possible.
   D. All of the above.

6. _____

PART IV: PROBLEMS/ACTIVITIES

1.

DIRECTIONS:
Using the modular grid below, draw the plan view wall framing plan for a 10'-0" x 12'-0" frame Storage Building with siding. (Be sure to apply the modular concepts presented in the text.) Provide an access door at least 36" wide and two windows in your design. The scale is 1/2"=1'-0".

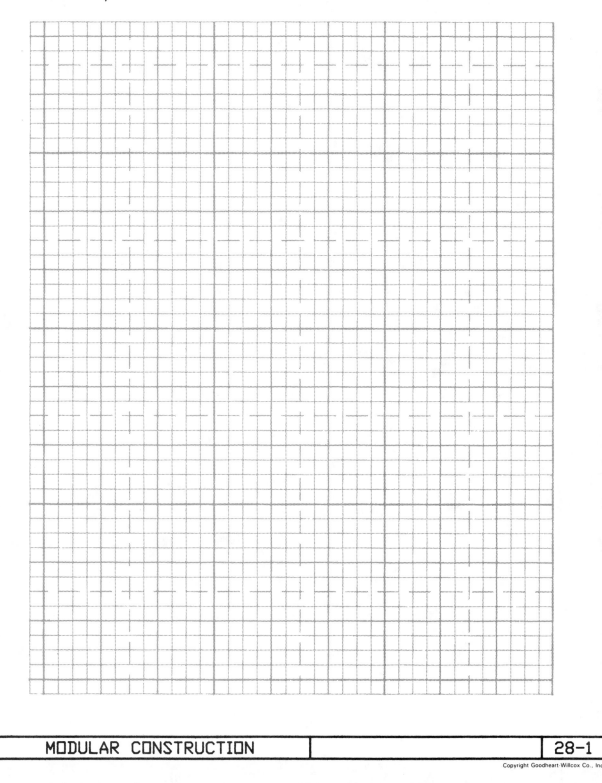

MODULAR CONSTRUCTION		28-1

x

x

Copyright Goodheart-Willcox Co., Inc.

Chapter 29

PERSPECTIVE DRAWINGS

Text Pages 429-452

Name _____   Course _____

Date_____   Score _____

PART I: MATCHING: Match the correct term with its description listed below. Place the corresponding letter on the blank at right.

A. Ground line
B. Horizon line
C. Perspective
D. Perspective grid
E. Picture plane

F. Plan view
G. Station point
H. Three-point perspective
I. True length line
J. Vanishing points

1. A type of pictorial drawing that gives a realistic view of the object.

1. _____

2. Also called an oblique perspective.

2. _____

3. Represents a horizontal plane which is called the ground plane.

3. _____

4. The place where the ground and sky meet.

4. _____

5. A vertical plane on which the perspective is drawn.

5. _____

6. The location of the observer's eye.

6. _____

7. A line used to project heights on a perspective drawing.

7. _____

8. Always located on the horizon line.

8. _____

9. Also known as roof view.

9. _____

10. Saves time and space in drawing a large perspective.

10. _____

PART II: SHORT ANSWER/LISTING: Provide brief answers to the following questions.

1. Name the three types of perspectives and indicate a typical use for each type.

A. _____

_____

B. _____

_____

C. _____

_____

2. List the three parts in a perspective layout.

A. _____

B. _____

C. _____

3. How many views of the station point are used in a one-point perspective?

_____

4. What are the angles on each side of the object with respect to the picture plane?

_____

5. List two factors that determine the height of the horizon line?

A. _____

B. _____

6. In a two-point perspective, should the picture plane, ground line, and horizon line be parallel or perpendicular to each other?

_____

7. Explain how the left and right vanishing points are determined in a two-point perspective.

_____

_____

_____

_____

_____

8. Explain how you would draw a chair with soft curves in perspective.

_____

_____

PART III: MULTIPLE CHOICE: Select the best answer and place its letter in the blank at right.

1. One-point perspectives are _____ perspectives.
   A. Oblique.
   B. Angular.
   C. Parallel.
   D. All of the above.

1. _____

2. When an object is placed behind the picture plane, and the station point is above the ground line:
   A. It must touch the ground line in the perspective of the object.
   B. The perspective of the object will be above the ground line.
   C. The object will extend below the ground line.
   D. None of the above.

2. _____

3. Two-point perspectives are good communicators because:
   A. They generate a photo-like drawing that is very accurate in detail.
   B. The objects are drawn true to size.
   C. They are quite simple to draw.
   D. None of the above.

3. _____

4. Generally, the station point is placed so that it forms a cone of vision between _____.
   A. 15 and 30 degrees.
   B. 15 and 22 1/2 degrees.
   C. 30 and 45 degrees.
   D. All of the above.

4. _____

Name _____

5. The most frequently used method for drawing one- and two-point perspectives is the:
   A. Common method.
   B. Office method.
   C. All of the above.
   D. None of the above.

   5. _____

6. The elevation should be placed on the _____ at the extreme right or left in a two-point perspective.
   A. Picture plane.
   B. Ground line.
   C. Horizon line.
   D. None of the above.

   6. _____

PART IV: COMPLETION: Complete each sentence with the proper response. Place your answer on the blank in the right column.

1. In perspectives, the _____ is the location of the observer's eye.

   1. _____

2. Any part of the object that is in front of the picture plane will appear _____ (smaller/larger) than scale.

   2. _____

3. If the _____ is placed too close to the picture plane, the drawing will be unrealistic and distorted.

   3. _____

4. To obtain a "bird's eye view" of the object, locate the station point or horizon line approximately _____ (5 to 6 ft./20 to 30 ft.) above the ground line.

   4. _____

5. When drawing a large two-point perspective, draw the _____ and elevation on separate sheets of paper.

   5. _____

6. The height of roof ridges, overhangs, and chimneys may quickly be determined by establishing a new _____ line.

   6. _____

7. The vanishing point _____ (is always/may not be) located in a one-point perspective.

   7. _____

8. Circular or oval objects may be drawn by locating several _____ on the surface to be drawn and then connecting them together.

   8. _____

1.

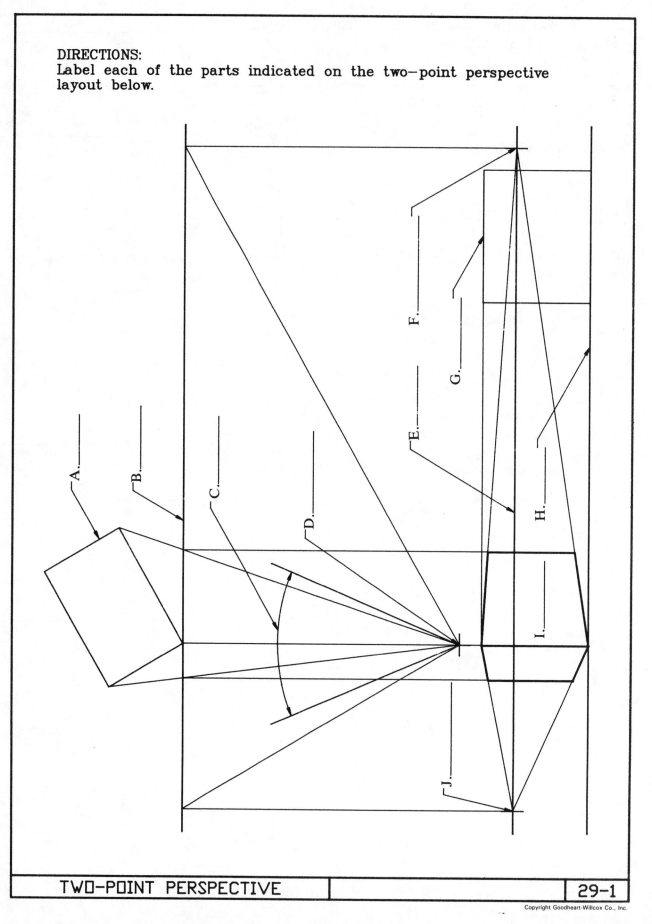

DIRECTIONS:
Label each of the parts indicated on the two–point perspective layout below.

TWO–POINT PERSPECTIVE

29–1

2.

DIRECTIONS:
Draw a two—point perspective of the object using the setup provided.
Show all construction lines, but darken in visible object lines. Omit
hidden lines from the pictorial.

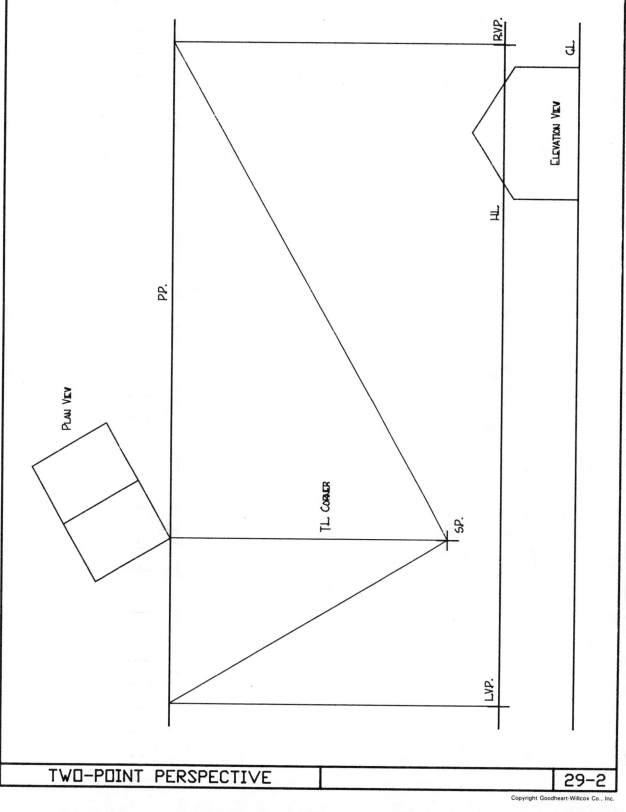

TWO-POINT PERSPECTIVE

29-2

3.

DIRECTIONS:
Draw a two—point perspective of the object as indicated. Show all
construction lines, but darken in the visible lines of the object.

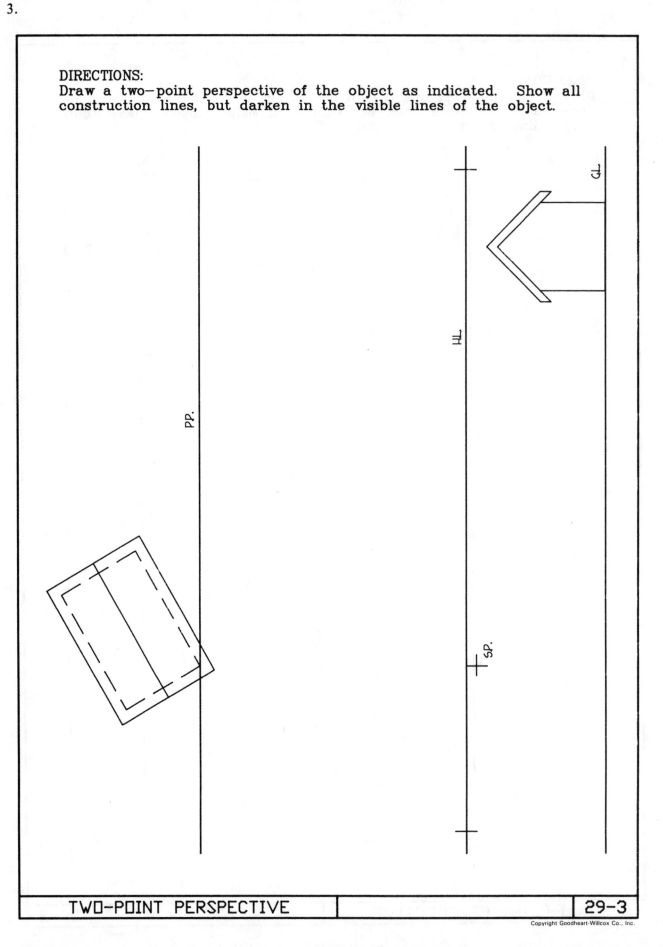

PP.

HL

GL

SP.

TWO—POINT PERSPECTIVE

29-3

Name _____

4. **Two-point perspective.** Using the elevations, floor plan, and foundation plan of the garage in Fig. 7-56 of the text, set up a two-point perspective layout on a "C" size sheet. Construct the perspective from an appropriate position. Follow the procedure described in the text. The solution will be evaluated on accuracy as well as the quality of the view.

5.

DIRECTIONS:
Complete the One–Point Perspective drawing below using the procedure described in the text. Show your construction using light construction lines. Darken the visible object lines.

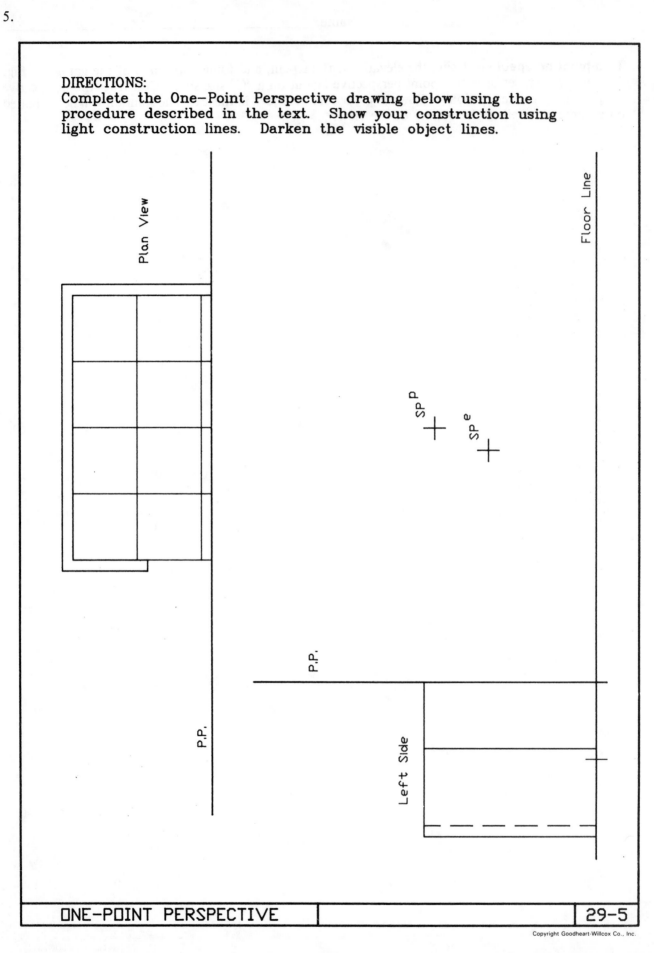

ONE-POINT PERSPECTIVE

29-5

6.

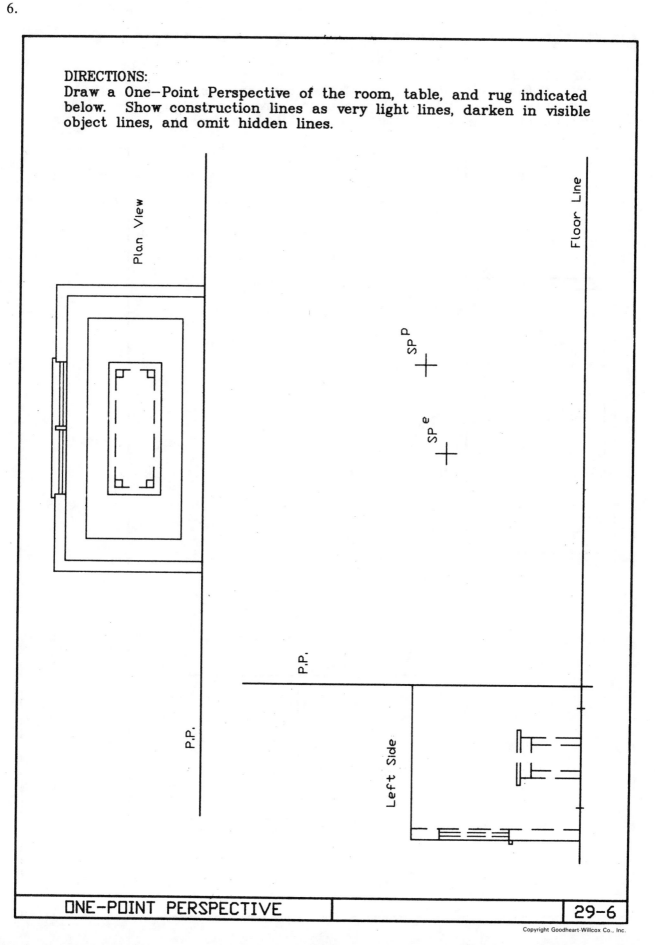

DIRECTIONS:
Draw a One—Point Perspective of the room, table, and rug indicated below. Show construction lines as very light lines, darken in visible object lines, and omit hidden lines.

Plan View

Floor Line

SP^p

SP^e

P.P.

P.P.

Left Side

ONE—POINT PERSPECTIVE

29-6

7.

DIRECTIONS:
Draw a One–Point Perspective of the room and contents (simplified furniture pieces) below. Show construction lines as very light lines, darken in visible object lines, and omit hidden lines.

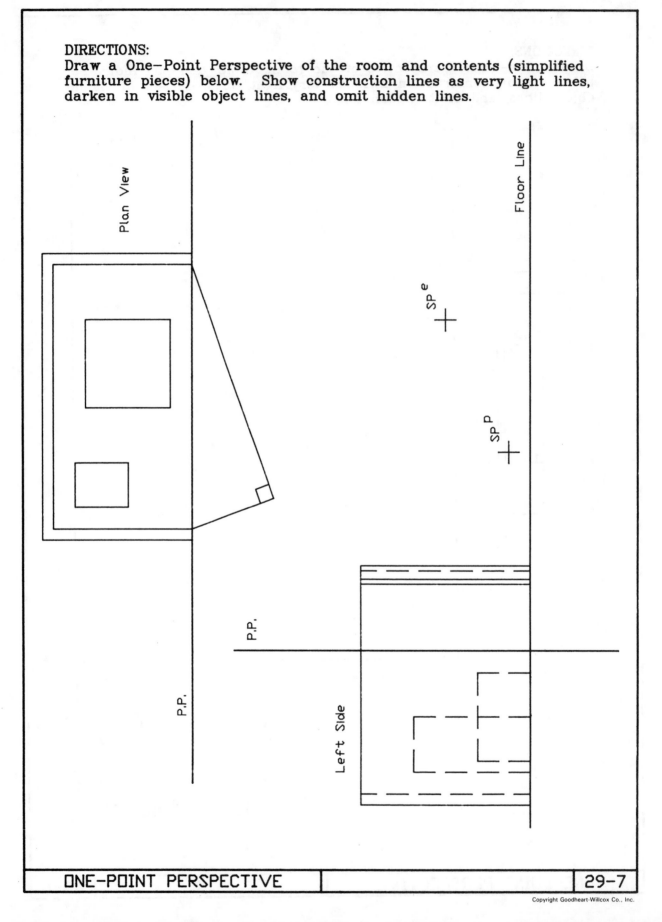

ONE-POINT PERSPECTIVE | | 29-7

Name _____

8. **One-point perspective.** Using the kitchen plan that you designed for Problem 7-3, set up a one-point perspective layout on "C" size paper. Draw a perspective which accurately communicates the features of your design. Follow the procedure described in the text. The evaluation will consider the communication of the drawing as well as accuracy of your construction.

Chapter 30

PRESENTATION DRAWINGS

Text Pages 453-470

Name _____ Course _____

Date_____ Score _____

PART I: SHORT ANSWER/LISTING: Provide brief answers to the following questions.

1. Why are presentation drawings made in addition to construction drawings?

   _____

   _____

2. Name eight methods typically used for rendering presentation drawings.

   A. _____ E. _____

   B. _____ F. _____

   C. _____ G. _____

   D. _____ H. _____

   ALSO: _____

   _____

3. What method of rendering is fairly easy to complete and can be varied in final appearance by adding water?

   _____

4. Describe appliqué rendering and explain how it might be used to render a presentation drawing of a living room.

   _____

   _____

   _____

   _____

5. List two ways an architectural firm might use presentation drawings in their work.

   A. _____

   _____

   B. _____

6. Why is accuracy so important in presentation drawings?

   _____

   _____

PART II: MULTIPLE CHOICE: Select the best answer and place its letter in the blank at right.

1. A method of rendering which is fairly easy to do and quite popular is:
   A. Water color.
   B. Pencil.
   C. Air brush.
   D. None of the above.

   1. _____

2. A color rendering which is transparent and very effective is:
   A. Water color.
   B. Pencil.
   C. Ink.
   D. All of the above.

   2. _____

3. A color technique that is vastly different in appearance and often used for presentation plot plans is:
   A. Pencil.
   B. Ink.
   C. Magic markers.
   D. Tempera.

   3. _____

4. Renderings that use ink or paint and require a great deal of practice to do successfully are:
   A. Scratch board.
   B. Appliqué.
   C. Tempera.
   D. Air brush.

   4. _____

5. An orthographic type drawing sometimes used in the place of a perspective is a:
   A. Presentation plot plan.
   B. Presentation elevation.
   C. Section.
   D. All of the above.

   5. _____

6. The primary purpose of the _____ is to illustrate interior features, such as furniture arrangement.
   A. Presentation elevation.
   B. Presentation plot plan.
   C. Presentation floor plan.
   D. None of the above.

   6. _____

PART III: COMPLETION: Complete each sentence with the proper response. Place your answer on the blank in the right column.

1. _____ rendering is highly suggested for reproduction purposes.

   1. _____

2. Color renderings that are opaque and often used for monotone renderings are done in _____.

   2. _____

3. Renderings that show much character and create attention are _____ renderings.

   3. _____

4. Features such as people, trees, and cars provide a more realistic setting for a presentation drawing and are referred to as _____.

   4. _____

5. A "bird's eye view" showing property boundaries, location of the structure, and topographical features is the _____ plan.

   5. _____

6. Rendered _____ provide an excellent method for illustrating the various levels of a complex dwelling.

   6. _____

1.

DIRECTIONS:
Make a pencil rendering of the contents shown in the photo below.
Use a piece of tracing vellum over the photo to produce your
rendering.   Use texture to add realism to the freehand drawing.

PENCIL RENDERING   30-1

2.

DIRECTIONS:
Make an ink rendering of the cast concrete structure below. Use a
piece of tracing vellum over the photo to produce your freehand
drawing. Add texture to the drawing to produce a realistic
appearance.

INK RENDERING		30-2

Name _____

3. **Rendering.** Use the front elevation that you drew for Problem 18-4 as the subject for this activity. Render it on the appropriate paper or illustration board in colored pencil, water color, tempera, or magic marker. This assignment will be evaluated based on realism and accuracy of the rendering.

Chapter 31

ARCHITECTURAL MODELS

Text Pages 471-480

Name _____   Course _____

Date _____   Score _____

PART I: MULTIPLE CHOICE: Select the best answer and place its letter in the blank at right.

1. A planned community of houses is often displayed using
   _____ models.
   A. Small scale solid.
   B. Structural.
   C. Presentation.
   D. All of the above.

   1. _____

2. The scale of structural models is usually _____.
   A. 1/4" = 1'-0" or 1/2" = 1'-0".
   B. 1" = 1'-0" or 2" = 1'-0".
   C. 1/2" = 1'-0" or 1" = 1'-0".
   D. None of the above.

   2. _____

3. Styrofoam® sheets are often used in building model structures
   because:
   A. They will not scratch or break easily.
   B. They can be finished to resemble various exterior building
      materials.
   C. All of the above.
   D. None of the above.

   3. _____

4. Before gluing the exterior walls of a presentation model, com-
   pare each wall with the _____ to insure accuracy.
   A. Floor plan.
   B. Foundation plan.
   C. Site plan.
   D. All of the above.

   4. _____

5. Interior walls of presentation models are typically _____
   in. thick balsa.
   A. 1/16.
   B. 1/8.
   C. 1/4.
   D. None of the above.

   5. _____

6. _____ paint is often used on model interior walls.
   A. Transparent stains.
   B. Enamel.
   C. Tempera.
   D. All of the above.

   6. _____

PART II: COMPLETION: Complete each sentence with the proper response. Place your answer on the blank in the right column.

1. The scale of small scale solid models may range from 1/32" = 1'-0" to _____.

1. _____

2. An architect would most likely choose a _____ model to show the most realistic appearance of a residential structure.

2. _____

3. A model building material which is easy to work with, lends itself to different kinds of finishes, and is strong is _____.

3. _____

4. The base of a _____ (rolling/flat) site may be built of 3/4" plywood.

4. _____

5. To obtain a more professional looking corner, use a _____ (butt/miter) joint.

5. _____

6. A material that is useful for windows in models is 1/16 in. thick _____.

6. _____

7. Putting the roof together on the _____ (model/plan) will produce a more accurate roof.

7. _____

8. Using 1/4 in. balsa for roof sheathing will approximately duplicate the thickness of the rafters and _____ on a house.

8. _____

9. Lichen may be purchased to represent _____ in the landscaping.

9. _____

PART III: SHORT ANSWER/LISTING: Provide brief answers to the following questions.

1. Name the three types of models commonly used to represent structures.

   A. _____

   B. _____

   C. _____

2. If you were a building contractor and decided to use a model to illustrate an innovative building technique, which type of model would you select?

   _____

3. What scale is commonly used for presentation models?

   _____

4. What materials could be used to build up elevated areas to represent a rolling terrain?

   _____

5. Name two types of plans generally required to build a model.

   A. _____

   B. _____

6. How thick should the exterior walls of a presentation balsa model be for a residential frame wall structure?

   _____

7. List four tools that are used by architectural model builders.

   A. _____

   B. _____

   C. _____

   D. _____

Name _____

8. What procedures or materials are sometimes used to simulate various types of exterior materials, such as siding and brick.

_____

_____

9. What procedure may be applied to give mortar joints an authentic appearance on an architectural model?

_____

10. What material can be used to represent roofing materials?

_____

PART IV: PROBLEMS/ACTIVITIES

1. **Architectural Model.** Using the Garden House (Problems 10-1 and 18-3), construct a solid wall presentation model of the structure at 1/4" = 1'-0" scale. Heavy illustration board, 1/8 in. plywood, balsa wood, or foam board may be used to construct the roof and walls. Sandpaper strips may be used to represent asphalt shingles. Supplies are generally available at a local hobby shop. Paint or stain the walls for realism. Mount the completed model on a base for protection and handling. Study the text for procedures and useful hints.

2. **Structural Model.** Construct a structural model of the Garden House described in Problems 10-1 and 18-3 at a scale of 1" = 1'-0". The purpose of this model is to show the actual construction. Therefore, leave sections of the framing members exposed to view. Balsa or poplar wood is generally used for framing members and balsa sheets are recommended for panel products. Mount the completed model on a 1/4 in. plywood base.

3. **Ranch House Model.** Construct a solid wall presentation model at 1/4" = 1'-0" of the ranch style home you designed for Problems 16-3 and 18-4. Your instructor will provide specific instructions for this assignment.

Chapter 32

MATERIAL AND TRADEWORK SPECIFICATIONS

Text Pages 481-488

Name _____   Course _____

Date_____   Score _____

PART I: SHORT ANSWER/LISTING: Provide brief answers to the following questions.

1. Which document lists the information on details and products concerning the structure?

   _____

2. Two documents form a contract which is binding for the client and building contractor. Name the two documents.

   _____

3. What can the client do to assure a certain level of quality workmanship in the house?

   _____

   _____

4. Where may specification forms be obtained?

   _____

   _____

   _____

   _____

5. What information on appliances is needed in the specifications?

   _____

   _____

   _____

6. Who is usually responsible for liability during the construction process?

   _____

PART II: COMPLETION: Complete each sentence with the proper response. Place your answer on the blank in the right column.

1. The _____ (a professional) helps his/her clients prepare the "specifications outline."

   1. _____

2. Generally, the _____ (architect/client) should have the greatest input on materials, while the _____ (architect/ client) will have more input on interior finishing, appliances, and fixtures.

   2. _____

3. The required _____ operations—excavation, masonry, carpentry, millwork, plumbing, electrical, and insulation—should be described in the specifications.

3. _____

4. Cash allowances are generally set up for items such as lighting fixtures. The _____ is usually responsible for any money spent above the allowance.

4. _____

5. The specifications should include type, material, _____, and brand name.

5. _____

PART III: PROBLEMS/ACTIVITIES

1. **Contract Specifications.** Using the Contract Specifications form shown in the text, fill out the form as completely as possible for the ranch home you designed in previous assignments, or use a set of working drawings provided by your instructor. Plan the specifications as though you plan to be the owner. Select items from current catalogs and manufacturers' literature.

Chapter 33

ESTIMATING BUILDING COST

Text Pages 489-496

Name _____   Course _____

Date_____   Score _____

PART I: COMPLETION: Complete each sentence with the proper response. Place your answer on the blank in the right column.

1. A systematic attempt to arrive at the cost of materials, labor, and other services needed to build a house is _____.

   1. _____

2. Since building costs per square foot vary from one section of the country to another, check with local _____ to determine the correct cost for your area.

   2. _____

3. In the square foot method, the cost is based on _____, while in the cubic foot method the cost is based on volume.

   3. _____

4. Two documents should be studied very carefully for use as the basis for estimating the cost of a structure. These are the construction drawings and _____.

   4. _____

5. To estimate the cost of a house using the cubic foot method, multiply the area by the _____.

   5. _____

6. Labor costs usually range from _____ to 80 percent of the total cost of the house.

   6. _____

7. Fees may be required for electrical, gas, telephone, water, and _____ hookup.

   7. _____

PART II: SHORT ANSWER/LISTING: Provide brief answers to the following questions.

1. Name the two methods used to estimate the cost of a home.

   _____

2. To find the area of a house in square feet, multiply the length by the width. Should wall thickness be included?

   _____

3. How will including an extra bath or a solid oak circular stairway affect the cost of a house?

   _____

4. Describe another way to estimate the cost of a home that is probably more accurate than the square foot method or cubic foot method.

   _____

   _____

   _____

5. What is the relationship between the headings on a materials list and the construction sequence?

_____

_____

6. The cost of permits should be included when estimating the cost of building a house. List the permits which may be needed.

A. _____

B. _____

C. _____

D. _____

PART III: MULTIPLE CHOICE: Select the best answer and place its letter in the blank at right.

1. Porches, garages, and basements are figured at _____ the cost per square foot of the living area.
   A. One-fourth.
   B. One-half.
   C. Three-fourths.
   D. The same as.

1. _____

2. Ranch style homes are usually _____, providing that you are estimating the same living area.
   A. More expensive to build than two-story homes.
   B. Less expensive to build than two-story homes.
   C. The same cost as two-story homes.
   D. None of the above.

2. _____

3. The document that indicates all the materials, fixtures, and finishes to be used in building the structure is the:
   A. Warranty deed.
   B. Building schedule.
   C. Materials list.
   D. All of the above.

3. _____

4. Prices of the building materials should be obtained from:
   A. The supplier to be used in the construction of the house.
   B. Taking an average of the prices in the geographic area where the house will be built.
   C. The supplier with the lowest prices regardless of quality.
   D. None of the above.

4. _____

5. The cost of labor in building a house varies around the country. To obtain the cost for your area:
   A. Consult local contractors and subcontractors.
   B. Check the Building Construction Cost Data Book.
   C. All of the above.
   D. None of the above.

5. _____

6. The builder usually provides insurance to cover _____. This cost is normally added to the cost of the house.
   A. Workers in the event of injury and materials against theft.
   B. Health care of tradeworkers.
   C. Flood loss.
   D. All of the above.

6. _____

1.

DIRECTIONS:
Prepare a Materials List for the Garden House used in Assignments 10-1 and 18-3 or another building provided by your instructor. Use the following headings in your Materials List: General Information, Masonry, Carpenter's Lumber List, Windows and Screens, Doors and Trim, Cabinets and Miscellaneous Millwork, Insulation, Weatherstripping and Caulking, Plastering or Drywall, Finish Flooring, Painting and Finishing, Hardware, Finish Hardware, Sheetmetal Work, Floor Finishing Material, Wall Finishing Material, Roofing, Plumbing, Electrical Wiring, Telephone Wiring, and Heating. Follow the complete list in the text.

MATERIALS LIST

MATERIALS LIST		33-1

2.

Page 2 of MATERIALS LIST

| MATERIALS LIST | | 33-1 |

3.

Page 3 of MATERIALS LIST

MATERIALS LIST		33-1

Page 4 of MATERIALS LIST

MATERIALS LIST		33-1

Chapter 34

COMPUTER APPLICATIONS

Text Pages 497-508

Name _____   Course _____

Date_____   Score _____

PART I: SHORT ANSWER/LISTING: Provide brief answers to the following questions.

1. What key factor has made computers more useful for architects?

   _____

2. List five broad areas of computer applications which are helpful to the architect.

   A. _____

   B. _____

   C. _____

   D. _____

   E. _____

   ALSO: _____

   _____

3. How is the computer quite valuable to an architect who plans subdivisions and multifamily complexes?

   _____

   _____

   _____

4. Structural analysis should be applied to non-traditional designs to assure proper construction. Name two residential non-traditional designs that benefit from computer-generated structural analysis.

   _____

5. Explain how a computer-aided drafting and design system can benefit the architect or designer.

   _____

   _____

   _____

   _____

6. List three advantages of using the computer to generate graphics as opposed to the traditional method of drawing the presentations by hand.

   A. _____

   B. _____

   C. _____

7. Name the three types of pictorial drawings that can be generated using the computer.

   A. _____

   B. _____

   C. _____

8. How can the information obtained from an energy analysis help an architect?

   _____

   _____

9. How can project management software benefit the contractor?

   _____

   _____

10. A PERT chart displays a plan of the operations to be performed and monitors the projects progress. What does PERT stand for?

    _____

PART II: COMPLETION: Complete each sentence with the proper response. Place your answer on the blank in the right column.

1. The architect will find a _____ to be useful in developing drawings and analyzing data for design and construction.

   1. _____

2. Water surface profile analysis and assessment of delays and congestion are _____ applications.

   2. _____

3. The architect may utilize the computer to design _____ components that accommodate unique stress and weight.

   3. _____

4. Elastic stability analysis, analysis of fixed arches and frames, and steel structure design are applications of _____ analysis.

   4. _____

5. Items such as standard symbols and shading may be generated from the _____ of a CADD system.

   5. _____

6. CADD systems use matrix printers or _____ to generate drawings.

   6. _____

7. Newly designed structures as well as remodeling projects may become more energy efficient due to computer software for _____.

   7. _____

8. An energy analysis benefits the _____ of the house by providing comfortable room temperatures, conserving _____, and saving money.

   8. _____

9. A software program for _____ is available to help plan the management, cost estimates, financial models, and scheduling for the structure.

   9. _____

10. The planner or designer is able to visualize the outcome of various design solutions through the use of computer _____.

    10. _____

Name _____

PART III: MATCHING: Match the correct term with its description listed below. Place the corresponding letter on the blank at right.

A. CADD
B. Computer graphics
C. Computer simulations
D. Energy analysis

E. Project management
F. Site planning and mapping
G. Structural analysis

1. Earthwork cost optimization.

2. Finite element analysis.

3. Creation and storage of drawings.

4. Generate color graphic visuals.

5. Heat loss calculation.

6. PERT, CPM, and PM network.

7. Perform parametric studies.

1. _____

2. _____

3. _____

4. _____

5. _____

6. _____

7. _____

PART IV: PROBLEMS/ACTIVITIES

1. **Computer Software Packages.** Use trade magazines, manufacturers' literature, or other sources, to prepare a report of software programs or packages available for residential and/or light commercial applications. Cover the following areas: Site Planning and Mapping, Structural Analysis, Computer-Aided Drafting/Design, Graphic Representation, Energy Analysis, Project Management, and Computer Simulation. Give a brief description of the capabilities of each package, cost, name of the product, and source of information.

Chapter 35

INTRODUCTION TO COMPUTER-AIDED DRAFTING AND DESIGN

Text Pages 509-522

Name _____   Course _____

Date_____   Score _____

PART I: COMPLETION: Complete each sentence with the proper response. Place your answer on the blank in the right column.

1. A _____ system replaces drawing instruments such as drawing boards, triangles, scales, and other traditional drafting equipment.

1. _____

2. Popular CADD systems produce a large variety of architectural, _____, and construction drawings.

2. _____

3. When selecting a computer, _____ speed is an important consideration.

3. _____

4. The element which controls program execution and keeps various system components synchronized and operating in harmony is the _____.

4. _____

5. A computer with a _____ chip can generate graphics approximately five times faster than one without the chip.

5. _____

6. Many dot matrix and daisy wheel printers connect to a _____ port.

6. _____

7. _____ is the sharpness of detail displayed on screen. It is an important consideration when selecting a monitor.

7. _____

8. A keyboard which is touch sensitive with no moving parts is the _____ type.

8. _____

9. When speed is a consideration, a _____ tablet with a menu overlay should be selected as the input device.

9. _____

10. The _____ plotter is popular with experienced drafters because it produces drawings similar to the way they produce them.

10. _____

11. The _____ at which the pen plotter runs is dependent upon the application, drafting medium, pens, and ink used.

11. _____

12. The _____ plotter may function as a plotter or printer and can produce drawings much faster than a pen plotter.

12. _____

13. Color prints, transparencies, or 35 mm slides can be generated by _____ recorders.

13. _____

14. To expand memory in a computer, _____ (often called cards) can be placed in expansion slots.

14. _____

PART II: SHORT ANSWER/LISTING: Provide brief answers to the following questions.

1. List two drawing processes that a modern CADD system can provide.

   A. _____

   _____

   B. _____

   _____

   ALSO: _____

   _____

2. Of the many functions which a CADD system performs, which offers the most time savings?

   _____

3. Name five components of a CADD hardware system.

   A. _____

   B. _____

   C. _____

   D. _____

   E. _____

4. What type of computers are self-contained units and are usually designed for a single user? Examples are: the Zenith series, Compaq series, Apple Macintosh series, the IBM PC and PS/2.

   _____

5. Many CADD software programs require that the computer contain a math coprocessor. What purpose does a math coprocessor serve?

   _____

   _____

6. A hard disk as well as floppy disks are recommended for use with a CADD system. In what ways are they used?

   _____

   _____

7. Two types of monitors—monochrome and color—are available. Which type is better suited for CADD operations?

   _____

8. A special printed circuit board is required by the graphics monitor. What is the name of this printed circuit board?

   _____

9. List five typical CADD input devices.

   A. _____

   B. _____

   C. _____

   D. _____

   E. _____

   ALSO: _____

Name _____

10. What are the two types of mice and how do they differ?

_____

_____

_____

_____

_____

11. What input device is commonly used with the digitizing tablet to locate points and select items?

_____

12. Name three hardcopy output devices.

A. _____

B. _____

C. _____

ALSO: _____

13. How do drum plotters operate?

_____

_____

PART III: MULTIPLE CHOICE: Select the best answer and place its letter in the blank at right.

1. Microcomputer-based CADD systems are:
   A. Very costly.
   B. Not user friendly and difficult to use.
   C. Easy to use and fast.
   D. None of the above.

   1. _____

2. Standard symbols as well as unique symbols used on drawings are stored in the:
   A. Symbols library.
   B. Symbols index.
   C. Monitor.
   D. All of the above.

   2. _____

3. A large computer system which can handle many users at the same time and still maintain speed is the:
   A. Mini.
   B. Mainframe.
   C. Super-minicomputer.
   D. Microcomputer.

   3. _____

4. Memory for short term storage, or RAM memory, should be _____ for microcomputers handling CADD software programs.
   A. 480K.
   B. 560K.
   C. 640K.
   D. None of the above.

   4. _____

5. One of the more popular size floppy disks commonly used for
   a CADD system is:
   A. 5 1/4 in.
   B. 3 1/4 in.
   C. 5 in.
   D. 8 in.

5. _____

6. Monitors with flat screens tend to produce:
   A. Curved lines.
   B. Straight lines.
   C. Wavy lines.
   D. None of the above.

6. _____

7. A keyboard which easily permits input of numeric data as well
   as text is the:
   A. Membrane.
   B. Typewriter style.
   C. Calculator style.
   D. All of the above.

7. _____

8. High resolution is a requirement for digitizing hardcopy draw-
   ings. A digitizing tablet capable of high resolution should be
   able to distinguish over _____ lines per inch.
   A. 5.
   B. 100.
   C. 500.
   D. 1,000.

8. _____

9. The output to the monitor—user prompts, instructions, and
   a visual record of the operations—is _____ output.
   A. Softcopy.
   B. Hardcopy.
   C. All of the above.
   D. None of the above.

9. _____

10. An advantage of flatbed pen plotters is:
    A. That it is easy to monitor the drawing while it is being
       drawn.
    B. That they take little space.
    C. They perform better than drum plotters.
    D. All of the above.

10. _____

11. Which of the following statements is true of laser printers?
    A. The quality of line drawings is better than with pen plotters.
    B. They can handle large sheets of drawings.
    C. They are efficient for desktop publishing.
    D. None of the above.

11. _____

12. When cost is a consideration, and the demand for quality is
    not so great, a _____ may be used for hardcopy output.
    A. Daisy wheel printer.
    B. Color impact printer.
    C. Electrostatic plotter.
    D. Pen plotter.

12. _____

Name _____

PART IV: MATCHING: Match the correct term with its description listed below. Place the corresponding letter on the blank at right.

A. CADD
B. CPU
C. Computer
D. Digitizing tablet
E. Keyboard

F. Minicomputer
G. Monitor
H. Mouse
I. Pixel
J. RAM

1. Computer-aided drafting and design.

1. _____

2. The heart of a CADD system.

2. _____

3. A self-contained computer system.

3. _____

4. Random Access Memory.

4. _____

5. Central Processing Unit.

5. _____

6. Permits the computer to communicate with the operator.

6. _____

7. Picture element.

7. _____

8. Used to input alphanumeric information.

8. _____

9. A pointing device for picking objects and identifying points on the screen.

9. _____

10. Uses a stylus or puck to convert graphic data or X-Y coordinates for entry into the computer.

10. _____

1.

DIRECTIONS:
Label each of the components of the modern microCADD system
illustrated below.

A. _____

B. _____

C. _____

F. _____

D. _____

E. _____

MICRO-CADD SYSTEM   35-1

Chapter 36

CADD SOFTWARE

Text Pages 523-538

Name _____   Course _____

Date_____   Score _____

PART I: SHORT ANSWER/LISTING: Provide brief answers to the following questions.

1. What is the purpose of a software package?

   _____

2. Schedules for windows and doors, cabinets, plumbing, and lighting fixtures may be generated using a CADD package. List an advantage of using CADD in this way over traditional drafting methods.

   _____

   _____

   _____

3. Explain how the CADD symbols library can save the designer time.

   _____

   _____

   _____

4. List five symbols or details typically stored in architectural CADD symbols libraries.

   A. _____

   B. _____

   C. _____

   D. _____

   E. _____

5. Identify the three basic categories of drawing dimensions offered by CADD systems.

   A. _____

   B. _____

   C. _____

6. A good CADD package will support more than one input device to move the cursor on the screen. List three devices commonly used.

   A. _____

   B. _____

   C. _____

7. General CADD packages may include 3D shading. How might a drafter use this application?

_____

_____

_____

8. AEC CADD packages are designed to do what kind of work?

_____

_____

9. Identify the modes commonly incorporated into AEC packages for 3D viewing.

A. _____

B. _____

C. _____

D. _____

E. _____

F. _____

G. _____

H. _____

I. _____

10. List the common plumbing symbols available for use in AEC packages.

A. _____

B. _____

C. _____

D. _____

E. _____

F. _____

G. _____

11. Explain how background drawings are used in AEC packages.

_____

_____

PART II: COMPLETION: Complete each sentence with the proper response. Place your answer on the blank in the right column.

1. _____ software allows a designer to communicate ideas about objects and structures in accurate computer-generated graphics.

1. _____

2. Changes are _____ (easy/difficult) to make using a CADD system.

2. _____

3. Symbols are drawn the same each time they are used with CADD software. This promotes a high degree of _____ among symbols and drawings.

3. _____

4. Mechanical drawings, as well as other general drafting requirements, are usually generated by _____ CADD packages.

4. _____

Name _____

5. Speed and flexibility are affected by _____ hardware, such as math coprocessors, digitizing tablet or mouse, plotter, or extra memory.

5. _____

6. General-purpose CADD packages have standard _____, such as continuous, dashed, hidden, center phantom, border, dot, and dashdot.

6. _____

7. Drawing interchanges allow CADD packages to communicate with other packages. Examples are IGES, _____, and DXB.

7. _____

8. Typical microcomputer programming languages are AutoLISP and _____.

8. _____

9. AEC packages normally generate _____ thickness from space diagrams, continuous walls, and from dimensions.

9. _____

10. A good AEC package _____ (will/will not) allow the designer to add user-drawn symbols to the symbols library.

10. _____

PART III: MULTIPLE CHOICE: Select the best answer and place its letter in the blank at right.

1. Mechanical, architectural, construction, and engineering drawings can be drawn with:
   A. Most computers.
   B. CADD systems.
   C. Wordstar programs.
   D. All of the above.

1. _____

2. A CADD system is flexible because it can generate drawings in different ways. Which of the following is true of a CADD system?
   A. A drawing may be developed in ordered steps.
   B. More than one drawing may be generated at a time.
   C. Drawings may be plotted at different speeds.
   D. All of the above.

2. _____

3. Less time and money are lost on the construction site because:
   A. The construction workers are paid extra if they come to work on time.
   B. Each worker has a complete set of drawings.
   C. The lettering and lines on CADD drawings are always clear and concise.
   D. The CADD system is usually taken to the job site.

3. _____

4. A number of questions should be answered before purchasing a CADD system. Which of the following questions is not relevant to the purchase of a CADD system?
   A. Is the program easy to use?
   B. Does the program require hardware uncommon to other packages?
   C. What are the specific features of the hardware?
   D. Will the CADD system function in a high dust environment?

4. _____

5. Which one of the following groups represents entity editing tools?
   A. Copy, erase, move, scale, rotate, trim, break, explode.
   B. Lines, points, circles, arcs, boxes.
   C. Polylines, fillets, chamfers, freehand sketching.
   D. None of the above.

5. _____

6. A CADD package may provide a number of systems for assigning linear units, including:
   A. Decimal degrees, degrees/minutes/seconds, grads, radians, and surveyor's units.
   B. Architectural, engineering, scientific, decimal, and fractional.
   C. All of the above.
   D. None of the above.

6. _____

7. Geometric analysis, such as _____, is helpful for some types of drawings.
   A. Lines, symbols, and notes.
   B. Linear, angular, diameter/radius, leader, and alternate units.
   C. Area, distance, and angles.
   D. None of the above.

7. _____

8. Hardware requirements for AEC packages are usually _____ those for general-purpose CADD packages.
   A. About the same as.
   B. Much more specific than.
   C. Less specific than.
   D. None of the above.

8. _____

9. Standard window types, furniture symbols, tree and plant symbols, and appliance symbols are characteristics of:
   A. General CADD packages.
   B. AEC CADD packages.
   C. All of the above.
   D. None of the above.

9. _____

PART IV: MATCHING: Match the correct term with its description listed below. Place the corresponding letter on the blank at right.

A. Display controls
B. Drawing aids
C. Entities
D. HVAC
E. Layers
F. Schedule generation
G. 2D drawing
H. Title symbols
I. 3D primitives

1. Basic elements used to create objects.

1. _____

2. Permit certain parts of the drawing to be placed on "sheets."

2. _____

3. Zoom, pan, view, redraw, regenerate, and fill functions.

3. _____

4. Grid, snap, ortho, axis, isoplane, dynamic location, and attach.

4. _____

5. Uses lines, rectangles, circles.

5. _____

6. Uses boxes, cylinders, cones.

6. _____

7. Heating, ventilation, and air conditioning.

7. _____

8. Include north arrow, revision triangle, drawing title, scale, and tags.

8. _____

9. Used for doors, windows, lighting, appliances, furniture, etc.

9. _____

PART V: PROBLEMS/ACTIVITIES

1.

DIRECTIONS:
Connect each of the general purpose CADD characteristics on the left
with the appropriate example on the right.

Basic System ☐   ☐ Math Co—processor

Supported Hardware ☐   ☐ Copy, Erase, Move, Scale

Number of Dimensions ☐   ☐ Transparent Drawing Sheets

Entities ☐   ☐ Decimal Degrees, Radians

Entity Editing ☐   ☐ 2.5 D

Layers ☐   ☐ Boxes, Cylinders, Cones

Standard Linetypes ☐   ☐ Linear, Angular, Arrow Styles

Angular Units ☐   ☐ Microcomputer

Display Controls ☐   ☐ Area, Distance, Angle

Drawing Aids ☐   ☐ Continuous, Dashed, Hidden

Dimensioning ☐   ☐ Lines, Points, Circles

Geometric Analysis ☐   ☐ Zoom, Pan, View

3D Primitives ☐   ☐ Grid, Snap, Orthosnap

GENERAL PURPOSE CADD		36—1

2.

DIRECTIONS:
Connect each of the AEC CADD characteristics on the left with the appropriate example on the right.

Data Base Dinensions   □   □   Gobal Viewpoint, Isometric

Space Diagram Generation   □   □   Mapping, Site Development

3D Viewing   □   □   Tub, Lavatory, Shower

Plumbing Symbols   □   □   Concrete in Section

Electrical Symbols   □   □   2D, 2.5D, 3D

HVAC Symbols   □   □   Structural Grid

Site Symbols   □   □   Switches, Outlets, Meter

Title Symbols   □   □   Automatic Wall Thickness

Hatch Patterns   □   □   Heating, Ventilating & AC

Background Drawings   □   □   Personal Font

Schedule Generation   □   □   North Arrow, Scale, Tags

Customization   □   □   dBaseII, Lotus

Database Interface   □   □   Window, Door, Lighting

AEC CADD CHARACTERISTICS		36-2

Chapter 37

CADD COMMANDS AND FUNCTIONS

Text Pages 539-554

Name _____   Course _____

Date_____   Score _____

PART I: SHORT ANSWER/LISTING: Provide brief answers to the following questions.

1. What purpose do drawing commands serve?

   _____

2. In what ways may commands be entered?

   _____

   _____

   _____

3. List five drawing commands.

   A. _____

   B. _____

   C. _____

   D. _____

   E. _____

4. Which command should be used to create contour lines on a plot plan?

   _____

5. When are edit commands used?

   _____

6. Which editing command should be used to permanently remove entities from the drawing?

   _____

7. Explain how the COPY command differs from the MOVE command.

   _____

   _____

   _____

   _____

8. What function does the PERIMETER command perform?

   _____

   _____

9. Name the three functions provided by the display control commands.

A. _____

_____

B. _____

_____

C. _____

10. Identify the display control commands typically found in CADD packages.

A. _____

B. _____

C. _____

D. _____

E. _____

11. List the six commands that relate to linear dimensioning.

A. _____

B. _____

C. _____

D. _____

E. _____

F. _____

12. What do layer, color, and linetype commands do?

_____

_____

_____

13. What purpose does the GRID function serve?

_____

14. The storage data for 2D software packages accommodates X and Y coordinates of all points. What are the capabilities of 2.5D and 3D storage data?

_____

_____

_____

_____

15. Which utility command provides user assistance for the current command?

_____

16. Identify utility and function command menus.

A. _____

B. _____

C. _____

D. _____

Name _____

PART II: MULTIPLE CHOICE: Select the best answer and place its letter in the blank at right.

1. Which one of the following commands may be used to modify drawings?
    A. COPY.
    B. AREA.
    C. DRAW.
    D. SKETCH.

    1. _____

2. Starting point, center, and end point is one method of drawing a(n):
    A. Line.
    B. Circle.
    C. Arc.
    D. Rectangle.

    2. _____

3. Picking a corner and dragging the opposite corner to the desired location is a method used to construct a(n):
    A. Polygon.
    B. Rectangle.
    C. Circle.
    D. Triangle.

    3. _____

4. The _____ function is used to visually "pull" an object to size or location.
    A. SKETCH.
    B. HATCH.
    C. TEXT.
    D. DRAG.

    4. _____

5. Relative displacement takes place when the _____ command is used.
    A. MOVE.
    B. ERASE.
    C. ROTATE.
    D. EXTEND.

    5. _____

6. The ROTATE command may be used to:
    A. Move entities to a new location on the drawing.
    B. Alter the orientation of entities on a drawing.
    C. Draw a mirror image of an object.
    D. All of the above.

    6. _____

7. The command that trims two intersecting lines back a certain distance and then connects the trimmed ends with a new line is the _____ command.
    A. FILLET.
    B. CHAMFER.
    C. ROTATE.
    D. SCALE.

    7. _____

8. The LIST command enables the drafter to:
    A. Examine the data stored for an entity.
    B. Measure the distance and angle between two points.
    C. Generate copies of a specific object.
    D. None of the above.

    8. _____

9. A magnification factor is an option in the _____ command.
   A. ZOOM.
   B. PAN.
   C. VIEW.
   D. REDRAW.

9. _____

10. The process of measuring lengths, distances, or angles between objects is:
    A. Finding area.
    B. Editing.
    C. Dimensioning.
    D. All of the above.

10. _____

11. The function of the LEADER command is to:
    A. Regenerate a program.
    B. Connect dimensions to objects.
    C. Add specific or local note.
    D. All of the above.

11. _____

12. Which of the following statements applies to layers?
    A. Layers are similar to opaque overlays.
    B. Most software packages provide six layers.
    C. Each layer has a different zoom factor.
    D. Drawing entities may be placed on one or more layers.

12. _____

13. A drawing aid helpful for connecting objects very accurately is:
    A. GRID.
    B. AXIS.
    C. SNAP.
    D. None of the above.

13. _____

14. The three axes of an isometric grid are:
    A. Vertical, 30 degrees, and 150 degrees.
    B. Horizontal, 30 degrees, and 150 degrees.
    C. Vertical, 60 degrees, and 150 degrees.
    D. Vertical, 30 degrees, and 130 degrees.

14. _____

15. A 3D representation that appears to be illuminated is:
    A. Solids modeling.
    B. Surface modeling
    C. Shaded solids modeling.
    D. All of the above.

15. _____

16. Which of the following is not a utility command or function?
    A. HELP.
    B. STOP.
    C. END.
    D. QUIT.

16. _____

17. To protect a drawing in the event of a power loss, use the _____ command often.
    A. WINDOW.
    B. STATUS.
    C. DRAW.
    D. SAVE.

17. _____

Name _____

PART III: COMPLETION: Complete each sentence with the proper response. Place your answer on the blank in the right column.

1. The attributes of a _____ are linetype, width, or color.

    1. _____

2. Center and diameter is one method used to draw a _____.

    2. _____

3. When the designer is ready to create walls on the floor plan, he/she uses the _____ command.

    3. _____

4. Rotated text _____ (is/is not) possible.

    4. _____

5. Calculating distances, areas, and perimeters is a function of an _____ command.

    5. _____

6. To move a certain part of a drawing while keeping the connections between portions of the drawing left in place, use the _____ command.

    6. _____

7. An entity may be lengthened to meet a boundary edge using the _____ command.

    7. _____

8. The _____ command copies objects in a circular or rectangular pattern to make a number of copies.

    8. _____

9. When it is necessary to quickly move back and forth between views on a drawing, the _____ command should be used.

    9. _____

10. Marker blips are removed by the _____ command.

    10. _____

11. LINEAR, ANGULAR, DIAMETER, RADIUS, and LEADER are basic types of _____ commands.

    11. _____

12. Dashes, dots, and blank spaces combine to form a _____.

    12. _____

13. Drawing aids include GRID, SNAP, _____, ORTHO, and ISOMETRIC drawing. They increase accuracy and save time.

    13. _____

14. Hidden line removal is possible in 2.5 and _____ packages.

    14. _____

15. A command that updates the drawing file and leaves the drawing screen is _____.

    15. _____

16. For the current date and time, consult the _____ command.

    16. _____

PART IV: MATCHING: Match the correct term with its description listed below. Place the corresponding letter on the blank at right.

A. ANGULAR
B. ARC
C. Blue
D. DIAMETER
E. FILLET
F. Green
G. HATCH
H. Line
I. OBJECT SNAP

J. PAN
K. PLOT
L. Polygon
M. QUIT
N. SCALE
O. Surface modeling
P. System variables
Q. Window

1. A command which tells the computer to make a hardcopy of the drawing.

1. _____

2. The basic element of most drawings.

2. _____

3. A command that draws partial circles.

3. _____

4. A shape with equal length sides and angles.

4. _____

5. A command that creates patterns for section lining.

5. _____

6. The size of a shape may be increased or decreased with this command.

6. _____

7. A command that produces a smoothly fitted arc of a certain radius between two lines, arcs, or circles.

7. _____

8. Used to place a box around one or more objects.

8. _____

9. Moves the display window from one area to another.

9. _____

10. A type of dimension that creates an arc to show the angle between two lines.

10. _____

11. Used to dimension circles and arcs.

11. _____

12. Color number 3.

12. _____

13. Color number 5.

13. _____

14. Connects new entities to points on existing objects.

14. _____

15. A 3D function.

15. _____

16. A command which returns to Main Menu and discards drawing changes.

16. _____

17. Sets modes, sizes, and limits.

17. _____

PART V: PROBLEMS/ACTIVITIES

1.

DIRECTIONS:
This assignment requires the use of a CADD system. Using a scale of 1/4"=1'-0" and an "A", "B", or "C" size drawing sheet, draw a border line 480" @ 90°, 348" @ 0°, 480" @ 270°, and 348" @ 180°. The space enclosed by this border is exactly the same as this page in your workbook. The title block is 12" high and the plate # box is 36" wide. Use the following drawing commands (or your program's equivalent) to generate the lines and shapes indicated.

LINE

ARC

CIRCLE

POLYGON

RECTANGLE

DOUBLE LINE

SKETCH

TEXT

HATCH

Add the title, assignment #, and your name to the title block.

DRAWING COMMANDS		37-1

2.

DIRECTIONS:
This assignment requires the use of a CADD system. Set the scale
to 1/4"=1'-0" and prepare a drawing sheet identical to the one
required for Assignment 37-1. This assignment deals with selected
Editing and Inquiry commands. Practice using all of these commands
that your program provides, but demonstrate the use of the
following:

Draw a circle at one location and MOVE it to another.

Draw a rectangle and make two copies of it.

Draw one-half of a geometric shape and MIRROR the
other side to complete the shape.

Draw a shape and then ROTATE it 15˚.

Draw a box and use FILLET to round the corners.

Draw a three-sided figure as shown and EXTEND it to
twice its original length.

Use ARRAY to create five circles around a center.

Use SCALE to change the size of a circle to half its
original size.

Draw a rectangle and use AREA to determine the area.

EDITING & INQUIRY COMMANDS | 37-2

3.

DIRECTIONS:
This assignment requires the use of a CADD system. Draw a border and title block as required for Assignments 37-1 and 37-2. Set the scale to 1/4"=1'-0". Draw a series of rectangles in the space below leaving room for dimensions. Using the DIMENSION command, dimension the length and width of each rectangle. You may wish to add other shapes to show angular, diameter, radius, and leader type dimensions as well.

DIMENSIONING		37-3

4. **Display Control and Utility Commands and Drawing Aids.** This assignment requires the use of a CADD system. Practice using the display control commands, drawing aids, and utility commands to develop your ability to use the CADD system. Study the documentation for each command before using it. Practice using the commands until you thoroughly understand their application.

Chapter 38

ARCHITECTURAL CADD APPLICATIONS

Text Pages 555-580

Name _____   Course _____

Date _____   Score _____

PART I: MULTIPLE CHOICE: Select the best answer and place its letter in the blank at right.

1. A factor that will influence the drawing sheet size is:
   A. Size of the drawing.
   B. Size of the monitor screen.
   C. Style of house.
   D. None of the above.

   1. _____

2. A number of CADD packages contain:
   A. An unlimited number of colors.
   B. Pens in two widths only.
   C. Designated colors and layers for certain drawing characteristics.
   D. All of the above.

   2. _____

3. The first step in drawing a floor plan would be to draw a _____ to see how the rooms will fit together.
   A. Bubble plan.
   B. Space diagram.
   C. Working drawing.
   D. None of the above.

   3. _____

4. Interior walls are dimensioned to the center of the wall. Exterior walls are dimensioned to:
   A. The outside of the rough frame wall.
   B. The inside of the rough frame wall.
   C. Include the weatherboard and the siding.
   D. None of the above.

   4. _____

5. Doors and windows in a frame structure should be dimensioned:
   A. Using exact measurements.
   B. Using multiples of 1 in.
   C. To the center of the unit.
   D. All of the above.

   5. _____

6. Standard symbols from the _____ are used in drawing bathroom fixtures.
   A. Fixture and appliance layer.
   B. Symbol layer.
   C. Symbols library.
   D. All of the above.

   6. _____

7. The height measurements required to draw the elevation are obtained from the:
   A. Floor plan.
   B. Wall section.
   C. Foundation plan.
   D. All of the above.

7. _____

8. The foundation walls and basement floor slab are drawn using _____ lines on an elevation.
   A. Hidden.
   B. Construction.
   C. Guide.
   D. None of the above.

8. _____

9. The grade line and foundation walls should be drawn on separate layers because:
   A. There would not be sufficient room to place them on one layer.
   B. The line widths and symbols are different.
   C. Each is drawn at a different scale.
   D. All of the above.

9. _____

10. The connecting "wire" used between the switch and the fixture it controls is represented by a:
    A. Short dashed line.
    B. Hidden line symbol.
    C. Long dashed line.
    D. None of the above.

10. _____

11. You can use a _____ to move the screen cursor for freehand sketching contour lines on a plot plan.
    A. Mouse.
    B. Stylus.
    C. Puck.
    D. All of the above.

11. _____

12. When drawing the plot plan, a _____ command should be used to terminate the end of each property line.
    A. TERMINATE.
    B. CIRCLE.
    C. DRAW.
    D. All of the above.

12. _____

13. To draw exterior walls and roof trusses on a wall section, use _____ sizes.
    A. Actual.
    B. Nominal.
    C. Seasoned.
    D. All of the above.

13. _____

14. The reference point for most elevations is the:
    A. Horizon line.
    B. True length line.
    C. Grade line.
    D. None of the above.

14. _____

Name _____

PART II: SHORT ANSWER/LISTING: Provide brief answers to the following questions.

1. What skills and knowledge should you possess in order to be successful with a CADD system?

   A. _____

   B. _____

   _____

   C. _____

   _____

   D. _____

2. Name the two basic types of drawing units common to architecture.

   A. _____

   B. _____

3. Two basic systems of paper size are used — architectural and engineering. What are the sizes of each system?

   _____

   _____

4. Why is it important to plan the layers, colors, and pen sizes before you begin to draw?

   _____

   _____

   _____

5. Two methods are commonly used to draw floor plans. One procedure automatically converts the space diagram into a floor plan. The other requires using the DOUBLE LINE command to draw walls. Which of the two methods requires less time to execute?

   _____

6. List the features of the stairs which should appear on the floor plan.

   A. _____

   B. _____

   C. _____

7. Should sliding glass patio doors be dimensioned?

   _____

8. List nine questions that should be answered before a wall section is drawn.

   A. _____

   _____

   B. _____

   C. _____

   D. _____

   E. _____

   F. _____

   G. _____

(Continued)

H. _____

I. _____

9. When drawing elevations, exterior materials, such as siding, may be placed on a separate layer. Name four other features which may be placed on separate layers.

    A. _____

    B. _____

    C. _____

    D. _____

10. What are some questions that need to be answered before drawing the foundation/basement plan?

    A. _____

    _____

    _____

    B. _____

    C. _____

    D. _____

11. Should room names be included on the electrical plan?

    _____

12. On which drawing is the electrical meter shown when underground service is provided to a home?

    _____

13. Before you begin to draw a plot plan, you should obtain the property line description. Where may this be obtained?

    _____

14. What type of drawing would be used to communicate a unique fireplace design?

    _____

15. Why is it necessary to have accurate dimensions for drawing details?

    _____

    _____

16. List the dimensions required on a typical wall section.

    A. _____

    B. _____

    C. _____

    D. _____

    E. _____

PART III: COMPLETION: Complete each sentence with the proper response. Place your answer on the blank in the right column.

1. Study the _____ which accompanies your software package to fully understand how the program operates.

    1. _____

2. Most average-size home drawings will fit on _____ size paper.

    2. _____

Name _____

3. Consider layers, colors, and _____ size together when planning your CADD drawing.

3. _____

4. The _____ plotter selects a different pen for each color or line width specified on the drawing.

4. _____

5. Interior walls should be drawn in the proper location and should be 4 1/2 in. thick. This permits _____ in. thick drywall on either side of the stud.

5. _____

6. Generally, walks, patios, and porches are drawn on the _____ plan.

6. _____

7. Notes should be added to the floor plan using the _____ command.

7. _____

8. Similar details should be placed on their own _____, which can be displayed or not depending on whether the information is needed.

8. _____

9. Time may be saved by developing and storing window _____ in the symbols library.

9. _____

10. The _____ command should be used to place the dimensions on the plans.

10. _____

11. For ease in handling, all the drawings in a set of plans should be on the same size _____.

11. _____

12. The roofline should be shown with long _____ lines on a plot plan.

12. _____

13. To differentiate between different parts of a wall section, draw them in different _____.

13. _____

14. A short lesson provided by the CADD program covering the program's operation is called a _____.

14. _____

PART IV: PROBLEMS/ACTIVITIES

1. **Computer-Generated Plans.** Using a pad of grid paper, plan a small garden house, detached garage, or other simple structure. This design will be used to generate your first CADD drawing. Follow the step-by-step procedures for drawing the floor plan, elevations, foundation plan, electrical plan, plot plan, and details. Seek approval from your instructor after each drawing is completed before proceeding to the next. Remember to use appropriate layers, colors, linetypes, and scale for each drawing sheet. Your instructor will set the evaluation process and guidelines for the design.

Chapter 39

CAREER OPPORTUNITIES

Text Pages 581-586

Name _____   Course _____

Date _____   Score _____

PART I: SHORT ANSWER/LISTING: Provide brief answers to the following questions.

1. Generally, what are the educational requirements to become an architect?

_____

2. If you are artistic and have studied architectural drawing, what career choice might you pursue?

_____

3. Is a college degree generally required to be a specification writer?

_____

4. What knowledge should an estimator have?

_____

5. List the four categories in surveying which the American Society of Civil Engineers has identified.

   A. _____

   B. _____

   C. _____

   D. _____

6. Explain the difference in educational requirements of a surveyor and surveying technician.

_____

_____

_____

_____

_____

PART II: COMPLETION: Complete each sentence with the proper response. Place your answer on the blank in the right column.

1. One of the many responsibilities of the _____ is to check on the progress of the construction. He/she must see that the contractor is complying with the drawings and specifications.

   1. _____

2. A number of architectural drafters prepare to become licensed as _____.

   2. _____

3. The selling price of a structure is generally based upon the conclusions of an _____.

   3. _____

4. Grade level, property lines, and site description are based on the _____ work.

   4. _____

5. For a _____ career at the high school level, you should pursue a bachelor's degree in construction or industrial technology.

5. _____

6. Purchasing, estimating and bidding, and site supervision are just a few areas of specialization of a _____.

6. _____

PART III: MULTIPLE CHOICE: Select the best answer and place its letter in the blank at right.

1. A registered architect is qualified to:
   A. Make copies of original drawings.
   B. Design structures which meet the standards for health, safety, and property.
   C. Make renderings and presentations.
   D. None of the above.

1. _____

2. To become an architectural drafter, you should have completed high school, possess a knowledge of architectural drawing, and:
   A. Be famiiliar with a CADD system.
   B. Have an art background.
   C. Possess an understanding of economics.
   D. All of the above.

2. _____

3. A specifications writer should have a knowledge of:
   A. Construction, building materials, and surveying.
   B. Building materials, hardware, and art.
   C. Hardware, construction, and building materials.
   D. All of the above.

3. _____

4. Responsibilities of the surveyor include:
   A. Preparing plats and maps of features above and below ground level.
   B. Preparing descriptions of property.
   C. Planning and subdividing property.
   D. All of the above.

4. _____

PART IV: MATCHING: Match the correct term with its description listed below. Place the corresponding letter on the blank at right.

A. Architect
B. Architectural drafter
C. Construction technologist
D. Estimator
E. Specification writer
F. Surveyor

1. A professional who creates a design based upon his/her client's requirements.

1. _____

2. He/she draws the details of working drawings.

2. _____

3. Prepares a description of materials, methods, and fixtures to be used in construction.

3. _____

4. Calculates cost of materials and labor.

4. _____

5. Establishes areas and boundaries of real estate property.

5. _____

6. Requires knowledge in science and construction methods.

6. _____

1.

DIRECTIONS:
Present a brief summary of the duties and educational requirements
of each of the jobs/positions listed on these two pages.

Architect--

Architectural Drafter--

Architectural Illustrator--

Specification Writer--

CAREERS		39-1

Estimator‑‑

Surveyor‑‑

Construction Technologist‑‑

Teacher of Architectural Drafting‑‑

CAREERS		39‑1